Northern Gospel, Northern Church

Reflections on Identity and Mission

— EDITED BY —

GAVIN WAKEFIELD & NIGEL ROOMS

Sacristy
Press

Sacristy Press
PO Box 612, Durham, DH1 9HT

www.sacristy.co.uk

First published in 2016 by Sacristy Press, Durham

Sacristy Limited, registered in England & Wales, number 7565667

British Library Cataloguing-in-Publication Data
A catalogue record for the book is available from the British Library

ISBN 978-1-910519-19-6

FOREWORD

John Sentamu, Archbishop of York

This book arises out of a day conference held at Bishopthorpe Palace in October 2013, itself an initiative which arose from a series of events hosted to devise a path "towards the re-evangelisation of the North of England". This book seeks to provide reliable and challenging material to inform this process.

The following year, in May 2014, the Bishops of the Province of York gathered on Lindisfarne to take time away to pray, to take counsel together, and to seek a common vision towards the re-evangelisation of the North of England. As the not so gentle spring breezes swept over the island, we sensed the Holy Spirit leading us into an ever more intentional and joyful approach to our shared mission, to make Christ visible amongst the people of the North. Out of this came our decision to join with a diocesan bishop, each year, to be leaders in mission together. We gladly responded to the Bishop of Sheffield's invitation to join together in what he called the "Crossroads Mission" in September 2015. Bishop Steven Croft has made the connection with these words of Jeremiah:

> Stand at the crossroads, and look, and ask for the ancient
> paths, where the good way lies; and walk in it, and find rest
> for your souls. (Jeremiah 6:16)

The ancient paths trod by Aidan and Cuthbert and their fellow missionaries, who in their day walked the hills and valleys of Northumbria speaking of the love of God to all they met, have been replaced in many cases by motorways, train tracks, and aeroplane routes. The context changes but the message remains essentially the same—God in Christ invites us to be his friends, to receive forgiveness, and to begin a new life and be filled with the Holy Spirit. This means we are all called to join in what God is doing in the world, giving us faith, hope, and love capable of transforming lives, communities, and nations.

Is there a specifically "Northern Gospel"? The writers of this book are not agreed on this—and I myself am not convinced. What I know, however, is that the Gospel of Jesus Christ is as relevant today as ever it was here in the North of England.

Article 34 of the *Book of Common Prayer*'s "Articles of Religion" stresses the importance of adapting the traditions and ceremonies of the Church to suit local needs: "It is not necessary that Traditions and Ceremonies be in all places one, and utterly like; for at all times they have been divers, and may be changed according to the diversity of countries, times, and men's manners, so that nothing be ordained against God's Word." If this is true of traditions and ceremonies, it is also true of modes, media, and methods of mission.

Today's evangelists in the North are out and about amongst the people, and, wherever I meet them, they are being creative about how they make Christ known—it has to fit the context. I find them doing this wherever I visit across the North. They are either engaging children and families through "messy church", working together to run foodbanks, or joining initiatives in their local community to address local or regional needs. They are in the streets as street pastors or simply gossiping the Gospel in pubs or on the bus. Mission today involves an increasingly wide range and network of pathways.

And yet, at the intersection, at the crossroads, the Gospel remains the same. For all of us it is all about Jesus and seeing God in Christ make all the difference, whether in the world of education, politics, healthcare, or business—wherever people are. Urban, suburban, rural, industrial, post-industrial—whatever the context, the followers of Jesus Christ, followers in the North of England, are strengthened by the Holy Spirit, and must be more and more actively engaged as they seek to bless this land with the truth, justice, righteousness, and love of God.

The North of England is known for the persistence of certain kinds of poverty, but also for the enormous potential and resilience of its people. It is doubtful whether any single narrative will do. What happens in Christ is "new creation"—a whole new world. (2 Corinthians 5:17) It is this new world of transformed lives and transformed communities, the Kingdom of God which Jesus proclaimed, which we seek today, and for which we live, hope, and pray.

The reflections shared in this book, examining a range of issues affecting people across the North of England, give a broad picture of the many and diverse contexts and factors which contribute to our common life. It is my prayer that they will in turn provoke deeper thought, and promote more purposeful, and ever more fruitful action.

+Sentamu Eboracensis

CONTENTS

CONTRIBUTORS

Steven Croft

Steven Croft was born and brought up in Halifax and has lived most of his life in the North of England working as a vicar in Ovenden in Halifax and Warden of Cranmer Hall in Durham. He became Bishop of Sheffield in 2009. He is the author of a number of books including *Ministry in Three Dimensions* (DLT, second edition 2008), *Jesus People: What the Church Should Do Next* (CHP, 2009), and *The Advent Calendar* (DLT, 2006), a novel for adults and children. He is also a co-author of *Pilgrim: A Course for the Christian Journey* (CHP, 2013, 2014).

David Goodhew

David Goodhew is Director of Ministerial Practice at Cranmer Hall, a theological college which is part of St John's College, Durham. He is also director of the Centre for Church Growth Research, a research centre based in Durham. David edited *Church Growth in Britain, 1980 to the Present* (Ashgate, 2012) and *Towards a Theology of Church Growth* (Ashgate, 2015). Prior to moving to Durham in 2008, David was vicar of two parishes in York.

Claire Dawson

Claire Dawson has been priest in charge of St John and St James Church Bootle in the Liverpool Diocese since 2010; she initially joined the parish in 2008 as Urban Missioner. Claire was ordained in 2004 in Southwell and Nottingham Diocese having previously worked as social worker in Nottinghamshire and Derby City, where she set up a project for young people who were being exploited through prostitution. Her ministerial training took place at the East Midlands Ministerial Training Course alongside her work with young people. Claire is currently studying for a Doctor of Professional Studies in Practical Theology at Chester University; she is researching issues relating to urban theology and mission.

James Newcome

Although he was born and brought up in the South of England, James has now worked in the North West for more than twenty years. After some time as Director of Ministry and Residentiary Canon in Chester Diocese he became Bishop of Penrith, and for the last six years has been Bishop of Carlisle. Carlisle Diocese has become the first "ecumenical county" where Anglicans are working closely with Methodists and the United Reformed Church in Mission Communities whose purpose is to "grow disciples of all ages." James Newcome is married with four grown-up children, and is co-chairman of the Rose Castle Foundation.

Catherine Pickford

Despite being born in Oxford, Catherine Pickford considers herself a committed Northerner. A vicar's daughter, Catherine spent the first part of her childhood in Wath Upon Dearne, a South Yorkshire mining town, during the miners' strike. When she was nine the family moved to inner-city Sheffield, just as the *Faith in the City* report came out. Both Wath and Sheffield had a significant influence on Catherine's faith and vocation. For the last eleven years, Catherine has served first as Team Vicar and then Team Rector in Benwell in inner-city Newcastle. She is now Vicar of Stannington and CMD officer in the Diocese of Newcastle.

Matthew Porter

Matthew Porter is Vicar of St Michael le Belfrey in York, a church with a vision to play their part in serving God's transformation of the North. The Belfrey established St Cuthbert's House of Prayer in 2014 as a prayer centre for York and the North. With strong northern roots, Matthew was brought up in Doncaster and has previously served in churches in Sheffield. He believes that nothing of lasting significance happens without prayer.

Mark Powley

Mark Powley is Principal of Yorkshire Ministry Course, which works with St Barnabas Theological Centre to train ordinands for the Church of England. He was born in Bury, Manchester, and has studied Theology at the University of Nottingham, University of Oxford, and Kings College London. He is the author of *4Life: God's Values for Living* (Cell UK, 2006) and *Consumer Detox* (Zondervan, 2010).

Su Reid

Su Reid grew up in Nottingham, where her father was an Anglican Lay Reader, and then read English at St Anne's College, University of Oxford. She lectured at Aberdeen University for seven years before moving with her husband, a sociologist, to Teesside University where she eventually became Dean of the School of Arts and Media. Su spent some years worshipping as a Quaker, but returned to Anglicanism after women were ordained as priests, and trained as a Lay Reader. She is now Sub-Warden of Readers in Stokesley Deanery in the Diocese of York.

Nigel Rooms

Nigel Rooms is an Anglican priest, practical theologian, and missiologist. He oversees lay and clergy development as the Director of Ministry and Mission in the Diocese of Southwell & Nottingham, and serves in a voluntary capacity in the Local Ecumenical Partnership of Bestwood Park with Rise Park in North Nottingham. He holds a Master's degree in theology from Nottingham University and a professional doctorate in missiology from the University of Birmingham. He is the author of *The Faith of the English* (SPCK, 2011) which explores the relationship between Christian faith and English culture. Born, brought up, and educated initially all in Yorkshire, he has been interested in contextual theology throughout his ministry beginning in Stoke-on-Trent and continuing in Tanzania before moving to the liminal East Midlands.

Michael Sadgrove

Michael Sadgrove was Dean of Durham from 2003 to 2015. He was born in London and educated at Balliol College, Oxford. Ordained in 1975, he has been lecturer in Old Testament studies at Salisbury and Wells Theological College, Vicar of Alnwick, Northumberland, and Canon Precentor and Vice-Provost of Coventry Cathedral. In 1995 he became Provost, then Dean, of Sheffield. He has written on the Bible, Christian ministry, spirituality, and religious art and heritage.

Stephen Spencer

Stephen Spencer began researching William Temple's life and thought for his doctoral studies at the University of Oxford. Since then he has combined parish ministry and teaching on theological courses with ongoing research and writing. He published *William Temple: A Calling to Prophecy* (SPCK, 2001). He has just published a set of extracts from Temple's writings: *Christ in All Things: William Temple and His Writings* (Canterbury Press, 2015). He is currently Vice Principal of the Yorkshire

Ministry Course based at Mirfield in West Yorkshire, and is engaged in research for a history of Anglican social theology from F. D. Maurice to Rowan Williams.

Mark Tanner

Mark Tanner is based in Durham where he serves as Warden of Cranmer Hall, training people for mission and ministry. Previously he has lead parishes in North and South Yorkshire, worked with the Army, with New Wine, and served as Area Dean of Ripon. He is passionate about people coming to a full and life-giving faith in Jesus, helping the Church to serve with loving confidence in the darkest of places, and seeing Christians set free to worship and witness to the "glorious liberty" that is ours in Christ.

John Thomson

John Thomson is the Bishop of Selby. Before this he was Director of Ministry in Sheffield Diocese, a vicar in Doncaster, a theological educator in South Africa, and a youth chaplain in Sheffield. His published works include *The Ecclesiology of Stanley Hauerwas: A Christian Theology of Liberation* (Ashgate, 2003), *Church on Edge? Practising Christian Ministry Today* (DLT, 2004), *DOXA: A Discipleship Course* (DLT, 2007), *Living Holiness: Stanley Hauerwas and the Church* (Epworth, 2010), and *Sharing Friendship: Exploring Anglican Character, Vocation, Witness and Mission* (Ashgate, 2015). He has lived in central and southern Africa for over sixteen years and in Yorkshire for twenty-five years.

Gavin Wakefield

Gavin Wakefield is Director of Training for Missional Ministry in the Diocese of York, overseeing a team responsible for lay and clergy development. Previously he has served in the dioceses of Sheffield and Chelmsford, and was, for ten years, Director of Mission and Pastoral Studies at Cranmer Hall, Durham. Although brought up in the South of England, he has happily spent most of his adult life in the North, seeking to contribute to the mission of the Church in this context. Among his publications are *Alexander Boddy: Pentecostal Anglican Pioneer* (Authentic Media, 2007), a biography of an unusual and influential vicar in Sunderland, and *Holy People, Holy Places* (Lion Hudson, 2008), a book for pilgrimage set in the North East.

John Wigfield

John Wigfield was born and educated in West Yorkshire, and has taught Modern Foreign Languages, mainly in northern towns, and English in Zimbabwe. Having served as Theological Consultant with the South American Mission Society in several countries in Latin America, he is currently Director of Pioneering Ministry at the Yorkshire Ministry Course, with responsibility for the Contextual Pathway. He enjoys combining an innate appreciation of the people and places of Yorkshire and the wider North, overseas experience, a training in missiology and contextual theology, and studies in Old Testament to train Anglican ordinands for mission and ministry in multi-faceted contexts within Yorkshire and beyond.

INTRODUCTION

Is there a gospel for the North of England? Does it make sense to talk of a gospel for a specific place when there is "one Lord, one faith, one baptism" (Ephesians 4:5)? Does it make sense to consider the North of England as an entity—does it have a particular identity? After all it is a region with great variety, and yet it clearly shares many features with the rest of England and, indeed, Western Europe. These are the kinds of questions faced by all who sought to share the gospel in new contexts: is there an essence of the gospel which must be kept? What are the tensions inherent in seeking the holy in a culture? Who decides?[1] There are differing answers to these questions throughout this volume and we hope it will help the reader to make up their own mind.

There is a considerable literature from many parts of the world where such issues have been debated, wrestled with, and lived out.[2] Missiologists and practical theologians of many persuasions have all contributed to global and local perspectives on the interaction between faith and culture. But it is all too easy in a land where the Christian faith has been embedded for many centuries to forget the assumptions we bring to this debate. The developing sense that we are now post-Christendom does mean that we having to ask these questions in Europe, and to ask them in the regions of Europe, each of which has its own historical and sociological story within the larger European perspective.

It was this awareness that led the editors (Gavin Wakefield and Nigel Rooms) to organise a day conference at Bishopthorpe Palace, the home of the Archbishop of York, in October 2013. It was a speculative venture which attracted a significant group of people from across the North of England, clergy and lay, mainly Church of England but with good representation from other denominations. The opening address was given by the Bishop of Sheffield, Dr Steven Croft, on "Searching for the Angel of the North", and we are pleased that he has provided a written version for this book. Croft argues for a distinctive understanding of the North and for essentially one understanding of the gospel. Our second contributor was Professor Kate Pickett from the University of York and co-author of *The Spirit Level*.[3] She shared the insights of that book on the importance of understanding inequality in nations and the impact this has across all classes in a nation. She was clear that England is a divided and unequal nation and this is not contributing to the common good amongst us. Participants chose their own topics for the following discussion. As a result, two further day conferences were held in autumn 2014. The first was on the specific issue of vocations to ordained ministry in the North of England, which Mark Powley picks up on later in the book. The other was with the 'father' of contextual theology worldwide, Professor Steve Bevans, where we discussed further the issue of mission in England and the question of a regional, northern gospel.

This book is largely the fruit of the 2013 conference: there was a strong desire expressed for further reflection and most of the contributors were present at the conference. The premise is simple: we wish to stimulate imaginative reflection on the place of the gospel in the North of England and to encourage appropriate action, especially in the light of Archbishop Sentamu's call for a re-evangelization of the North.

We have taken a multi-disciplinary approach, with contributions drawing on biblical studies, systematic theology, history, social geography, empirical sociological research, and reflection on practice. Alongside this variety and depth of reflection the authors have acknowledged their personal commitments to working out the implications of the gospel in the North, often in very moving ways.

We are also very conscious of our limitations: this book is partial and only a beginning—all the contributors are from the Church of England; it is provisional—we have not tried to formulate a comprehensive picture; it is provocative—we have not imposed a single framework on the authors, but encouraged them to write of what they know and long for. The view from other denominations will be different, not least given the Church of England's general failure to engage effectively with working-class communities while retaining Establishment rights and privileges. There is more to say about the major cities of the North as well as the changing patterns of rural life, but we believe we have a made a start on developing a missiology for the North of England and we hope that readers will be provoked into responding, whether in agreement or disagreement.

In the next part of the Introduction we make a case for the proposition that there is a continuing North-South divide in England, and after that we briefly introduce the contributions.

ESTABLISHING THE NORTH-SOUTH DIVIDE IN ENGLAND[4]

The aim of this section is simple, to establish as factually as possible that a demographic divide exists in England between the North and the South. In addition, given current research, it can be shown that the unequal divide is neither being overcome nor good for the nation as a whole on the basis of a set of human outcomes such as health, education, social mobility, and work availability.

The source material comes from two books, both written by human geographers working in an academic setting. Danny Dorling uses population and census data alongside cartography to map the whole of the UK around birth, education, identity, politics, inequality, health, work, and home.[5] Kate Pickett and Richard Wilkinson have a much larger project working on a worldwide scale to show that the greater the inequality in a nation the worse are a wide range of human outcomes for people in that nation.[6] The now influential discipline of Social Epidemiology, within which their work is situated, barely existed thirty years ago. Epidemiology studies what causes diseases and ill-health in populations. Social Epidemiology has been described as the study of the causes of the causes—how social factors influence the health of individuals.[7] In making economic inequality a pivotal focus of its research, *The Spirit Level* serves to advance the conversation, taking the findings of its own discipline of Social Epidemiology to the discipline of Economics.[8]

The key to understanding the mapping that Dorling undertakes is the method of cartography that he introduces in his unique book for the first time. Using European electoral constituencies, as they contain roughly the same number of people and "combine those electors who had most in common geographically",[9] he is then able to draw a "gridded UK population cartogram" which maps the human geography and which therefore looks quite unlike the usual physical geography map. The map is drawn by giving every person the same amount of space. By dividing the physical space up into grid cells the map then reflects the number of people living in that space in relation to the other grid cells.

Thus the major urban populations loom very large on the map and thinly populated rural areas almost disappear when looking at the whole. As Dorling notes, the problem with a conventional map is that "those areas that are home to most people are obscured in comparison to sparsely populated places which appear most prominent."[10] Overall, this new approach provides a much more objective and fairer picture of the human geography of the nation.

We can now draw out of Dorling's work those points at which the North-South divide is most prominent.

Birth rates

Striking, first of all, is the almost complete reversal in data between babies born to teenagers and those born to the over-35s. Apart from two areas of central London, all the other fifteen-plus areas with more than 6,000 births to teenagers exist north of a line drawn from the Bristol Channel in the West to the Wash in the East. In complete contrast, mapping the number of babies born to mothers over 35 shows the way in which "older mothers and their children are crowded into London and the Home Counties of England".[11] Dorling also demonstrates how this demographic mirrors university entrance rates such that "everywhere where there were more than 6,000 births to teenagers had a university entrance rate below 30 per cent".[12]

Education

Children receiving no qualifications through school education and those achieving low qualifications show a clear predominance in the exactly the same area—north of a line from Bristol to the Wash.[13] While all educational achievements have improved across the board over the last twenty years, Dorling points out that this is largely illusory as increased qualifications (graduate and post-graduate) are required at the other end of the ladder for professional jobs. Thus the map showing where university graduates aged 21 or over live demonstrates a clear concentration in London and the South East, as does one showing the highest level of qualification gained.[14] Consequently, London and places immediately west of it have the greatest numbers of areas where holding a degree is the largest group in an area, whereas north of the usual line it is no qualifications which is often the largest group. Perhaps not unrelated is a map showing children attending private schools at age 15: again all the areas with more than 15 per cent attending are in London and the South East.[15]

Politics

It might be expected then that there is a political divide in the nation as well and this is indeed the case. As Dorling concludes emphatically: "there is a very strong geographical pattern to voting in Britain, a clear North-South divide".[16] Conservative and Liberal Democrat voters have much higher concentrations in the South East, apart from central London, and the increase in share of the Conservative vote in the 2000s is also concentrated there. Disaffection from politics, that is the proportion of the electorate abstaining from voting, also increases in the North West.[17]

Inequality and Poverty

Inequality and the related question of poverty are perhaps the most important indicators of a North-South divide in the country. On a map showing "people living on below half of average income", the lowest level of less than 14 per cent of people is represented in all of the areas surrounding London with only Cornwall in the South having a higher rate. While central London does have some areas with greater than 20 per cent of people in this bracket, all the other areas are in the Midlands and the North. Dorling puts it another way:

> In no area where more than 4 per cent of the population earn over £60,000 does income poverty exceed 20 per cent. In all areas where those living in income poverty exceed 20 per cent of the population, high earnings do not exceed 3 per cent [of the population].[18]

The only exception to this is central London where income poor and income rich people live side by side. So, with London as the exception (in this and many other indicators), Dorling states clearly:

> There are high rates of income poverty in the North because there are low average incomes in the North. There are high rates of great affluence in suburban parts of London and the Home Counties because there are high average incomes there.[19]

There are different ways of mapping and measuring poverty but the results are always much the same. Other related indicators of inequality also pile up in the same way. Functional illiteracy is less in the South, and it has the lowest rates of adults dying by the age of 60 as a proportion of the population.[20] Dorling does not research the most recent indicator of poverty—the prevalence of food banks—since they have only really been in existence since 2010–11 when the austerity measures of the coalition government were first instigated. A map is available showing the distribution of those food banks sponsored by the Trussell Trust around the country (<http://www.trusselltrust.org>)—though it is not drawn like one of Dorling's maps, a clear concentration in central London followed by many more outlets north of the Bristol-Wash line confirms all his data.[21]

Health

Having mentioned death rates by the age of 60, we turn now to health indicators. The pattern we have established (without the exception this time of central London) is repeated in relation to death by heart attack and stroke.[22] Dorling comments succinctly:

> mortality rates in parts of the North are simply too high to
> be purely a reflection of behaviour and social conditions
> there; rates in the south of London, through Hampshire to
> the coast, are too low for local environments to be simply
> the cause of these patterns.[23]

Rather the rates are explained partly by migration of the richer and healthier people away from the North to the South (a pattern Dorling notes regularly in the book). The low rates in London serve as evidence for this since it is the fit and healthy who are able to migrate there, however poor they may be. The other factor is clear: the distribution of poverty. Being poor is bad for your health.

Work

When it comes to the question of work, Dorling draws the maps around growth and decline of various industries. Starkest is the finance sector which has shown the greatest growth and the greatest concentration in the South East of England since the 1990s—and while the more recent crises in the sector showed its weakness, the fundamental structure of the industry has not changed.[24] Once a pattern like this is established it is very difficult to change it as wealth attracts more wealth—not least since the number of "service" sector or menial jobs required to support the wealthy is higher in those areas:

> . . . buoyant, financially secure and successful companies
> are more able, in theory, to choose where they locate. But
> they want to locate within reasonable distance of an able

workforce, for their workers to be able to travel easily to where they need to go to carry out that work, to be near large international airports and other amenities of capital, and they want a housing market in which the high salaries they can afford to pay can compete. Given all this the finance industry is bound to concentrate in the South Most importantly, when you can partly choose where to locate your industry, then why place it among the decaying remnants of former industries in areas suffering all the problems of depopulation, illness and worklessness that result?[25]

Housing

Dorling states that population in mainland Britain is concentrated in a line that runs down the west coast from Manchester to Birmingham and then to London. Housing density was high in the past in the North and it remains so in contrast to the South, barring the exception of the capital once again. People are moving south from the North and there is major evidence for this from the numbers of people living in flats as opposed to houses, since this tends to be the abode of choice for the socially mobile.[26] Size of house and the number of cars owned also both increase in the South whereas "car ownership tends to be lower in the North, even where there is space to park vehicles".[27] In the North, people are much more likely to have to give up 50 or more hours a week caring for a relative or neighbour whereas this is not required in the South as there is resource to pay someone to do it for you.[28]

What can we conclude from this abundance of evidence? Of course we can find rich and poor everywhere, yet they are most likely to live side by side in London; inequality is clearly present in England either side of a line from the Bristol Channel to the Wash. This includes, in most cases, an extension to an extremity like Cornwall. The South East, therefore, dominates the nation demographically on the majority of indicators. The gap, since the introduction of austerity measures, has been getting wider. The Archbishop of Canterbury has also drawn attention to this gap: "the

UK now has the largest variation in living standards between regions in the European Union", and goes on to call for a "common vision and solidarity of purpose which covers the whole country".[29]

Inequality

It is time then to think about the implications of inequality for a nation. Pickett and Wilkinson claim that we in developed late modern capitalist societies have material success and social failure, given the levels of isolation, mental illness, and general anxiety that exist in these societies.[30] They put this down to the "end of economic growth" as a driver of a better society and show how inequality is behind many of the ills of society, not least because health and social problems are strongly associated with the level of income. They show how the UK has one of highest rates of inequality in the developed world based on the gap between the richest 20 per cent and poorest 20 per cent of people. Japan and the Nordic countries are at the other end of the scale. We can make the connection here with Dorling's work and state that the UK's inequality manifests itself typically in differences between the South East and the rest of the country.

Health and social problems associated with the bottom 20 per cent in any country are also correlated to the level of inequality in a country.[31] The UNICEF index of child wellbeing is inversely proportional to income inequality.[32] Inequality also has important psychological effects around anxiety, self-esteem, and questions of status.[33] The evidence is damning, and yet it remains controversial that the more unequal a society is, the more problematic its social life will be. Pickett and Wilkinson then systematically work through the effects of inequality on nine outcomes, including mental and physical health, obesity, educational performance, teenage births, violence, and social mobility. In each case they make the link between inequality and the prevalence of negative results within that outcome.

While Pickett and Wilkinson do offer some solutions to making societies more equal, this is clearly a political question beyond the scope of this Introduction. Nevertheless, the fact that more equal societies with better outcomes do exist would point to the fact some very concrete things can be done about inequality.

What we are left with is a stark reality which is not being addressed in any systematic way by the UK government or Church. We rarely talk about inequality and the North-South divide, though there is some reference to the need to address inequality in the recent pastoral letter *Who is my neighbour?* from the Church of England bishops, and in a book of essays arising from a series of symposia called together by Archbishop Sentamu.[34] Continuing questions for the Church include: How prophetic should she be in a divided nation? How can she be counter-cultural and present a gospel which addresses the darkness inherent in an increasingly unequal society? What can we do in concrete terms to reverse the trend of concentrating power, population, and resource in London and the South East?

This book makes the case that within the nation of England there is a continuing divide between North and South, wherever the line is drawn exactly, and the gospel of Christ calls us to address that in a multiplicity of ways. Our present contributions are offered as variegated starting points for what this might mean, not the final answers.

THE CONTRIBUTIONS

Steven Croft sets the agenda for the book with his personal and ministerial reflection on life in the North of England and the implications for sharing the good news of Christ. Like the other contributors, he is conscious of wider perspectives and is looking for what is distinctive about the North rather than setting up an opposition. Nigel Rooms responds warmly to Croft's lecture and paper, though has another angle on the relationship between gospel and context, drawing especially on the work of Stephen Bevans. A short personal reflection by Catherine Pickford explores what it might mean to be Geordie and Christian.

The historical context is referenced and investigated in many of the essays, showing the importance of the long story of Christianity in the formation of identity across the region. Gavin Wakefield contributes a piece explicitly on some prominent stories and key themes in the history, linking them to present concerns over the use of power and powerlessness, and the relationship of the North to the rest of the England. John Wigfield takes up the challenge of *The Spirit Level* and, in an imaginative and detailed study of the Book of Deuteronomy, shows the resonance of the authors' call for greater equality with this biblical perspective.

John Thomson looks at Anglican mission in the light of Stanley Hauerwas' concern for churches to be aware of their distinctive Christian identity in contexts where their experience is often of fragility. James Newcome alerts us to a specific piece of work developing reconciliation via a new foundation in Carlisle.

The influence of the North in the life and ministry of William Temple is well brought out by Stephen Spencer, showing how one region can relate to others, in this case through the personal history of a remarkable individual. Su Reid explicitly brings some of Temple's concerns up to date in the first of her two essays: Letting the Poor Speak is a passionate and well-thought-out reflection on the lives of those who are poor and dependent on welfare, using Middlesbrough as a case study. In "Considering Northern England and Biblical Samaria" Reid makes helpful connections between the historical and contemporary sense of marginality in the North and the biblical material on Samaritans at the time of Jesus. Between these is a vivid reflection by Claire Dawson on the gospel in Bootle.

Contrasting in style is an initial report on a research project led by David Goodhew on the growth of new churches in the North East, put in the context of the secularization and resacralisation debate. There is more going on than is often realized! Both positive and challenging, Matthew Porter's short piece is on praying for God's transformation of the North, describing the call to re-evangelize and to pray for the North.

After a long and fruitful ministry in northern cathedrals, Michael Sadgrove explores the northerness of Durham Cathedral, making use of personal and shared history, leading to what he calls "mission with a north east accent" in a significant exploration of the links between mission and identity. Also set in Durham is Mark Tanner's report on micromissions undertaken by students at Cranmer Hall in Durham.

The final, longer essay by Mark Powley looks at issues around the calling and deployment of clergy in the North. He draws on his personal and professional experience, as well as a day conference held on this issue in November 2014. Nigel Rooms rounds off the book by challenging the myth of "It's Grim up North", arguing that Jesus was found in a liminal location, Galilee, and so there is an imperative for the two halves of our nation to relate together to find him today.

Our hope is that you will be stimulated and provoked by what you find helpful and what you dispute so that the good news of Jesus may be loved and experienced across our nation.

Gavin Wakefield and Nigel Rooms
Easter 2015

NOTES

1. A classic text has been Reinhold Niebuhr, *Gospel and Culture* (Faber & Faber, 1952), while a helpful development is Robert J. Schreiter, *Constructing Local Theologies* (Orbis, 1985), especially Chapter 7.

2. For example, Gerald A. Arbuckle, *Earthing the Gospel: An Inculturation Handbook for the Pastoral Worker* (Orbis, 1990); Stephen B. Bevans, *Models of Contextual Theology*, Revised and Expanded Edition (Orbis, 2002); Laurenti Magesa, *Anatomy of Inculturation: Transforming the Church in Africa* (Orbis, 2004); Robert J. Schreiter, *Constructing Local Theologies* (Orbis, 1985); Clemens Sedmak, *Doing Local Theology: A Guide for Artisans of a New Humanity* (Orbis, 2002).

3. Kate Pickett and Richard Wilkinson, *The Spirit Level: Why Equality is Better for Everyone* (Penguin, 2010).

4. This section is especially the work of Nigel Rooms.

5. Danny Dorling, *The Population of the UK*, Second Edition (Sage, 2013).

6. Pickett and Wilkinson, *The Spirit Level*.

7. Further background on Social Epidemiology can be found in a programme treating that subject in the BBC Radio 4 *Analysis* series "Sick Society?",

broadcast 24 September 2012; <http://www.bbc.co.uk/programmes/ b01mw15s> (accessed 16 December 2014).

8. "Postscript: Research Meets Politics", in Pickett and Wilkinson, *The Spirit Level*, pp. 273–298, replies to the principal critiques it has received, some of which are from those with economic interests in negating its findings.

9. Dorling, *Population* p. 3.

10. Ibid.

11. Ibid., p. 28.

12. Ibid., pp. 26–28.

13. Ibid., pp. 35–37.

14. Ibid., p. 43 and p. 60.

15. Ibid., p. 40.

16. Ibid., p. 85.

17. Ibid., pp. 75–76.

18. Ibid., p. 91.

19. Ibid., p. 93.

20. Ibid., pp. 94–97.

21. Go to <https://www.google.com/maps/d/viewer?mid=zsvX5ePkig24. kQ9wAa9s4al8&msa=0> (accessed 16 December 2014). Some expansion of the original scale is needed to see the full picture.

22. Dorling, *Population*, p. 115ff.

23. Ibid., p. 116.

24. Ibid., p. 131.

25. Ibid., pp. 145–146.

26. Ibid., p. 153.

27. Ibid., pp. 156–157.

28. Ibid., pp. 158–159.

29. Justin Welby, "Building the common good", in John Sentamu (ed.), *On Rock or Sand? Firm Foundations for Britain's Future* (SPCK, 2015), pp. 29–30 and p. 51.

30. Pickett and Wilkinson, *The Spirit Level*, p. 4. Much of this material was presented at the 2013 Bishopthorpe conference.

31. Ibid., pp. 18–20.

32. Ibid., p. 23.

33. Ibid., on anxiety, p. 33; self-esteem, p. 36; and status pp. 40–41.

34. *Who is My Neighbour* (2015), <https://www.churchofengland.org/ media/2170230/whoismyneighbour-pages.pdf> (accessed 31 March 2015),

especially paragraphs 75–77; and Welby, "Building the common good", in Sentamu (ed.), *On Rock or Sand?*, pp. 29–32.

1. SEARCHING FOR THE ANGEL OF THE NORTH

Steven Croft

1.1. A NORTHERN GOSPEL?

This introductory chapter and this book arose out of a day conference at Bishopthorpe Palace for interested parties from the North of England. The question we came together to address was: "Is there a gospel for the North?"

It is one of those questions which has made me think a great deal before and after the day conference. One of my memories as a teenage Christian was Archbishop Donald Coggan's "Call to the North". I helped to deliver special copies of Mark's gospel from door to door in the place where I lived.

Although the question has made me do some hard thinking, I do not have too many clear answers to the questions. Briefly, I do think that there is something distinctive about the North of England; I do not think that there is a "northern gospel". But I do believe that contextualization is vital in any communication of the Christian faith. I think it is vital to encourage this kind of reflection together on how we share and communicate that gospel to the North of England at this particular moment in history. I'm delighted to see the reflection which began at Bishopthorpe continue through this book of essays.

My own roots in the North of England are deep. I was born and brought up in Halifax, as were my parents and my grandparents. One of my grandfathers claimed to have crossed the Pennines from Lancashire when he was 6. My grandmother, Elizabeth Croft, was born in 1900 and survived until 1998, so I knew her the best of the four. She left school at 12 and began work in Dean Clough mills at 14. She spent her working life as a weaver. Her husband Jack was a labourer. Elizabeth was never a regular churchgoer but she had a strong faith. She claimed to pray every night of her life. She knew significant hardship but that faith never dimmed.

My father, Jim, Elizabeth's only surviving child, lived until he was almost 91, dying shortly after this address was written. He left school at 15 and again worked in the textile industry, this time as a warp twister (someone who sets the looms). In its day, this was a highly skilled trade and he served a seven-year apprenticeship. Apart from RAF service during and just after the war, he lived his whole life in Halifax.

I was born and raised in Halifax and lived there until I was 19. I went south to university but came north again to Durham for my theological college training. My curacy was in Enfield in north London, but then I came back to Halifax to be the Vicar of Ovenden, where my grandmother still lived and where I served for nine very happy and fulfilling years.

I remember still a conversation with a parishioner in Enfield just after it was announced I had been made a vicar which sums up for me some of the attitude of the South to the North:

> "Congratulations. Where is your new parish?"
> "Halifax", I said.
> "Oh dear!" they said. "I am sorry!"
> "Actually, it's my home", I said.
> "Well they do say some of these northern towns can be very nice."

After nine years in Halifax, my family returned to Durham for eight years, where I was Warden of Cranmer Hall. We then had a further brief sojourn in the South, in Oxford, while I was the national team leader of Fresh Expressions, before returning to Yorkshire when I came to Sheffield in 2009. The Diocese of Sheffield, where I serve, covers most of South Yorkshire and some parts of East Yorkshire around Goole.

1.2. WHAT IS DISTINCTIVE ABOUT THE NORTH OF ENGLAND?

For me, the North of England is distinctive in a wide range of ways and also contains many distinctive features within its regional and urban identities. One of the particular features of the North is the cherishing of regional identity—not only Northern but identities particular to the cities and towns.

There are economic attributes distinctive to the region determined in part by evolution of a variety of different industries which came to shape the landscape, the economy, and the culture: mining in Durham and the Yorkshire coalfields; cotton in Lancashire; textiles and heavy engineering in West Yorkshire; farming determined by the climate and the soil across much of the region; the steel industry in Sheffield and Rotherham. These heavy industries which shaped the regions within the North do have something in common: they were characterized in the nineteenth and twentieth centuries by the majority of the workforce in any particular town working within a single industry and for a relatively small number of large employers. This led in turn to the stratification or layering of society and, in some cases, to the deeply ingrained idea that everything would and should be provided by someone else. The Working Men's Clubs and bowling greens in Halifax were provided by the large textile and engineering firms, in Doncaster by the Miner's Welfare.

Each of those industries has evolved, of course, in different ways. The economy of the North of England is much more diverse now that a generation ago. But the industry has not all gone. The textile industry has changed both east and west of the Pennines. A great deal of steel is still made in Sheffield, especially at the high value, innovative end of the market. Manufacturing requires fewer people and the companies are part of international corporations in the main, not locally owned. Mining is, of course, almost all gone and has left a painful legacy in what are, generally speaking, stable communities which therefore have very long memories. The Rector of Maltby near Rotherham can take you to estates built for migrant workers three generations ago where you will still find a Welsh, Scottish, or Weardale version of a Yorkshire accent. He can also take you to families and neighbourhoods still divided by the miners' strike of the 1980s.

From the perspective of the Church, and especially the Church of England, we are still dealing with some of the legacy of generations of engagement with landowners and gentry rather than the artisans or working classes. This is more focused in the North than in the South. I was involved some years ago in leading an Anglican-Methodist mission team to Sedburgh in Cumbria. The team was briefed in advance that certain families and sorts of people were part of the Anglican Church and certain families and sorts of people were part of the Methodist Church. Class remained a determining factor in churchgoing. I sat in on a seminar some years ago in Durham about the legacy of the extraction of minerals and coal in Weardale to the profit of the Church and its clergy and the legacy of resentment against the Church in that community which had been perpetuated through many generations.

There are clear economic differences between the North of England and parts of the South of England but, when you look more closely, these are not as marked as they seem. As the Introduction to this book makes clear, the contrasts in many ways are not simply between "North" and "South" but between London and parts of the South East and the rest of the United Kingdom in terms of economic growth, employment, and prosperity. Many of the poorest dioceses in the Church of England, in terms of per capita income, are in the Northern Province but the poorest, Birmingham, is in the Midlands, and several others in the "South" are not far behind. As we all know, there are areas of significant wealth and relative prosperity in the North of England as well. I served on the Sheffield Fairness Commission last year. One of the reasons Sheffield is one of the less equal cities in the country is that our wealthy areas really are very wealthy indeed relative to other cities.

The cultural identity of the North, and the regional identities within that northern identity, is significant. As Stuart Maconie says in his book, *Pies and Prejudice*,[1] there is a clear northern identity in a way there is no clear "southern" identity. The BBC has no "South of England" correspondent. It is one of the mysteries of English life that the miles are much longer travelling north than travelling south: people in London are always expecting me to pop down for meetings but the idea of convening a similar meeting in Sheffield raises eyebrows. In exactly the same way, people in Doncaster are often expected to travel to Sheffield but when the same events are held in Doncaster, the people in Sheffield say that it is too far. Lack of awareness of the North of England is one of the principal things which offends people in the North—including within the Church.

Those regional identities are carefully nurtured and reinforced by the local press, by the BBC and ITV regional television, and local radio. The Yorkshire version of Look North is, in my view, the best BBC local television programme in the quality of its journalism and its connection with the region. My wife and I often amuse ourselves by counting the number of times the word "Yorkshire" appears from beginning to the end of the programme. It simply does not happen in other places.

1.3.   THE CHURCH OF ENGLAND IN THE NORTH

For the Church of England, the division between North and South is, of course, underlined and reinforced by the historical reality of the northern ecclesiastical province which has existed (in more or less the same form) from the time of Paulinus in the sixth century. The ancient boundary between Mercia and Northumbria is marked by an ancient stone in Dore churchyard, on the south-west rim of Sheffield. If anyone is puzzled about where the North of England begins, it begins in Dore.

When I was consecrated bishop in York Minster six years ago, the most moving moment in the process was the evening before at night prayer in the chapel. The Archbishop said to the assembled guests, "Archbishops of York have been consecrating bishops to carry the gospel into the North of England for hundreds of years, and since the twelfth century those bishops have knelt to pray before their consecrations in this chapel." There was a tremendous sense of connection with the past and of a distinctive northern identity.

Part of what makes Christianity distinctive in the North of England is that sense of both history and community. In terms of history, the North was evangelized both from the north, from Ireland via Scotland through

Holy Island, and from the south, from Canterbury via Rome. The first history of the Church in England and the first history of England, that of Bede, was written partly to preserve that northern perspective. The northern saints, particularly Hilda, Aidan, Cuthbert, and Bede, continue to have resonance. Even today the fact that the bishops of the North gather around the Archbishop of York preserves a distinctive ecclesial identity to the Church of England in the Northern Province. That gathering happens symbolically at the consecration of a new bishop, when most bishops normally attend in a very different way from in the South.

What are some of the characteristics of the northern identity and the identity the Church shares? Most people would put honesty and bluntness somewhere on the list. People in the North of England, we like to think, say it like it is. When I first went back to Halifax as Vicar, a number of people in the parish clearly thought I might have gone soft because of my sojourn in the South. So they came up to me to warn me that, "We tell it as it is in Yorkshire", and, "We speak as we find." I swiftly discovered what that meant was: "We want to tell you exactly what we think of you but we do not like it when it's the other way round." Learning to be blunt in the right way is one of the keys to communicating the gospel in the North.

Attitudes to money are vital in the North of England in the Church because there is not a lot of it around. Good stewardship is vital. Waste is abhorred. The pennies are still counted in many church vestries. We were interviewing for a senior lay post in the Diocese a couple of months ago and asked the candidates to talk about what they would bring to the post. One talked about her ability to make a lot out of a little: "My colleagues describe me in this way: give her a shilling and a couple of conkers and she'll soon sort it out." It was a very northern sentence. She got the job.

Pomposity does not go down well in the North. There is a due respect for authority but not for swank and show. That rings very true with the gospel of Jesus Christ, of course. But it does not always ring true with the culture of the Church of England. Hard work is respected. Common sense is valued. There is a wariness of Church politics and parties. I do not think that the lay people of the Diocese of Sheffield care very much about what vestments are worn or the style of the Eucharist that is offered or what happens at General Synod. They do care about the integrity of their ministers as evidenced in their life and character. When I travelled around the Sheffield Diocese holding a series of deanery meetings in 2009, I expected to inherit a bit more positional authority—that people might listen to me because I was the Bishop. In fact, the meetings were much more like hustings. People had come with an open mind to check me out and to determine whether or not to give their trust and assent. There was no automatic right to respect based on position.

Beneath the bluster, self-confidence is generally low, in my observation, across the North of England and across the Church in the North of England. I think this is a cultural legacy, and I am not exactly sure why but I recognize it to be true. As a city, Sheffield is remarkably understated. So are many of our great northern cities. People in them doubt what we have to offer to the rest of the nation and to the world. There is a tendency to look on the bleak side of life. If you say nine encouraging things to a congregation or a person and one which may be less than encouraging, which one will they remember and feed back to you?

There is always a need for gentleness in the mediation of Church authority but I think that it is needed even more in the Church in the North. Aidan stands out as a model and exemplar from Bede's history. Cormán, the first person sent by the Irish to preach in Northumbria, was "a man of a more austere disposition". The English refused to listen to him and he returned home, reporting that he had been sent to "an ungovernable people of an obstinate and barbarous temperament". In the Irish conference which followed his return Aidan spoke:

> Brother, it seems to me that you were too severe on your ignorant hearers. You should have followed the practice of the Apostles, and begun by giving them the milk of simpler teaching, and gradually nourished them with the word of God until they were capable of greater perfection, and able to follow the loftier precepts of Christ.[2]

Aidan himself is distinguished in his ministry above all as a man of outstanding gentleness, holiness and moderation.

The Church in the North is not helped in its efforts to change by being repeatedly shown downward sloping graphs of church attendance and by being told it will be extinct by 2030. There is, generally speaking, no difficulty confronting that reality. People are not daft: if anything, we believe it to be slightly worse than it is. The difficulty is believing the positive evidence that growth is possible. The fundamental shift needs to be in our theology of hope to create the capacity for change and in developing consistent and wise strategies to encourage growth. Hope needs to be practiced consistently as a virtue rather than a mood, perhaps especially in the North of England and above all by bishops and church leaders.

I have found the concept of congregational narratives developed by James Hopewell and Martyn Percy very helpful, particularly their analysis of the way communities tell their stories according to a romantic or a tragic template[3]. The former narrative carries the danger of excluding some of the difficult realities of the present situation. The latter, in excluding the positive signs of growth and adjusting reality to our expectations of decline. There is a constantly developing northern narrative which tends towards the second of these paradigms. The myth which needs profound challenge is that we are simply managing decline in the life of the Church. I believe that the challenge is beginning to be effective.

Finally, there is, I believe, in much of the North of England (though not all) a parochialism which inhibits development and the sharing of ideas. That parochialism is in part the product of a lack of social and geographical mobility. Congregations have the same families at the heart of them for generations. This produces resilience and stability but it can make those congregations resistant to change and very, very fractious when change is introduced. A wider vision is vital, which is why I believe the bishop and the diocese have a vital role to play in enabling local churches to develop and move forwards.

1.4.   IS THERE A NORTHERN GOSPEL?

I do not believe that there is a specific gospel for the North of England or for anywhere else in the world for that matter. I believe that there is one gospel, one Lord, one faith, one baptism, as we declare often in the liturgy, which faith the Church is called upon to proclaim afresh in each generation. However, I do believe that this gospel needs first to be rediscovered and understood anew by the Church in the North of England. It then needs to be incarnated, to take flesh, in the lives of individuals and communities, and it needs to be contextualized in and for the different regions of the North of England.

The search for the Angel of the North is firstly about this recovery of the heart of the gospel and stripping back its cultural and ecclesial accretions. It is, secondly, about learning to incarnate and express that gospel in the lives of ministers and churches. Thirdly, it is about the contextualization of the gospel in the communities of the North.

One of the features of Paul's epistles which we need to ponder is how quickly the early Christian communities lost their hold on the life-transforming power of the gospel for their own lives and the life of the Church. Over and over again, Paul reminds the first churches in his letters of the need to return to that gospel and to its first principles, and to keep them at the very centre of their personal lives and of their ecclesial life.

The letter to the Colossians turns around an appeal to keep the gospel central and to guard it against accretions:

> As you therefore have received Christ Jesus the Lord, continue to live your lives in him, rooted and built up in him and established in the faith, just as you were taught, abounding in thanksgiving. See to it that no-one takes you captive . . . (Colossians 2:6–8, *NRSV*)

The letter to the Romans is, of course, a single great exposition of the gospel in which Paul proclaims the power of God for salvation to those who believe. The letters to the Corinthians are a pastoral interpretation of the gospel to a Church which has become fractious and divided within itself (in 1 Corinthians) and from Paul's leadership and authority (in 2 Corinthians). Both letters treat the symptoms of disunity with the medicine of the gospel: the good news of Jesus Christ, his life, ministry, death, and resurrection. These epistles are an indispensable guide in our task of recovering the heart of the gospel, stripping back its accretions, understanding it afresh and proclaiming it effectively in the communities of the North of England.

We should take both encouragement and warning from the universal tendency reflected in the New Testament for the Church to drift away from the central truths of the gospel and to find a new centre and, in effect, a different gospel. The encouragement is that, when we fall into this error, others have been there before us. The warning is that the Church in our own day is highly likely to fall into this error if even the New Testament churches were not immune.

One of the fundamental challenges for the Church across the North of England, I believe, is that the life-giving power of the Christian gospel has become submerged under the accretions of church life, of Christendom, and parochial structures, and needs to be recovered and to be the focus of our attention and to be made central again in our church life.

My own journey in this has been a slow, steady, and repeated learning curve over perhaps twenty years. The heart of the learning is focussed on the question of how we can best encourage the Church in the North of England to make disciples and to grow healthy churches again.

Here are two patterns of diagnosis and response. The first is that the Church across the North retains a clear grasp of the gospel but has lost the motivation and the skill to share it and proclaim it. The response to that diagnosis would be to teach the Church again how to evangelize and proclaim the gospel it already understands. And so we would offer courses on initial proclamation and catechesis, and on forming fresh expressions of church to equip more of the Church in these aspects of mission.

The second pattern of diagnosis and response is much starker. It is to acknowledge that the Church across the North needs to not only recover its grasp of the gospel but also the centrality of the gospel of Jesus Christ and the vision of the kingdom which Christ proclaims and inaugurates. The beauty of the gospel has become submerged beneath a shallow, cultural veneer of Christianity, the vestiges of Christendom. The response to that diagnosis will be to recover and proclaim the gospel afresh within as well as beyond the Church in the next generation and to equip others in that proclamation. And so we would proclaim, over and over again, in the church and beyond the Church the call to saving faith in Christ, the attractiveness of Jesus, the meaning of his death and resurrection as the centre of our faith.

Across the Diocese of Sheffield, the part of the North I know best, I would say that both diagnoses are correct and both are needed. Some parts of the Church understand the gospel and need support in learning again how to proclaim it. Other parts of the Church have, frankly, lost the sense of what the gospel is about and need to return to very centre of the faith to be renewed and to move forward. My sense of where we need to place the stress in our preaching and teaching is on the second diagnosis, not the first. Theologically, this is what I sense the Church in every generation is called to do and what I see happening in the New Testament. Historically and culturally, I believe this is the particular calling of the Church in our generation as we emerge from Christendom. We need to recover again the sense of the gospel as the centre of our faith. We need ministers and teachers and preachers who will re-evangelize the Church in the North of England and re-evangelize England.

1.5.   INTENTIONAL EVANGELISM

In 2013, I was asked to draft with others a document on evangelism to set the scene for a major debate in the General Synod of the Church of England. The document is called *Intentional Evangelism*.[4] The major question for me was the starting point, the theological introduction to the paper. The structure of the paper is rooted in the diagnosis I have just explored.

The first two sentences of *Intentional Evangelism* are as follows:

> The Church is renewed in evangelism only through being renewed in love for Jesus Christ and love for God's world.
> The first step in this renewal is, therefore, for the Church to focus once again on the wonder of God's love revealed in Jesus Christ.[5]

The first section of the paper carries the title of "The Pearl" and this, in essence, is Jesus and his gospel.

Here are some of the paragraphs which attempt to describe the gospel:

> The good news of Jesus Christ is not a human invention but the revelation of God's grace to humankind.[6]
>
> This gospel of Jesus Christ offers forgiveness for sin for those who are alienated from God and a renewed relationship with our creator and with one another.[7] The gospel offers guidance for the lost, spiritual food for the hungry, healing for the broken in spirit, freedom for those who are captives, order and safety for those whose lives are in chaos, fruitful living for those whose lives are barren.[8] The gospel offers the gift of life in all its fullness[9] and fellowship in the life of God the Trinity both now and for all eternity.[10] The gospel offers the rich gift of resurrection and life beyond death for, in Christ, the power of death itself has been vanquished and resurrection life is offered to all.[11]
>
> The gospel offers hope for the transformation of the world both through the witness and actions of the people of God, as agents of change, and, most of all, in the promises of God that the kingdom will come in all its fullness and that Christ will be Lord of all.[12] The Church is a sign and instrument of God's kingdom on earth, a channel of peace and reconciliation in a world divided, a witness to God's purpose for humanity and an agent of God's compassion in the world.
>
> This gospel, with all its profound benefits, is offered by God's grace, as God's gift, free of charge[13] to every man, woman, and child in creation. Each person is invited to respond to God's offer of new and eternal life in Christ Jesus and to receive these gifts through repentance and faith in God's Son.[14] Each person is called by God to find and grace through offering their lives in return to God's service as part of God's household, the Church.[15] The gospel is good news for all people, of whatever race, gender, background or social class.

This is the gospel which the Church explores, rehearses and celebrates in her worship, in her engagement with the Scriptures and through the celebration of the Sacraments of Holy Baptism and Holy Communion. This is the gospel which the Church is called upon to proclaim afresh in each generation, including our own generation in this present age.

"Woe to me if I do not proclaim the gospel," writes St Paul.[16] The Church is compelled to proclaim the gospel with imagination and perseverance out of love for God, whose gospel this is, and out of love for the world. We have nothing more, and nothing less, to offer to the world around us than this pearl of inestimable value. The world around, at different times, may ridicule, scoff or reject the message. But the response of the world does not invalidate the gospel or excuse the Church from the call to proclaim it. We have been entrusted with the words of love and of eternal life. We need continually to recall one another to a fresh vision of Jesus Christ, a fresh vision for the gospel of God's kingdom, and a persistent and imaginative proclamation of the whole gospel to the whole world in this generation in the power of God's Spirit.[17]

The second section of *Intentional Evangelism* is entitled "The Vision". It begins with this sentence:

To proclaim the gospel of Jesus Christ is also to proclaim the vision of Jesus Christ for God's world, for humankind and for the whole creation.[18]

That vision is focused in the concept and phrase "the kingdom of God", which the section explores in the Old and New Testaments. The proclamation of the gospel is inextricably linked with this fresh vision for society. Quoting again:

Our present world is thirsty for a vision for creation and human society which cherishes peace, freedom, justice, reconciliation, and care for the earth. This vision is at the heart of the Christian gospel and all the Church proclaims.

Evangelism is not simply the attenuated proclamation of a formula to draw individuals to salvation. To evangelise is to announce at one and the same time both the coming of the Saviour and this rich vision of the kingdom of God. True evangelism invites the response of personal repentance and faith and a call to whole life discipleship following the pattern of Christ and lived in response to this vision of the world.

For this reason, for Anglicans, evangelism can never be separated from other aspects of the mission of God: from loving service to our neighbours, from social action, from proclaiming God's desire for peace and justice, from care for creation. Although there is real merit in considering evangelism as a distinctive activity in order to allow for due focus and reflection, it must also, always be considered as part of the whole which is God's mission to the world.[19]

1.6.   *THE JOY OF THE GOSPEL*

One of the key experiences which led to the writing of *Intentional Evangelism* and these paragraphs in particular was the privilege of being invited to be the Anglican Fraternal Delegate to the Synod of Bishops in Rome in 2012. The Synod was on the theme of the new evangelization and the transmission of the faith. More than 400 bishops and others assembled from all across the world to reflect on the theme of the gospel and its transmission. The following year, the new Pope, Francis, published *The Joy of the Gospel*, the apostolic exhortation arising from the Synod of Bishops.

The Joy of the Gospel begins in exactly the same place as *Intentional Evangelism*, with the need for a fresh encounter with the living Christ who is at the heart of the gospel. These are the opening paragraphs:

The joy of the gospel fills the hearts and lives of all who encounter Jesus. Those who accept his offer of salvation are set free from sin, sorrow, inner emptiness and loneliness. With Christ, joy is constantly born anew ... I invite all Christians everywhere, at this very moment, to a renewed personal encounter with Jesus Christ or at least an openness to letting him encounter them; I ask all of you to do this unfailingly each day.[20]

Francis too talks of a stripping away of the accretions of religion to return to the heart of the gospel:

I prefer a Church which is bruised, hurting and dirty because it has been out on the streets rather than a Church which is unhealthy from being confined and from clinging to its own security. I do not want a Church concerned with being at the centre and which then ends by being caught up in a web of obsessions and procedures ... More than by fear of going astray, my hope is that we will be moved by the fear of remaining shut up within structures which give us a false sense of security, within rules which make us harsh judges, within habits which make us feel safe, while at our door people are starving and Jesus does not tire of saying to us: "Give them something to eat" (Mark 6:37).[21]

1.7.   INCARNATION AND CONTEXTUALIZATION

The search for the Angel of the North is, firstly, about the recovery of the heart of the gospel and stripping back its cultural and ecclesial accretions. This is, I believe, where we need to focus.

Secondly, it is about learning to incarnate and express that gospel in the lives of ministers and churches. As in the very message of the incarnation, the Word is made flesh through the individuals and through communities living a distinctive life. This presents a particular challenge to Anglican mission and identity at the present time. Bishops and other Church leaders live their lives at the intersection of the challenges of stewardship and mission. Stewardship is about the prudent management of the resources entrusted to us. Mission is about the creative and hopeful engagement with the world in order to make disciples, to serve our communities and to seek to be salt and light. The demands of prudent stewardship are pressing the Church to do less with a decreasing resource. The call of God's mission is pressing the Church to do more in what is a moment of significant opportunity.

There is no easy way to resolve that tension which everyone who reads this book will be familiar with. It is perhaps focussed in the dilemma of how and whether to spread our resources in people and finance as evenly as possible across the dioceses or whether, on the other hand, to seek to create focused centres of excellence, mission, and growth which can be catalysts for change. Clearly, there will need to be a balance. I am personally convinced that we need those focused centres of strength and excellence as well as places and sources of renewal of the Church in the wider region.

One such focus is encouraging the growth of larger churches and their engagement with dioceses and the wider communities. The deaneries on the west of Sheffield contain some of the largest Anglican churches outside London. They have grown largely through becoming centres of excellence within particular Anglican traditions, through the formation of students in discipleship and then through the formation of ministers. Large churches are sometimes viewed with suspicion by their dioceses and often do not feel loved and cherished. Yet, over many years, these churches have produced ordinands and other ministers for the Diocese of Sheffield and beyond who go on to serve in many different places and communities. These large churches often provide informal and formal networking, training, and support for clergy and congregations across the region, and have done for many years, supporting growth. A key part of my learning as a vicar in Halifax used to be travelling across to St Thomas Crookes in Sheffield two or three times a year to sit at the feet of Robert Warren and his team. Centres of excellence and informal networks of support are key. They need the active support of dioceses and an economy of church life in which they can develop.

A second means of focus is the encouragement and development of institutions and communities which are not parochial but have the capacity to strengthen and resource the wider church. The North is not well resourced with religious communities, with retreat houses, with theological colleges and training institutions, or with other kinds of institutions which can deepen Christian life and formation here. Over the whole of my ministerial life I have cause to be grateful to the Community of the Resurrection at Mirfield, for their prayers, spiritual direction, and hospitality in different seasons. Cranmer Hall and St John's College Durham have played, in my view, a vital role in strengthening the Church in the North, as do Alnmouth and Holy Island. This year sees the beginning of St Mellitus North West, a theological training hub, as well as the St Barnabas Theological Centre which are both fragile new institutions. Others are needed.

In Anglican polity at the present time, I believe bishops and dioceses have a critical role in articulating a theological vision for the re-evangelization of the North of England and in leading the reshaping of the Church for that purpose. In 2014, the Archbishop of York invited the bishops of the Northern Province to a 24-hour retreat on Holy Island to take further the re-evangelization of the North. One of the fruits of our time there in prayer will be that between fifteen and twenty bishops are coming on mission together to the Diocese of Sheffield in September 2015, many bringing teams of young people. There are plans to repeat this idea of Bishops in Mission Together across the North in the coming years.

Many of the northern dioceses are developing creative responses in mission leading to growth which have lessons for the whole Church of England and indeed the worldwide Church. The way the bishop and the diocese lead in relation to mission and growth is becoming more, not less, important in the formation of disciples, of church life, and of ministers.

1.8.   THE ATTITUDE OF THE CHURCH IN THE NORTH TO THE CHURCH IN THE SOUTH

Finally, I want to say something about the relationship between the Church in the North to the Church in the South. All of us who work in the North are irritated by ignorance and prejudice from South to North. All of us need to break that down.

I am, however, becoming increasingly aware of a growing resentment in the North of England that clergy in particular are reluctant to come and serve in the northern dioceses. There is no doubt that this is statistically accurate and I believe the Church of England does need to challenge ideas of deployability among its ordinands and clergy.

However, it all too easily tips over into a visible chip on the shoulder, a self-pitying projection that "it's grim up north and if only people from the South would come and help us all would be well", which actually reinforces the attitude we are trying to combat. It is, and it remains, a privilege to serve the Church in the North of England.

1.9.   IN CONCLUSION

The Church in the North of England ministers and serves to particular cultures and in a particular geographic and historical context. We are at a key moment in our history with significant opportunities before us. We need the perspective of Christian hope in all we do and gentleness in the way we serve.

Our primary calling, I believe, is to deepen our understanding of Jesus Christ and of the gospel of Jesus Christ and to proclaim that gospel within the church and beyond the Church. We further need to continue to incarnate and contextualize that gospel in the parishes of the North of England. As we do that, we need our strong centres of excellence as well a spread of presence. We need to cherish our pioneers and entrepreneurs and keep them connected to the wider body. We need to be bold and hopeful in our dioceses in developing a positive vision for the growth of the Church and its impact on our wider society.

In the North of England, as in the rest of the world and the rest of human history, "The Church is renewed in evangelism only through being renewed in love for Jesus Christ and love for God's world."[22]

QUESTIONS FOR CONVERSATION

The Church is renewed in evangelism only through being renewed in love for Jesus Christ and love for God's world.

- Do you agree with the diagnosis that the Church needs to focus on engaging again with the gospel of Jesus Christ and proclaiming the gospel with the Church as well as to the world?
- What is distinctive about the Church in the North of England?
- How can we cherish points of strength and distinctive Christian engagement and enable them to shape the wider Church?
- What are the challenges for the contextualization of minsters and ministry in the North of England?
- How should the Church in the North build creative and fruitful partnership with the Church in the South?

NOTES

1. Stuart Maconie, *Pies and Prejudice* (Ebury Press, 2008). A good read in parts, but contains far too much detail about the counties west of the Pennines and not enough about those to the east.

2. Bede, *The Ecclesiastical History of the English People* (henceforth *EH*), tr. E. T. Leo Sherley-Price (Penguin, 1968), III 5.

3. James Hopewell, *Congregation Stories and Structures* (Fortress Press, 1987); Martyn Percy, *Shaping the Church* (Ashgate, 2010).

4. *Intentional Evangelism* (GS Misc., 1917), available at <http://www.churchofengland.org>.

5. Ibid., p. 2.

6. Galatians 1:11–12.

7. Ephesians 1:13–22.

8. See, for example, Psalm 107 and Mark 5–7 for these great gospel images of salvation.

9. John 10:10.

10. 2 Corinthians 13:13.

11. 2 Corinthians 15:20–28.

12. Philippians 2:9–11.

13. 2 Corinthians 11:7.

14. Acts 2:38–39.

15. Ephesians 2:19; Romans 12:1–2.

16. 1 Corinthians 9:16

17. *Intentional Evangelism*, p. 3–4.

18. Ibid., p. 5.

19. Ibid., p. 6.

20. Pope Francis, *Evangelii Gaudium* (Catholic Truth Society, 2013), pp. 1–3.

21. *Ibid.*, p. 49.

22. *Intentional Evangelism*, p. 2.

# 2.	BIAS TO THE NORTH? THE MEANING OF THE NORTH AND ITS GOSPEL

Nigel Rooms

> "You're so southern you're almost in France!"
> *A chant from Hull City AFC supporters heard on*
> *Wembley Way and directed at the Arsenal FC fans*
> *in advance of the FA Cup Final, 17 May 2014.*

## 2.1.	INTRODUCTION

This chapter has several aims. First, to respond in part to Bishop Steven Croft's paper "Searching for the Angel of the North" published elsewhere in this volume. Second, to think about some definitions—just where and what is the "North" anyway? Then to develop the theme of inculturation, or, more broadly, contextual theology in the North, which may lead us to think about how the North elicits particular gospel themes out of its own particularity. Finally, to wonder about the implications of this study for the Church today.

2.2.   THE QUESTION OF A NORTHERN GOSPEL

We were very grateful to Bishop Steven for his input at a day conference on the theme of the title of his paper at Bishopthorpe Palace in York in 2013 and for his permission to publish that paper in this volume. What was surprising to me from the outset was the emphasis that Croft places on contextualization, stating categorically several times, even in is opening comments, that "I do not think there is a 'northern gospel.'" We are treated, however, to a full review of the context of the North, its distinctives and values, many of which are immediately recognizable. Both I and others on the day were drawn to the suggestion he makes about the North and romantic/tragic narratives of itself and the way in which we must challenge any "tragic" narrative. We will return to this theme later in the chapter. Croft emphasizes a theology of hope and states his position clearly on how the context of the North is to be dealt with:

> The search for the angel of the North is firstly about this recovery of the heart of the gospel and stripping back its cultural and ecclesial accretions. It is, secondly, about learning to incarnate and express that gospel in the lives of ministers and churches. Thirdly, it is about the contextualization of the gospel in the communities of the North.[1]

Thus we have a clear statement of what Steve Bevans calls the "translation" model of contextual theology.[2] This model "takes seriously the message of Christianity as recorded in the scriptures and handed down in the tradition",[3] just as Croft does when he recommends we return to the New Testament Epistles and recover the "good news of Jesus Christ, his life, ministry, death and resurrection".[4] The strength of this model, as Bevans points out, is that it offers a clear message to a world in need, it does take the context seriously and can be adjusted quickly when first coming into contact with a new culture. However, there is a serious critique of this approach as an exclusive model over and against others. Questions are raised as to whether it really takes the receptor culture seriously enough—has real, deep listening gone on? The example of a re-evaluation of polygamous marriages in African Christianity is offered as one example.[5] More importantly perhaps, this model can treat the "gospel" as above and beyond culture. It understands the gospel, as Croft does, as "the heart", while others use the idea of the kernel of a seed. The problem here is a deeply philosophical one as this model seems to separate "form and content" and, while I do not agree with everything in their book on Fresh Expressions, the first chapter of Davison and Milbank's *For the Parish* deals clearly with this question.[6]

The translation model may not take the incarnation seriously enough, with my own view being that the gospel cannot exist apart from culture— just as, in fact, a heart cannot live and beat without a body.[7] I prefer the term "inculturation" to "contextualization" when discussing questions of culture and gospel as, for me, it represents a dynamic movement (rather than static images like kernels) between the two "poles" of faith and culture which always need to be held in vibrant tension. This position arises from the work of Andrew Walls[8] and Lamin Sanneh[9] who discuss at length what the universal elements of the gospel might be when it has been "translated" through the whole history of the growth of the Christian faith as a missionary movement. Sanneh is clear that the context is always an evangelizer of the evangelist:

> Thus if we ask the question about the essence of Christianity, whatever the final answer, we would be forced to reckon with what the fresh medium reveals to us in feedback. This locates the message in the specific and particular encounter with cultural self-understanding.[10]

Walls understands the essential continuity in Christianity is to be found in "continuity of thought about the final significance of Jesus, continuity of a certain consciousness about history, continuity in the use of the Scriptures, of bread, of wine, of water", while all of these elements can be "cloaked with such heavy veils belonging to their environment" such that different expressions of the faith are unrecognizable from each other.[11] The gospel is, therefore, "infinitely translatable" rather than having any fixed, universal content—it contains the possibility of finding life and roots in the most unlikely of places, even northern post-industrial social housing estates.[12]

Bevans and Schroeder develop this idea further, naming six "constants" which, while not being the content of the gospel, are the questions which the gospel, in dynamic interaction with a cultural environment, has to answer at any one time in history.[13] They are the questions of Jesus Christ, the Church, salvation, human nature, culture, and the end of time. They show how these have been dealt with over the centuries of missionary endeavour and propose a mission theology for today based around "prophetic dialogue". This approach seems to take the context utterly seriously, being open to being changed by it while not denying the transformative and prophetic nature of the good news which sometimes stands over against the culture. I like the idea they take from Orthodox theologian Michael Oleksa: we can never be sure where Christ is not.[14] A double negative which ensures that missionary work is always a task of spiritual discernment.

These approaches have much more in common with three of Bevans' other models of contextual theology—the anthropological, the synthetic, and the counter-cultural. Vincent Donovan's work amongst the Masai in Tanzania[15] in the 1960s is often held up as a *sine qua non* example of mission work for contemporary Fresh Expressions in the UK (and is the basis of many an academic course on mission today), and is classified by Bevans as an example of his anthropological model.[16] That is, it moves to the other "pole" of the faith-culture spectrum and takes utterly seriously the human context and culture. Donovan goes to the Masai confident in the translation model, but, for all sorts of reasons including the fact that they do not have a word for sin (how contemporary does that sound?), he has to lose his faith in order to "re-discover" it in dialogue with the Masai and their culture. The categories and content of the faith he carried with him were inadequate for the context he now found himself called to as an evangelist. Thus I question whether the translation model favoured by Croft is adequate for our missionary purpose in a post-Christendom context in the North of England today. This is not least because the gospel is not one thing, a heart or kernel, but, like love, is a "many-splendoured thing" able to meet people where they are with the reality of God who deeply and profoundly desires relationship.

For all sorts of historical reasons rehearsed elsewhere in this volume, the Church (of many denominations, perhaps apart from Methodism and that only temporarily) has always been weaker in numbers, finance, and resources in the North than the South. Despite the effectiveness of the Irish mission from the seventh century onwards, one wonders whether the gospel, as it was preached, has ever been adequate for the North, given its level of acceptance. Anton Wessels raises the same question for the whole of Europe, where the identical issues of faith and culture that we have been discussing played out in the first evangelisation.[17] Malcolm Lambert, in his historical work on the conversion of Britain, shows clearly how both the Irish and Roman missions worked under the auspices of Christendom.[18] Yes, there was competition from pagan ideas, but access to kings and the powerful was afforded to evangelists by the establishment of Christendom after Constantine,[19] a fact that John Finney, in his otherwise very helpful book connecting the original conversion of Britain with mission today, misses.[20] I believe we probably have to go back to Patrick's evangelism in Ireland to find an evangelism in these islands where the evangelist was "a stranger, with no lord and without kin".[21] I think it makes a difference that Britain was evangelized in Christendom and now that we are in its twilight we are unsure of ourselves, the gospel, and how to respond.

So what is it about the possibility of a northern gospel that repels? Are we resistant to going back to first principles as Donovan did and starting with listening and dialogue again, before we make any move to the prophetic, having earned the right to it? Perhaps dividing the country into North and South, as I suppose we are attempting here, somehow undermines a sense of nationhood and unity, our essential Englishness and "being in it together". And yet I cannot help but feel that we are missing something if we homogenize and overlook the fundamental demographic and cultural differences in our land. Perhaps it is just too big a project, and I definitely feel that pressure as I write this essay, realizing it can only just be a start, a first word rather than the last, to quote the strap line of the well-known Grove Books series.

2.3. TOWARDS THE MEANING OF THE NORTH AND ITS GOSPEL

Nevertheless, it is time to have a go. Not many others have attempted such a project: the only other Christian work I could find in my nearest and best theological library was a book called *The Kingdom of God and North-East England*.[22] After an introductory essay by the editor, James Dunn, there is a description of twelve different projects which illustrate different aspects of the Kingdom. There is, however, no sense of the northern context (other than via economic poverty) portrayed in the book. We may not be able to delineate a northern gospel in the short space and time available, and, in any case, that can only be done on the ground or at the coal face, as we might say. A couple of celebrities have attempted a kind of autobiographical tour of the North from their own perspective: Morley combines personal anecdote, history, and place without really coming to any concrete conclusions;[23] Maconie is better as he ranges widely and works in relation to the South.[24] Some of the case study stories in this volume fill out the picture and here we start the task of working on a regional theology of the North which will begin, we hope, to elucidate some dimensions of the gospel within the North. Before we move to that, however, some definitions might be appropriate.

At this point I can introduce some data into this paper since I have aired the question of the North and its meaning at two further day conferences in 2014.[25] What I noticed at these events is that, when I suggested a notional boundary for the North, this generated enormous energy, argument, and discussion which, at the very least, shows that the issue is a real one. I offered at the first event the idea that the line between North and South stretches from the Bristol Channel to the Wash. This is the clear demographic delineator of Dorling's UK human geography project as described in the introduction to this volume. The room erupted! Of course this ignores the Midlands altogether, both East and West, and yet it does usefully isolate the South East with its unique position of power and resources from the rest of the country. Perhaps it is no surprise that the early Roman road, the Fosse Way, that runs from Exeter to Lincoln, and which may have been a boundary for what the early invaders could control of the country, follows much the same line.

Their power and resources lay in that region too and historian Mike Ibeji believes every ruler of the country since then has been trying to recover the glory of what the Romans did.[26] Nevertheless, I do think we have to take the Midlands seriously, not least because I currently live in them.[27] I have written elsewhere of the liminal space the Midlands provide as neither North nor South, evidenced by the placing of the foundational English story of Robin Hood in between Sherwood Forest and the City of Nottingham in the East Midlands.[28] Robin Hood, in whatever era his story is told, has remained a liminal or "in-between" figure, and I believe the story lands where it does as it is sufficiently far way from London (and north of the Fosse Way?) for him to get up to his subversive derring-do. This makes the River Trent perhaps a significant boundary between South and North, and it is no surprise that it formed the boundary of the Anglo-Saxon Kingdom of Northumbria and it virtually marks the limit of the Anglican Northern Province of York.

It is not quite as simple as this, however, since when discussing where the North is I notice people (alongside their engagement and animation with the subject) trying to negotiate away the question in interesting ways.

I have heard the following objections:

- "The North can't be defined as it is relative—for example, Sheffield is in the South if you are a Geordie"
- "There are massive regional and local variations in the North, so you can't lump it all together in one"
- "In any case, there is poverty and deprivation in the South too, so why are we just focusing on the North?"
- "While we are at it, there are plenty of places that are well off and more 'southern' while being in the North—just think of Harrogate!"
- "Or is it just an English class thing and much less to do with the geographical North?"

So I wonder, what is the cause of this seeming embarrassment about having to talk about the North? It is a real question given the energy it rouses, but is it the old English hypocrisy and "polite egalitarianism" asserting itself here?[29] Eventually though, I noticed if we stayed with the conversation, what emerges is something that we might call a "consciousness" of the North which contains all sorts of elements including geography but ranging much more widely into attitudes, values, and culture. A possibility might even emerge of understanding the North as a verb rather than a noun such that it is about a dynamic formation in the Northerner rather than some static geographical notion. There is fluidity and dynamism in the idea of the North which is not restricted to a specific place. Maconie agrees in his conclusion:

> I'm not sure that northernness is geographical. It's philosophical . . . northernness is a cast of mind, not a set of co-ordinates . . . It's about realising that the best place to drive a Range Rover is Cumbria not Islington. It's about embracing that life is short and work is hard and that London is not the answer to everything.[30]

We therefore come to a dynamic cultural understanding of the "North" which is geographically based, created through beliefs, attitudes, and values, and expressed in a myriad of ways.[31] It is important to note here, given this cultural understanding of the concept of the North, an axiom of anthropological study that *culture is always formed at its boundary.* An example might help: when the football team of my childhood city of Hull plays away outside of their home county, one of the chants they use against the opposition is "Yorkshire, Yorkshire!", yet, when they play Leeds, a whole other set of chants comes into play as what I call the "Samaria" effect takes hold. It seems the other who is just over the nearest border is often the most disliked, even hated. On the other hand, if people from Hull and Leeds found themselves in the South (or indeed Lancashire) they no doubt would quickly recover their common Yorkshire identity. The word *almost* in the opening chant at the top of this chapter is highly significant as with it the Hull fans still recognize their common English identity (all too well, perhaps!). Thus when we speak of the dynamic cultural understanding of the North we recognize that it is formed at its boundaries with recognizable internal differences within the North itself right down to a very local level.

2.4.   A NORTHERN CONTEXTUAL THEOLOGY

Clemens Sedmak, in his helpful book on developing local theology, offers fifty theses for this task.[32] He suggests that it is possible to work on both regional theology and "little theologies"—perhaps our task in this book lies somewhere between these two as follows:

> Thesis 37: Regional theologies try to do justice to the key features of a regional context. They pay special attention to key events, persons and features. Regional theologies look at the social realities in which people live and try to highlight the core constitutive elements of the regional social setting.
> Thesis 38: Little theologies are theologies made for a particular situation, taking particular circumstances into account, using local questions and concerns, local stories as their starting point. People should be able to recognize themselves in little theologies.[33]

So, taking our cue from Sedmak, we can begin to outline a northern theology. Once again, we recognize this as simply a beginning; much more will need to be said.

In terms of key events and persons, we can remember that the North has been the North since the Roman invasion took place from the south (and is the reason why Scotland is "somewhere else" since it was never conquered or "pacified" by the Romans). The North seems to take on a slightly different place and meaning when engaged from the west and north, as in the Irish mission and its influences, through Aidan, Cuthbert, and their companions, or when invaded from the east by the Vikings and Anglo-Saxons. The Normans re-establish the Roman pattern by invading from the South and very quickly "harrying" the North in 1069–70 in order to "pacify" it.[34] Historically, when the South has been dominant, as in the current era, the North has been used variously as a buffer zone to the far north (Scotland) or understood as a problem to be pacified.

More recent events must include the rapid industrialization of the North in the nineteenth century and its equally rapid decline in the twentieth. Perhaps the culmination of this was the 1984–5 Miner's strike and the subsequent closure of coal mining operations all over the North. Only Manchester, with perhaps Liverpool and Leeds not far behind, seems to have emerged from this period with any strength. One of Anthony Gormley's best known works of public art is the Angel of the North, placed strategically by the A1 motorway in the North East. He says this about it:

> Is it possible to make a work with purpose in a time that demands doubt? I wanted to make an object that would be a focus of hope at a painful time of transition for the people of the north-east, abandoned in the gap between the industrial and the information ages.
>
> The work is made of corten steel, weighs 200 tonnes and has 500 tonnes of concrete foundations. The mound near the A1 motorway which was the designated site of the sculpture was made after the closure of the Lower Tyne Colliery, out of the destroyed remains of the pithead baths. It is a tumulus marking the end of the era of coal mining in Britain.
>
> The Angel resists our post-industrial amnesia and bears witness to the hundreds and thousands of colliery workers who had spent the last three hundred years mining coal beneath the surface. The scale of the sculpture was essential given its site in a valley that is a mile and a half wide, and with an audience that was travelling past on the motorway at an average of 60 miles an hour.[35]

Here then is a first pointer to a theology of the North resonating with Croft's call for a theology of hope—that perhaps is now based on the sight of a transitional object offering hope of a post-industrial identity in the North.[36]

What then are the cultural distinctives that characterize the North? We noted some of these as delineated earlier by Bishop Steven in his chapter and we can add others. First, and at the expense of repetition, is a strong local identity over and against the other (both the South and the neighbour)—perhaps encapsulated by the Red Rose of the House of Lancaster, and therefore England, and the White Rose of Yorkists. At the same time, out of this sense of identity comes an openness, friendliness, and hospitality in which "what you see is what you get". Given the recent history of the growth and decline of industry, a grudging acceptance of authority alongside honesty, plain-speaking, and even bluntness is also emergent. The ability to work hard and to be careful with money—what is called "graft" and its companion thrift.[37] A pragmatic value placed on common sense, not over-complicating things. In these values is the giftedness of the North which can be understood as gospel, good news when contrasted over against any tendency to succumbing to the tragic narrative of the North that Croft refers to.

At the heart of the North-South divide is a mutual fear and suspicion encapsulated in the saying which presumably emanates from the South— "It's grim up North"—the other side of which is the Northern "chip on the shoulder". The sense of inferiority inherent in being from the North often provokes anger and dispute, just as on the occasion of an FA Cup final between a northern and a London team. To use the language and theory of Transactional Analysis, this could easily triangulate the Church as the "rescuer" between the persecuting South and victim of the North.[38] A transformation of the drama triangle takes place where the victim takes up a proper vulnerability, the persecutor offers their power and resources to the whole, and the rescuer takes responsibility for their own in-between position without attachment to either. The misplaced emotional energy of the chip on the shoulder can then be released to use the power and resources offered by those who have them to create something quite new and even beautiful. A robust gospel of reconciliation in the English Church will therefore be able to address the North-South divide. On the one hand, identity in Christ will raise the horizons of the Christian (this has been my own experience) while not denying culture and rootedness. I believe it is proper then for the Church to call for a "bias to the North" just as David Shepherd called for a bias to the poor in the 1980s.[39] This goes far beyond the subsidy to poorer Northern dioceses known as Ministry Support Funding from the Church Commissioners in London. Everyone knows money can't buy you love.[40]

So we come to the importance of another of Bevan's models of contextual theology—the praxis or liberation theology model. We have spent no little time describing and reflecting on the reasons for the North-South division in our nation which is also one of inequality in power, resources, and status. The gospel, it seems, is always on the side of the weak and vulnerable from Abel through to King David, and the second son in Jesus' story of the Prodigal Father (as it is alternatively known). If this is the case then there will be concrete action we can take in reconciliation between North and South. The tales of Robin Hood present a liminal figure standing between the rich and poor, the city and greenwood, the North and the South. As such they represent a latent hope of a fairer world (not unlike the Kingdom of God),[41] so the national Church might stand out as a body that is committed to advocacy for a fairer and more equal nation. She will need to model this in her own life.

A further aspect of a northern theology is a celebration of place, the local and the landscape. Jacob's experience of arriving in no particular place and it becoming Bethel, the house of God and gate of heaven (Genesis 28), combined with the Word being made flesh (John 1:14) makes every place a potential site of revelation. This is no less the case in the North than anywhere else, and perhaps more so. Is it really arrogant to claim Yorkshire as "God's own country" where "it's only a local call from here" as the joke goes? Perhaps not, if we can also understand every other place as blessed in the same way.

Finally, and perhaps arising from the landscape and the toughness of life for many northern people, is an ability to pay the "cost of discipleship"—to develop a spiritual robustness and toughness in the face of life's knocks and difficulties. Meeting with the Living God has never been something to be entered into lightly or without thought. It requires strength and courage along with straight talking. Perhaps this aspect of northernness elicits an aspect of the gospel that has been hidden for too long.

2.5. QUESTIONS FOR FURTHER DISCUSSION AND ACTION

Are there practical implications of this study and actions we might take as a result of this study to address the North-South divide both in Church and nation? Here is a list of initial suggestions offered mainly as questions for further discussion:

- Naming the issue—is there some evidence that simply bringing the question of the North out into the open brings the transforming light of Christ to it?[42]
- Where might we ask the question of how we can be biased to the North beyond Ministry Support Funding? What might vulnerability in the North in relation to the offering of the power and resource of the South look like?
- Some years ago there was a half-hearted attempt to "twin" Church of England dioceses together. Perhaps this fell foul of the "Samaria" effect. We are all very happy to partner with dioceses overseas. Could northern and southern dioceses develop meaningful relationships that allowed mutual celebration, learning, and challenge of each other?
- Why do we have two provinces? Is this an historical Christendom anomaly which is no longer actually useful for us a national church? What purpose does it serve? Of course if there were to be one province its seat would need to be somewhere other than Canterbury or York, and it could entrench the difference even further. However the BBC interestingly recently split its operations between London and Manchester, while remaining one organisation.
- What prophetic voice and action can we both offer and model to an increasingly divided nation?

NOTES

1. See above, p. 23.
2. Stephen B. Bevans, *Models of Contextual Theology,* Revised and Expanded Edition (Orbis, 2002), pp. 37ff.
3. Ibid., p. 42.
4. See above, p. 23.
5. Ibid., p. 43.
6. Andrew Davison and Alison Milbank, *For the Parish: A Critique of Fresh Expressions* (SCM, 2010), pp. 1–27.
7. Nigel Rooms, *The Faith of the English: Integrating Christ and Culture* (SPCK, 2011), p. 11.
8. Andrew F. Walls, "The Gospel as Prisoner and Liberator of Culture" in James A. Scherer and Stephen B. Bevans (eds.), *New Directions in Mission and Evangelization 3: Faith and Culture* (Orbis, 1999), pp. 17–28.
9. Lamin Sanneh, *Translating the Message—The Missionary Impact on Culture* (Orbis, 1989).
10. Sanneh, *Translating the Message,* p. 53.
11. Walls, "The Gospel as Prisoner", p. 21 (both quotations).
12. Rooms, *Faith of the English,* p. 12.
13. Stephen B. Bevans and Roger P. Schroeder, *Constants in Context: A Theology of Mission for Today* (Orbis, 2004), pp. 35–37.
14. Bevans and Schroeder, *Constants in Context,* p. 297.
15. Vincent J. Donovan, *Christianity Rediscovered: An Epistle from the Masai* (SCM, 1978).
16. Bevans, *Models of Contextual Theology,* pp. 65–69.
17. Anton Wessels, *Europe: Was it ever really Christian? The Interaction between Gospel and Culture* (SCM, 1994).
18. Malcolm Lambert, *Christians and Pagans: The Conversion of Britain from Alban to Bede* (Yale University Press, 2010).
19. I am using the term Christendom here in a slightly narrower sense than the dictionary definition of a place or time where the majority of people are Christian, to mean that period either where Christianity is the State-sponsored religion of the Roman Empire, which implies in most cases varying amounts of coercion for the people to be Christian, or where the prevailing culture (often dictated by the State) encourages regular Christian worship from citizens.

20. John Finney, *Recovering the Past: Celtic and Roman Mission* (DLT, 1996).
21. Lambert, *Christians and Pagans*, p. 139. Even Patrick had been preceded by an earlier Papal mission under Palladius—see ibid., p. 135.
22. James D. G. Dunn (ed.), *The Kingdom of God and North-East England* (SCM, 1986).
23. Paul Morley, *The North (and almost everything in it)* (Bloomsbury, 2013).
24. Stuart Maconie, *Pies and Prejudice: In Search of the North* (Ebury Press/ Random House, 2007).
25. On 7 October 2014, in the presence of Steve Bevans himself, we engaged with the topic of this chapter with around 25 mission thinkers and practitioners from around UK. On 26 November 2014 in Leeds, we discussed northern vocations with representatives from every Anglican diocese in the Northern Province.
26. Mike Ibeji, "An Overview of Roman Britain", at <http://www.bbc.co.uk/ history/ancient/romans/questions_01.shtml> (accessed 31 December 2014).
27. At this stage it is probably worth pointing out my own reflexivity in this study. I was born of one local, northern and one southern parent and raised on the outskirts of Hull in the East Riding of Yorkshire until 18 years of age. I attended the University in Leeds, which was about as far as my horizons reached at that stage. A working visit to South Africa at the age of 20 helped me discover my Englishness, and I have not returned to Hull, apart from an annual trip to watch the football team and visit family, since turning 21. I thus find myself in between North and South in all sorts of ways.
28. Rooms, *Faith of the English*, pp. 73–92.
29. Ibid., p. 48.
30. Maconie, *Pies and Prejudice*, p. 337.
31. It is, therefore, possible to have a northern mind-set in Devon, as pointed out in Maconie, *Pies and Prejudice*, p. 337.
32. Clemens Sedmak, *Doing Local Theology: A Guide for Artisans of a New Humanity* (Orbis, 2002).
33. Sedmak, *Local Theology*, p. 111 and p. 119.
34. Historically, there is some dispute as to how severe the harrying was; the memory it left, however, was deep enough for the pain and hurt to linger for many centuries, even perhaps until today. See Robert Wilde, "The Harrying of the North, 1069–70", <http://europeanhistory.about.com/od/ NormanConquest/a/The-Harrying-Of-The-North-1069-70.htm> (accessed

6 January 2015), and the brief discussion in Wakefield, "The Ebb and Flow of Power", pp. 61–62 of this volume.

35. Anthony Gormley, "Angel of the North, 1998", <http://www.antonygormley.com/sculpture/item-view/id/211> (accessed 5 September 2014).

36. The angel, in Christian theology, negotiates the boundary of heaven and earth from the perspective of the place of hope—heaven. In addition, like many of Gormley's sculptures, the Angel is deliberately made to rust over time thus underlining its transitional nature.

37. A joke I heard in Nottinghamshire (which borders on Yorkshire on its northern edge) goes like this: "Why does Notts have the greater claim on Robin Hood over those Yorkies?", "It's obvious—if Robin Hood had been a Yorkshireman he would have taken from the rich and kept the money!"

38. This might be a further reason for the reluctance I have experienced to speak about and name the North, lest we simply get lost in the emotions associated with the subject.

39. David Shepherd, *Bias to the Poor* (Hodder and Stoughton, 1983).

40. It is worth noting an encouraging recognition of the needs of poorer dioceses in terms of financial and human resourcing in the various Anglican Review reports, such as *Resourcing Ministerial Education* (GS1979) published in 2015.

41. Rooms, *Faith of the English*, p. 92.

42. A conversation I had with Matthew Porter, Vicar of St Michael Le Belfry in York, at the Vocations Day Conference revealed the naming of the North in their vision statement: "To play our part in Serving God's Transformation of the North." This has had an impact, at the very least, on vocations to ministry in the North.

3. INHERITED STORIES: GROWING UP GEORDIE AND CHRISTIAN

Catherine Pickford

My first encounter with the Angel of the North was when I was in my early 20s, travelling by train from Cambridge to Newcastle. I did not know the North East, and was on my way to be interviewed for a curacy in a Newcastle suburb. The Angel was a shock, a formidable mixture of man and machine glowering brownly over a landscape he claimed as his own, with a fierceness which was almost malign. I suddenly wondered what I was doing here, with my student rucksack and my Yorkshire vowels. What could the proud, industrial people of the North East possibly want with me?

Despite my early stand-off with the Angel, I did move to Newcastle and it has been my home for 14 years. I met my husband here and we have had three Geordie children. I never had cause to examine my continued uneasy relationship with the Angel until last summer. We were returning by coach from the annual parish outing. As the Angel came into view, one of the men on the bus put his arm round our eldest son Jack, who was six, pointed to the Angel, and said, "There he is lad. You see him, you know you are home." This was a significant moment for Jack and something he referred to several times afterwards. I think he had been made to feel very grown up and accepted as a Geordie male. The incident has led Jack to have the special relationship with the Angel which many Geordies share. Jack's and my different reactions to him made me reflect on what it means to belong to a region. The guardian angel looks very different, depending on where you are standing. Is he warning you off, or welcoming you home?

Regional identity is an elusive thing. Some people live in a place all their lives and never feel that it is home. Others live somewhere for a relatively short space of time and it already feels part of who they are. Geordies have several advantages when it comes to "catching" regional identity. The first is that "Geordie" is a well-known and established description of the people of this part of the North East. Geordie celebrities like Ant and Dec and Cheryl Cole celebrate their local identity. The comedian Sarah Millican has almost made a career out of being a Geordie. Having a football team in the Premiership is also a great source of pride. There is a prevailing sense here that to be a Geordie is something to be proud of.

Second, Geordie is not just an accent, it is a dialect. There are Geordie words which are actually used, not just in books about the history of the region. Geordie songs like the "Blaydon Races" and "Cushy Butterfield" are known and sung, celebrating the inherited memories of the region.

Third, geography is a friend to Geordie identity. Newcastle is a long way from London, and any other major city, and so is a centre for a wide geographical area. People from all over the North East come to Newcastle to shop, work, and be entertained. The city of Newcastle provides a vital core to the Geordie region.

Finally, Geordies are drawn together by adversity. The parts of the Geordie story which get told most frequently reflect a sense of struggling against the odds, and often against the stronger and richer South: the Jarrow march, when the people of the North East walked all the way to London to campaign for fairer pay, the fact that the famous coal from Newcastle lined the pockets of the London traders much more than the Newcastle workers, the miners' strike, the closure of the ship yards, and most recently, the disproportionately large cuts made to the budget of Newcastle city council by central government.

All of these things, the dialect and songs, distance from London, regional pride, and stories of uniting in adversity work together to make the Geordie sense of regional identity very strong.

So what is it like to grow up a Geordie and a Christian? I asked this question of the Sunday school of St James' Benwell, in inner city Newcastle, where I am Rector. The children found it impossible to answer because, as someone pointed out, they don't know what it would be like to be anything else. A particularly thoughtful nine-year-old said that, although she could not answer the question, she would like to tell me her favourite Bible story. It was the one where Jesus says it is easier for a camel to get through the eye of a needle than a rich man to enter the kingdom of God. I asked her what she thought it meant and she said, "People who are rich and powerful have to take it off to get into heaven." So she chose, above all the others, a story in which Jesus speaks of the personal cost of power and wealth. She had begun to articulate key similarities between the gospel stories and the stories of her region. I also wonder whether the way she chose to address the question was significant. Perhaps regions steeped in stories tend to produce storytellers, skilled in absorbing and understanding stories of faith and history.

Adult Geordie Christians often possess a tenacity born, in many ways, out of their regional identity and faith. In Benwell, there were riots in the 1990s which were so serious they hit the national press and threatened to destroy the community. The congregation of St James' responded by planting a community project at the heart of the worst affected estate. The planning group received threats of violence from some sections of the community and many people thought they should start the project in a safer area. Pat Young, one of the group, recalls, "We were scared, but we asked ourselves, where would Jesus choose to be? We thought he would want to be alongside the people on that estate, who were suffering the worst of the violence." That sense in many Geordie Christians, that struggle is an accepted and acceptable part of life, often creates characters of great resilience, able to face opposition, doubt, and fear, and do it anyway.

4. THE EBB AND FLOW OF POWER: STORIES TOLD ABOUT THE NORTHERN CHURCH IN MISSION

Gavin Wakefield

Retelling the story of the Christian faith in the North of England is second nature to many of us: the essays in this book were not deliberately intended to have strong historical references yet time and again the authors have felt the need to make historical connections explicit. There is a long history of both faith in the North and of a sense of difference to the South, and so a book like this needs an historical chapter, exploring which histories are remembered and retold.

Recent political rhetoric seeking to better balance economic development across the country has used the term "northern powerhouse" to encapsulate what this might mean.[1] Highlighting the term "power" reveals it to be a longstanding and multi-faceted theme in the history of northern England. The North was the battleground for power between the Roman Empire and "barbarian" northerners and the locus of power for successive Anglo-Saxon overlords in the seventh century. In the medieval period, much of that power moved south, the northern border with Scotland suffering constant dispute. In the modern period, it saw the birth of the Industrial Revolution powered by new machines, the demise of heavy industry in the twentieth century with the loss of power in several senses, and now the desire to create a "northern powerhouse".

This essay takes a broad concept of power as a lens through which to view some of the history of the Church's mission in the North. It does so in three movements: first, the period of political power in the seventh century when Christianity became deeply established and was associated with the ruling classes of the Anglo-Saxons, and in the work of Bede with his proposition of an English nation under God. The second and third movements are dealt with more briefly: in the second movement we touch on periods when political and economic power and influence were lost and the Church needed a new direction, referring to the renewal of monasticism and its aftermath in the sixteenth-century Reformation and especially the rebellion of the Pilgrimage of Grace. In the third, the subject is the challenge to the Church of the Industrial Revolution, changing social structures, and, above all, the rapid growth of large cities. In each movement, it is in the stories that continue to be told that we find evidence of identity in the North rather than in precise detail. Stories of the Church are not the only ones told in the region, but some remain very powerful reminders of history and are referenced in popular culture, not just academic treatises.

As the Introduction to this book discusses, the boundaries of "the North" are not fixed or agreed. In this account, I take it to be the area from Chester and Yorkshire (roughly the southern boundary of the old kingdom of Northumbria) northwards to the Scottish border. This gives some coherence to the early part of the story, referring to Aidan, Cuthbert, and their followers. Periods of violent disruption such as the Viking raids and settlements, the Norman Conquest and the harrying of the North, and later the dissolution of the monasteries all impacted this region in distinctive ways and often more deeply than in the South of England. My choosing of these stories was done independently of Nigel Rooms, and yet he has also referenced an almost identical list.

In recent centuries coherence has been found in significant centres of industrialization which reinforced one another: the proximity of water supplies, coal, iron ore, and developing transport infrastructure all played into this, leading to the North of England being at the heart of the industrial world in the nineteenth century, though of course never to the exclusion of other major centres in Britain and beyond. The approximate southern boundary of this region is still seen in the importance of the "M62

Corridor" stretching from Liverpool in the west, via Manchester, Bradford, and Leeds, to Hull in the east, linking what were major industrial centres.

So how has the Church in northern England lived with this ebb and flow of power? What are the stories which still make sense of the history today?

4.1.   POWERBASE: A GOLDEN AGE?

A major strand in the identity of northern England, and especially the North East, is found in its Christian heritage: the Holy Island of Lindisfarne, Durham Cathedral,[2] and York Minster are among the most visited and loved sites in the whole country, and help to shape both self-understanding within the region and perceptions from outside it. Cuthbert, the seventh-century monk-bishop of Lindisfarne, now buried at Durham, was long regarded as the pre-eminent saint of the Anglo-Saxon period. The Lindisfarne Gospels, made in his honour on Holy Island, have national and international significance and remain a source of pride for the North East. The mid-seventh century to mid-eighth century has often been described as Northumbria's Golden Age in both promotional literature and more serious works of historical interpretation.[3]

Taking the issue of identity further, it is worth noting that the North West and North East government regions had the highest levels of reported Christian affiliation in England in the 2011 Census, at over 67 per cent, well above the national average of 59 per cent, though paradoxically alongside some of the lowest rates of churchgoing, especially for the Church of England.[4] Bringing together the issues of heritage and self-identity suggests that part of the way into finding a gospel for the North of England is to look at its origins and to see how this continues to influence people today.

The earliest history of Christianity in this most northerly frontier of the Roman Empire remains elusive. Even in the south of the Roman province, clear evidence for Christianity is sparse, and in the north it is even more so: for example, we know of a bishop of York in AD 314,[5] but not the name of another until 625.[6] Recently uncovered archaeological evidence has suggested the existence of a late fourth-century church at the garrison of Vindolanda (just south of Hadrian's Wall) and, at Binchester, a Christian ring has been found from the third century, but these are rare and limited finds.[7]

It is likely that Christianity hung on in the lives of Romano-British people after the ending of the Roman Empire in Britain, though many of the structures which had supported this faith were diminished. There was, for example, enough energy in this British Christianity for Patrick to evangelize Ireland.[8] Augustine, the missionary bishop sent to England by Pope Gregory in 596, began his mission supporting the Frankish Christian princess Bertha in her marriage to the pagan king of Kent, Ethelbert. Augustine encountered British bishops in a meeting misunderstood by both sides,[9] and he was instructed to send a bishop to York,[10] presumably on the grounds that this was known to be an ancient centre of government and church.

A generation later, Paulinus was sent from Canterbury to York to be the chaplain and bishop for Ethelberga, daughter of Ethelbert and Bertha; here again we find a Christian princess marrying a pagan king, Edwin, king of the Northumbrians.[11] As had happened at Canterbury, the arrival and then adoption of Christianity were bound up in marriage alliances and political considerations; as kingdoms were secured in this period, kings widened their understanding of kingship by drawing on at least three external and prestigious exemplars, namely the Roman Emperor, Merovingian kings,[12] and Hebrew monarchs. The historian Kenneth Hylson-Smith noted that the need to develop "a distinctly Christian concept of kingship was one key to the future establishment and consolidation of the Christian faith throughout the length and breadth of the land".[13]

Ethelbert and Edwin feature in Bede's list of English overlords, third and fifth respectively.[14] Both kings had personal and dynastic reasons for converting to Christianity: they each chose to marry a Christian princess from a powerful royal family, knowing that doing so would mostly likely imply a change of religion, contrary to the opposition of some of their supporters. In Edwin's case, it took a complicated sequence including an assassination attempt, the premature birth of his and Ethelberga's child, and victory in battle against the West Saxon perpetrators of the assassination attempt before he was baptized at York on Easter Day 627.[15]

In 633 Edwin was killed in battle against Mercian pagans and Christian Britons, and the Anglo-Saxon Christians were attacked, many of them fleeing south.[16] In the confusion that resulted the upper hand was eventually won by Oswald, a member of a rival branch of the ruling family. Oswald had been baptized on Iona while in exile (Edwin had killed his father) and, after winning the battle of Heavenfield, he turned to Iona for missionaries.[17] The introduction of the Irish-based mission led by Aidan from Lindisfarne highlighted differences in religious practice in the Church of the seventh century, nowadays caricatured as a clash between Celtic and Roman visions of Christianity and of how to see the world. While much modern comment on the Synod of Whitby overstates its significance,[18] it does represent something of a power struggle between rival visons and understandings, with king Oswy of Northumbria making himself the arbitrator for outcome in his kingdom. The benefit to Oswy, brother of Oswald (and both of them also on Bede's list of overlords), was described by Bede in religious terms: aligning himself with Peter who holds the keys to the gates of heaven, but Oswy also was aware of the political benefits associated with links to Rome and the continental Church.

The results of the Synod were mixed: many on the Irish side in the debate chose to leave the region and return to what they saw as their motherhouse on Iona, and others went to Ireland. But others stayed and sought to integrate the Irish and Roman interpretations of Christianity, including exemplary characters such as Hilda, Chad, and Cuthbert. This opened the way to glories such as the Lindisfarne Gospels with their multiplicity of influences[19] and the international scholarship of Bede,[20] and helped to trigger the energetic missionary zeal of Anglo-Saxon Christians across England and northern Europe.

Throughout much of this "Golden Age", the kingdom of Northumbria was a major—and perhaps *the*—powerbase of the emerging English nation, in which political and spiritual power were intertwined. Politically, three kings who ruled from 616 to 670, Edwin, Oswald, and Oswy, were described by Bede as overlords of lands both north and south of the Humber, other than Kent. The exact nature of this overlordship, called *bretwaldas* in the ninth-century Anglo-Saxon Chronicle, is unclear and still disputed,[21] but, alongside the complex intermarriage of royal houses across the country, it suggests that authority over a wide area was more than nominal.[22] The wealth of Northumbria at this time is evident in the resources devoted to building churches and monasteries, and in producing artefacts like the Lindisfarne Gospels and the Codex Amiatinus at the Wearmouth-Jarrow monastery.

Spiritual power lay most obviously with bishops and the more important abbots, most of whom (possibly all) were from aristocratic backgrounds. It is likely that Bede, a monk of Wearmouth-Jarrow upon whom we depend for much of our knowledge, was also from a similar background, given his concentration on the conversion of the upper strata of his society and his familiarity with them.[23] Leading figures in the Church (such as Cuthbert, Wilfrid, Hilda, abbots like Benedict Biscop and Ceolfrith, and scholars like Bede and later Alcuin of York) were part of an elite cohort that spread its influence not just to other parts of Anglo-Saxon Britain but also across Western Europe, either through their own physical journeys or via correspondence.

The intertwining of political and spiritual power is well illustrated by the Synod of Whitby. Although it was but one of a sequence of Synods in the British Isles resolving issues between the Roman and "Celtic" Churches, it did hold some extra significance , being convened by King Oswy when he was overlord. Other kingdoms will have noted the decision to follow Roman customs. The flow of spiritual power and leadership was not all one way: the importance of Theodore of Tarsus, archbishop of Canterbury from 668–690, in bringing order and harmony to the Church in England following the Synod of Whitby is hard to overstate. But to achieve this he needed to travel to the North and engage with the leaders of the Church in the region, for example, dedicating a church on Lindisfarne, an event recorded by Bede at the start of his long chapter on the Synod.[24]

Does all this long-ago history matter today? The plethora of books, retreats, pilgrimages, and videos on the (exaggerated) conflict between Roman and Irish Christianity suggests people still look back this era for inspiration. The admiration and affection for sites such as Durham and Lindisfarne, York and Whitby, suggest that identity is still bound up in some way with the people that made these places significant; their stories continue to be told. Regional identity, most strikingly in the North East, but diffusing through much of the wider region here called the North of England, still draws on these elements of its Christian origins.

4.2.   POWER LOSS

This section covers a 1,000 year period in a similar number of words: its purpose is therefore not a detailed account but to note other layers of history which have shaped the story of the northern Church in ways that are somewhat distinct from the South of England.

The end of the "Golden Age" was followed by many centuries in which the main centres of political and religious power across England shifted south. The Viking invasions, beginning at Lindisfarne in 793, led to a period in which political power shifted from the by now established Anglian rulers to Vikings, especially in the north and east of what was becoming England. The new centre of power became the kingdom of Wessex, most prominently under Alfred and his successors. The Church did not disappear in the North, but it was considerably weakened and the formerly strong network of monasteries was largely wiped out. A revival in the tenth century led to a new network of monasteries, but another wave of Danish attacks meant that, by around 1000, there were no regular monasteries north of the River Trent. The uneven distribution of religious houses across England mapped the reality of Anglo-Saxon royal power.[25] A few collegiate churches remained in the North, most notably the Community of St Cuthbert, based around his shrine established in Durham in 995, and there was a scattering of minster churches, but there were none of the monasteries renewed by a stricter observance of their monastic rule to be found further south.

Assessing the impact of the Norman Conquest led by William in 1066 is notoriously difficult: to what extent was it a radical break with the past? How far were institutions allowed to continue and develop? For the purposes of this essay, let it suffice to say that leadership in Church and state clearly passed to Normans. Anglo-Saxon priests continued to work in parishes, overseen at a considerable social and political gulf by Norman bishops. This was true throughout England. Of special note here is the series of uprisings in Yorkshire and Durham from 1067–69, and William's decision to engage in what many have called genocide over the winter of 1069–70. The harrying (or harrowing) of the North left whole villages burnt to the ground, populations forced off their land or slaughtered, and fields salted so they would be unproductive for years to come. The exact magnitude of the devastation remains unclear, but the account has endured as part of the long story the region tells of itself. A contemporary example of its shocking effect is seen in the story of a Norman knight Reinfrid: having seen the destruction at first hand, he left soldiering to become a monk. Encountering refugees fleeing south to the safety of his monastery in Evesham, he returned north, eventually helping to re-found monasteries on ancient Anglo-Saxon sites, including at Whitby.[26]

In the centuries that followed there was a renewal of church life throughout the North, beginning with an energetic building programme under the Normans and leading to the re-establishing of monastic life across the region, and a transparent assertion of their power. Great parish churches and large-scale monasteries were developed, exceeding anything imagined by the Anglo-Saxons in the previous millennium. The story of the next 400 years and more is not uneventful, but Church life was brought into line with wider trends in England and the rest of Western Europe. The region's northern border with Scotland saw regular fighting, but the religious context was similar on either side of the shifting border.

It was the Reformation of the sixteenth century, and especially the English version of the Reformation, which saw a period of profound disjuncture between much of the North and the South, or more accurately between those against or in favour of the reform. The desire of Henry VIII for a male heir, concerns about Papal corruption, and theological scruples about Church teaching all became bound up with the benefits to the king of transferring power and wealth from the Church to direct royal control. The suppression of some monasteries, beginning in 1536 in England, was not unique to this period or to England, indeed Henry and his advisers were probably inspired by what they knew was happening across northern Europe. However, the scale and speed of closures in what became known as the Dissolution of the Monasteries was unprecedented. In many parts of the North the local economy and provision of welfare via schools and hospitals for ordinary folk were highly dependent on the effective functioning of monasteries. Discontent at changes in religious practice in parish churches together with the first closures of monasteries led to an uprising in Louth, Lincolnshire in October 1536, and within days this spread north to the Humber and across into the East Riding of Yorkshire.

Over the next few months commoners and gentry were caught up in an increasingly violent protest, under the leadership of Robert Aske.[27] This series of uprisings, which became known as the Pilgrimage of Grace, came close to defeating the king's forces, when 30,000 "rebels" confronted 10,000 of the king's men near Doncaster at the end of October 1536. Men had arrived from both sides of the Pennines ready to fight for the "old religion" but desperate negotiations from the king's side prevented a battle, and gradually Henry regained the initiative through a combination of false promises and harsh punishments, including mass executions. This was not the only religiously inspired rebellion faced by a Tudor monarch,[28] but it was the most serious in Henry's reign and the one that came closest to toppling him. It led him to impose excessive cruelty and punishments across the northern counties, and a speeding up of the monastic closures, even when there was no evidence of involvement in the uprising.[29]

Does it still matter? Rather like the harrying of the North, the story continues to be told in the region in local histories and it is given a place in school history teaching.[30] In both the school syllabus and the popular local accounts, there is a recognition of economic, political, and religious causes in the rebellion which can resonate with some twenty-first-century concerns about the centralization of economic and political power. More broadly, it may be interpreted as an example of the tension between conservatism and innovation in periods of rapid change: there was loss of power among the gentry as Henry centralised political power, while common people resented religious changes imposed by far off authorities. It is precisely the difference in attitude to the Reformation between much of the south-east of England and the peripheries, especially the North, that makes this episode an important part of the overall story. The strength in the North in later centuries of the recusant and then emancipated Roman Catholic Church was only partly a result of large scale migration; it also had deep roots in the resistance of the commoners and gentry in the sixteenth century.

4.3.   POWER SURGE: THE CHALLENGE OF
THE INDUSTRIAL REVOLUTION

Passing over the religious wars of the seventeenth century, it is important to remember the huge changes in society brought about by the Industrial Revolution of the eighteenth and nineteenth centuries. While much of the northern landscape was, and continues to be, more rural than in other parts of England, the bulk of the population shifted to urbanized and industrialized areas in the course of these centuries. An extreme example of population growth was Manchester which experienced a six-fold increase in its population between 1771 and 1831.

There is not space here to give a detailed account of the response of the Churches to industrialization in the North, for each place has its own particularities as well as commonalties. Some of the nuanced differences between towns and denominations, and over time, are detailed by Robin Gill, demonstrating the complexity of making sweeping comments about the growth and decline of the Churches.[31]

However, the usual tale that is told is of the failure of the Church of England to keep pace with an urbanizing England, in contrast to the relative progress of other Churches, especially the Methodists amongst artisans and the Roman Catholics amongst the immigrant populations in, for example, Lancashire and Middlesbrough. One version of this tale goes: "When did the Church of England lose the working classes?" Answer: "It never had them."

On the whole, I agree with this assessment. The impact of being a largely rural Church is still being felt two hundred years on. According to a recent report on the rural Church :

> Rural parishes make up two-thirds of the Church of England (there are 10,199 rural church buildings), almost all of which are within multi-church groups of varying sizes and structures. 42 per cent of clergy serve rural parishes. Using the measure of average weekly attendance, 40 per cent attend parishes in rural communities.[32]

This large preponderance of parishes serves the less than 18 per cent of the present population that live in these rural areas. This imbalance in the locations of the assets, both people and buildings, of a Church that aspires to serve every community is true across England. It has a particular resonance in the North where many of the industrial cities grew in the nineteenth century and the Church of England struggled. How does the Church show faith with its rural heartland and yet fulfil its sense of calling to the large populations living in towns and cities?[33]

And yet this is not the whole story. The detailed work of Robin Gill also shows that some of the time the Church of England did grow churches in towns during periods of industrialization, not just in absolute numbers but remarkably as a proportion of the burgeoning populations. Unusually good data on church attendance from the first half of the nineteenth century is available from Visitation returns in the diocese of Chester, which at the time included the growing cities of Liverpool and Manchester and rural areas in Lancashire and the south of Cumberland. Using this data Gill has shown that the familiar story of the Church of England's urban failure is not entirely accurate. When taken across denominations, rates of church attendance were similar in rural districts, large towns, and conurbations (meaning Liverpool and Manchester). The rates of church attendance increased slightly between 1821 and 1851, at a time when the large towns doubled in population and Liverpool and Manchester tripled. Finally, even in the large cities, attendance in the Church of England in 1851 was a little higher than all the Free Churches combined, reversing the position of 1821.[34]

Gill describes what lay behind these figures as "an extraordinary burst of energy across denominations".[35] Chester had the fastest growing population of any diocese in England,, from less than 87,000 people in 1801 to almost two and half million by 1851. At one stage Manchester was a single parish with a population of 200,000 people. So what happened?

Certainly there was growth through the stimulus of evangelicalism but alongside this went structural changes initiated by the visionary Bishop of Chester, John Bird Sumner. In his first Charge to the clergy of his diocese in 1829 he noted there "are many who imagine, that if the people are not in the established churches, they are in the dissenting chapels, and are therefore not destitute of religious instruction. The truth is not so . . .

The mass of the ADULT manufacturing population is, in point of fact, without religious instruction of any kind."[36]

Over the next 20 years he set in place structural changes which still sound familiar: systematic lay visitations, home instruction in the Christian faith, and the building of many more churches and schools for the population. Sumner was convinced that what today we call church planting was essential to cope with the rapid growth in population. The figures back him up: in town after town he saw churchgoing multiply many times over, even increasing faster than the population. He recognized that, for some people, churchgoing might be a big leap, so he argued that a school-room might be "an important step between the indifference which is too general among the working classes, especially of a town population, and an established habit of church-going. It is at first a substitute for the church, to those who either could not enter one for want of seat-room, or would not, from long habit of neglect."[37]

Structural change and imaginative leadership from Sumner—as a bishop he was certainly able to exercise power—provided a framework within which devoted clergy worked hard in appalling conditions, but did see fruit from their labours. James Boddy was a typical clergyman of the early nineteenth century, reading Classics at Cambridge, but deeply influenced by the evangelical movement. He was inspired by William Carey's book on working for the conversion of "the Heathens" to write his own book on mission in the cities of England.[38] He was one of Sumner's new clergy, placed in the poor parish of Red Banks, Cheetham in 1844, to grow a new church amongst the people drawn to the city. He lived and worked for 27 years in a parish of slums and polluted air and water, growing the church and bringing up a family of three boys.[39]

This uplifting story is told against a backdrop in which church attendance has since mostly declined across the country. The energy and vision of Sumner and those like him was insufficient to deal with the intellectual and social changes taking place. Too little attention was paid to structural issues in the ordering of the Church of England and church growth tended to be isolated, sporadic and little understood.

Although we do not face that level of population growth in northern England today, we inherit large industrial and post-industrial cities where parish populations are many times larger than the rural ones, making the building of relationships much more difficult. A significant part of Sumner's strategy was to substantially increase the personnel available for mission, both clergy and lay, in order to create many more opportunities for personal relationships. This insight has been re-discovered in cities around the world as churches develop small groups in which people can find identity and belonging in the midst of anonymity on a vast scale. It remains an important lesson for us.

4.4. SOME EMERGING THEMES

In re-telling these stories and connecting them to issues of power and powerlessness, what themes emerge? From each movement I have picked just one theme that emerges for me together with questions to ponder:

- The power exercised by the kings of Northumbria and used by early Church leaders has given rise to a longstanding sense of regional identity. Within it there is both the exercise and subversion of power: kings who fought battles in the name of Christ and clergy, nuns and monks who deliberately gave away power and possessions and yet gained huge influence by their example.

  What are our contemporary uses of power and what can we let go of by way of example? How does the Church do mission now that Christendom has crumbled, a new situation in England?

- The relative loss of power in the medieval period highlights the tensions that arise in periods of rapid change, tensions between conservatism and innovation in religion and social structures, tensions between North and South, and developing tensions between urban and rural worldviews.

  In situations of loss of power today, how do we provide proper support for one another, retaining the dignity of all, whatever their economic position?

- The development of power in the industrial sense was combined with the shift to an urban world, where individuals lived in very differently shaped and sized communities. The old ideas of power and social structure were overturned.

  As we now shift to a post-industrial and networked world of services and information, how do we share power and resources?

NOTES

1. The Chancellor George Osborne seems to be the originator of the term but it has gained wider acceptance as a useful phrase, especially since the May 2015 General Election. <https://www.gov.uk/government/speeches/chancellor-we-need-a-northern-powerhouse> (accessed 8 March 2015).

2. See the chapter by Michael Sadgrove for a reflection on the place of Durham Cathedral; below, pp. 179–198.

3. For example, Jane Hawkes and Susan Mills (eds.), *Northumbria's Golden Age* (Sutton Pub, 1999).

4. <http://www.ons.gov.uk/ons/rel/census/2011-census/key-statistics-for-local-authorities-in-england-and-wales/rpt-religion.html#tab-Religious-affiliation-across-the-English-regions-and-Wales> accessed 2/1/15, and <https://www.churchofengland.org/media/2112070/2013statisticsformission.pdf> p. 21 (accessed 5 March 2015).

5. Kenneth Hylson-Smith, *Christianity in England from Roman Times to the Reformation* (SCM, 1999), p. 54.

6. *EH* II 9.

7. For Vindolanda excavations, see <http://www.vindolanda.com/Default.aspx?PageID=13621443&A=SearchResult&SearchID=1782556&ObjectID=13621443&ObjectType=1>; for Binchester, see David Petts' blog, <http://binchester.blogspot.co.uk/2014/07/binchester-2014-early-christianity-at.html> (accessed 14 July 2015).

8. See Thomas O'Loughlin, *Discovering Saint Patrick* (DLT, 2005) for a readable and careful examination of this British Christian.

9. *EH* II 2.
10. Ibid., I 29.
11. Ibid., II 9.
12. Though they fluctuated greatly over this period, the lands of the Merovingian kings encompassed much of modern France.
13. Hylson-Smith, *Christianity in England*, p. 109.
14. *EH* II 5.
15. As recounted in substantial detail in EH II 9–14.
16. Ibid., II 20.
17. Ibid., III 2–3.
18. I have written a short polemical essay on this; see Gavin Wakefield, *Holy Places, Holy People* (Lion Hudson, 2008), pp. 123–6.
19. Michelle Brown, *The Lindisfarne Gospels* (The British Library, 2003) analyses the many influences in considerable detail.
20. Clare Stancliffe, "British and Irish Contexts", in Scott DeGregorio (ed.), *The Cambridge Companion to Bede* (Cambridge University Press, 2010), pp. 69–83.
21. The difficulties are well set out by Patrick Wormald in an essay somewhat dismissive of the usefulness of the term *bretwalda*; Patrick Wormwald, *The Times of Bede* (Blackwell, 2006), pp. 106–34.
22. James Campbell, "Secular and Political Contexts", in DeGregorio, *Companion to Bede*, pp. 27–8.
23. Ibid., pp. 25–6.
24. *EH* III 25.
25. Janet Burton, *Monastic and Religious Orders in Britain, 1000–1300* (Cambridge University Press, 1994), pp. 4–5.
26. A short account of his life can be found in Wakefield, *Holy Places, Holy People,* pp. 117–8.
27. The event is well told in Geoffrey Moorhouse, *The Pilgrimage of Grace* (Weidenfeld & Nicolson, 2002).
28. The wonderfully evocative account in Eamon Duffy, *The Voices of Morebath* (Yale, 2001) includes a significant West Country rising against the 1549 Prayer Book in the reign of Edward VI.
29. Moorhouse gives details of suppressions in Yorkshire, Northumberland, Lancashire, and Westmoreland; Moorhouse, *The Pilgrimage of Grace* pp. 278–308.

30. For example, an internet search finds plenty of support for A-level students, as well as local information, especially in the East Riding of Yorkshire.

31. Robin Gill, *The 'Empty' Church Revisited* (Ashgate, 2003). Many of his case studies come from northern England, including Cumbria, Lancashire, Liverpool, Manchester, Sheffield, Hull, Newcastle-upon-Tyne, and especially York; see Gill, *'Empty' Church Revisited, passim,* and the tables of data at pp. 220–236.

32. "Growing the Rural Church" (Archbishop's Council, GS Misc 1092, 2015), p. 5.

33. The chapter by John Thomson wrestles with these questions in more detail; see below, pp 93–104.

34. Gill provides extensive detail in figures and narrative; see Gill, *Empty Church Revisited*, pp. 71–80, with tables on pp. 222–3.

35. Gill, *Empty Church Revisited*, p. 86.

36. John Bird Sumner, *Charges Addressed to the Clergy of the Diocese of Chester,* (Hatchard & Son, 1841), 1.96, cited in Gill, *Empty Church Revisited*, p. 86.

37. Sumner, *Charges*, 4.62, cited in Gill *Empty Church*, p. 88.

38. James Boddy, *The Christian Mission* (William Smith, 1838).

39. His ministry and the context of Manchester is described in Gavin Wakefield, *Alexander Boddy* (Authentic Media, 2007), pp. 4–13.

5. THE SPIRIT LEVEL AND DEUTERONOMY: EVOKING A MISSIOLOGICAL CONVERSATION

John Wigfield

This article responds to a presentation given at a recent conference by Professor Kate Pickett of the University of York,[1] co-author of *The Spirit Level* (henceforward *TSL*).[2] Just as, through *TSL*, the discipline of Social Epidemiology has engaged the discipline of Economics in conversation,[3] so the conference began a conversation between *TSL* and the further discipline of Theology, and its offshoot, Missiology. Missiologically focused interaction with *TSL* is the goal of this paper. A number of studies of inequality and health had already shown "that more egalitarian societies tend to be healthier"[4] before Richard Wilkinson published an influential article in the *British Medical Journal* in 1992. Further confirmative evidence from subsequent studies elicited this editorial comment:

> The big idea is that what matters in determining mortality and health in a society is less the overall wealth of that society and more how evenly wealth is distributed. The more equally wealth is distributed the better the health of that society.[5]

Within the on-going debate as to how to define Missiology, the interaction between Theology and the Social Sciences is recognized as a significant element.[6] How *TSL*'s big idea impacted upon the question "Is there is a gospel for the North?" appeared to be exercising the conference conveners. The main aim here is to address a related prior question: might the book of Deuteronomy offer to the discipline of Missiology an appropriate framework and approach with which to connect with categories intrinsic to *TSL*'s own method and findings, and so meaningfully to engage with and reflect missiologically on *TSL*'s big idea? This might subsequently be helpful in offering a missiological perspective on the societal inequalities in England, which Rooms argues have a North-South dimension.

The New Testament articulates theologies of mission to which economic solidarity is intrinsic, perhaps most systematically in Luke-Acts.[7] So, a missiological reading of Deuteronomy may appear, *a priori*, a less obvious approach, especially since the practice of grounding missiological reflection in the Old Testament is still not widespread.[8] Nevertheless, in seeking to interact with *TSL*, this approach yields uniquely fresh perspectives, making connections not only with *TSL*'s advocacy of greater economic egalitarianism because of its relationship with human health (the "big idea"), but also with the methodology on which this advocacy rests. The common methodological factors include international comparison, national exemplarity in the socio-politico-economic spheres, and the ability of nations to perceive the superior wisdom inherent in systems which excel in social justice. Questions of politics, ideology, and democracy also offer significant points of contact. In pursuing these elements here, I draw on Christopher Wright's commentary on Deuteronomy, which specifically aims to bring out the "missiological significance" of the book.[9]

5.1.   METHODOLOGICAL CONNECTIONS; INTERNATIONAL COMPARISON AND EXEMPLARITY

The defining feature of *TSL*'s methodology is that evidence in favour of the social benefit to a nation of practising greater economic egalitarianism is acquired through engaging in international comparison. It is then noteworthy that a key text in Deuteronomy makes the international comparison of societies methodologically instrumental in its presentation of how Israel is to realize its vocation. Deuteronomy 4:5–8 reads (in my own translation):

> 5 See, just as the LORD my God has charged me, I now teach you statutes and ordinances for you to observe in the land that you are about to enter and occupy. 6 Observe these laws diligently, for this will show your wisdom and understanding to the peoples who, when they hear all these statutes, will say, "Surely this great nation is a wise and understanding people!" 7 For what great nation has a god so near to it as the LORD our God is near us whenever we call to him? 8 And what great nation has statutes and ordinances as just as this body of law (*torah*) that I am setting before you today?[10]

This passage achieves its goal, *telos*, via a four stage process. Stage 1 invites Israel to compare her own body of law/socio-political system with those of other "*great* nations" (*goy gadol*), not the lesser ones (vv. 6, 8). Similarly, *TSL* observes, "Everything we have seen comes from comparisons of existing societies, and those societies have not been particularly unusual or odd ones. Instead, we have looked exclusively at differences between the world's richest and most successful economies . . . "[11]

This comparison aims first to persuade Israel of the superiority of the justice inherent in its system (v. 8) so as to ensure (stage 2) Israel's diligent practice of that system (v. 6),[12] thus visibly demonstrating this entire societal system before the international community (stage 3), intrinsic to which is an economic aspect. Wright remarks,

But by suddenly introducing the nations as observers and commentators, the text opens up the whole significance of Israel's law to a much wider horizon. The nations will hear about these decrees, that is, they will notice and inquire and take an interest in the phenomenon of Israel as a society, with all the social, *economic*, legal, political and religious dimensions of the Torah.[13]

Similarly, whilst its focus is most specifically on the interrelationship between health and economics, intrinsic to *TSL*'s methodology is the visibility of contemporary societies on the international stage.[14]

Deuteronomy's *telos* is reached in stage 4, when Israel's visibility serves to persuade other great nations of the superiority of the wisdom inherent in the *torah* system (v. 6). Deuteronomy's connections with *TSL* on this *telos* appear under "Missiological Implications" below.

For Braulik, the text implies that the nations' admiration of the "practical validity"[15] of Israel's system will cause them to adopt it themselves. The ultimate goal of this virtuous circle is thus to transform the practice of nations by their adoption of a system which Israel knows to be incomparably just, and the international community recognizes as wise. As such, it can be referred to as Deuteronomy's Proposed International Narrative (PIN). Wright thus observes that PIN envisages "Israel as a model for the nations":

Its point is that if Israel would be shaped and characterized by the laws and institutions of the Sinai covenant, then they would be a highly visible exemplar to the nations . . . as to the quality of social justice embedded in their community. This seems to be a deliberate linking of Israel's role among the nations to the socio-ethical structure of their corporate life.[16]

Similarly, the point of *TSL*'s comparison of societies is to demonstrate that the more egalitarian ones merit being held up as exemplars to others. "Internationally, at the healthy end of the distribution we always seem to find the Scandinavian countries and Japan."[17]

5.2.   CAN DEUTERONOMIC SOCIETY BE COMPARED TO CONTEMPORARY SOCIETIES?

5.2.1.   Democracy and Constitutional thought

Whilst Deuteronomy and *TSL* share similar methodologies, a further methodological question must first be addressed if a missiological reading of Deuteronomy is to inform contemporary missiological practice. To what extent is it legitimate to compare contemporary societies with that of Deuteronomy's presentation? The implications of recent scholarship offer some justification. Prompted by the discovery of the texts of vassal treaties from the Hittite and Assyrian empires of the first and second millennia respectively, recent scholarship has recognized in the structure of Deuteronomy the marks of the regular form of ancient Near Eastern treaty texts. Drawing also on Josephus (see below), this has led to an interpretation of Deuteronomy as a polity or constitution which describes a socio-political order.[18] McBride calls this "A social charter of extraordinary literary coherence and political sophistication."[19] His political reading of Deuteronomy has the "comprehensive social charter"[20] of Deuteronomic *torah* set out in the "decrees" (Decalogue—chapter 5) which offer constitutional principles or guidelines for all spheres of life. The "statutes and ordinances" (the detailed stipulations of the Code— chapters 12–26), deemed "constitutional articles",[21] specify and illustrate the force and meaning of these guidelines.[22]

The section 16:18–18:22, which sits at the centre of the Code, treats social authority, thus illustrating the fifth commandment which focuses on those whom children encounter as the initial form of social authority: parents.[23] Known as The Constitutional Proposal because it sets out Deuteronomy's distinctive constitutional arrangement,[24] this section gives the people responsibility for choosing their political (17:15) and judicial (16:18) leaders, and describes the separation of powers into four office holders (judge, king, priest, and prophet), who are all subject to law (*torah*). This contributes to Deuteronomy's reputation for embracing democracy and democratization, thus radically countering the prevailing political arrangement in the ancient Near East which, by placing all forms of authority in the king, tended to make kingship "an office all too prone to despotism".[25] Levinson thus maintains, "it may well be that Deuteronomy . . . lays the foundation for western constitutional thought more broadly",[26] concurring with McBride's view that Deuteronomy is "the archetype of modern western constitutionalism".[27] It is then likely that the contemporary societies studied in *TSL*, which are largely western, and all "enjoy democratic institutions",[28] stand in recognizable continuity with the society envisaged in Deuteronomy.

5.2.2.   Justice—a comparative criterion throughout history

Implicit in the invitation to comparison in the rhetorical questions in 4:7–8[29] is the claim in v. 8 that, among the great nations, there is none with a body of laws more just than that of Deuteronomic *torah*. This claim itself appears to be a polemical response to that of Mesopotamian kings in the renowned and long-standing Hammurabi Code, dating to the early second millennium BCE. Through their profound wisdom, they claimed to have established "just laws" which contained a divine quality of social righteousness.[30] Meticulous comparative studies in ancient law have considered Deuteronomy's social and legal system to be, objectively, outstanding in its social justice and humanitarianism.[31] Moreover, Hammurabi's claim and Deuteronomy's counter-claim are not unique. Subsequently, Polybius and Cicero tirelessly made the polemical claim that Rome exhibited "a manifest pre-eminence among the world's nations in the cultivation of virtue, the exercise of rational governance and the practical implementation of social justice."[32] Significantly, it was these claims which prompted Josephus, one of the oldest interpreters of Deuteronomy, to refer to Deuteronomy as a divine *polity* (Gk. *politea*, not *nomos*), thus indicating his conviction that Deuteronomy set forth the socio-political order for Israel's life. This subtle choice of referent would not have been lost on his educated audience,[33] and his implicit instinct to compare the later Roman system with Deuteronomy's earlier presentation need not be lost on us.

Similarly, Wright maintains that Deuteronomic society can be compared with our own present-day societies. On an international stage crowded with other claimants, the claim of Deuteronomy 4:8:

> explicitly invites, even welcomes public inspection and comparison . . . It grants to the nations, and to the readers of this text, including ourselves, the liberty to analyse OT law in comparison with other social systems, ancient *and modern*, and to evaluate its claim.[34]

Throughout history, societies have, then, claimed their social systems to be incomparably just, much as through instinct, or a perceived biblical precedent, some commentators on Deuteronomy have considered it legitimate to compare Deuteronomic society with societies in their own or previous historical periods. Moreover, whilst one must heed the scholarly insistence that the "gap" between then and now is sizeable,[35] legitimacy is added to the task engaged in here through the growing recognition that Deuteronomy stands in recognizable continuity with our contemporary democracies and constitutional thought.

5.2.3.   Limitations

Nevertheless, even accepting these premises, some inherent discontinuities in the present enterprise must be acknowledged. In pursuit of its international comparisons, under the heading "The Costs of Inequality", Part 2 of *TSL* cites empirical research carried out in the developed nations on nine inter-related indicators from Community Life and Social Relations, through Teenage Births to Social Mobility: Unequal Opportunities.[36] Clearly, Deuteronomy has no empirical interest in teenage births, drugs use, or obesity. The social world of Deuteronomy has indeed been analysed,[37] but the book does not address these specific questions. Moreover, in contrast to *TSL*, Deuteronomy's rationale is theologically underpinned and predicated on the *torah* whose incomparable justice is presented as the expression of the character of Yahweh (4:8; cf. 32:4).[38] Nevertheless, in demonstrating convincingly that the more economically egalitarian countries such as Norway, Sweden, Finland, Denmark, and Japan are in fact healthier, *TSL* advocates economic egalitarianism, which appears to resonate with a key Deuteronomic value. It is this value, and its links with human health, that I seek to demonstrate, and to situate within the framework of a missiological reading of the book.

5.3.   DEUTERONOMY'S PERSPECTIVE ON ECONOMIC EGALITARIANISM

Two key passages from Deuteronomy are considered (15:1–11; 17:14–20). Both are set within the Deuteronomic Code (chapters 12–26). 15:1–11 forms part of a wider section (usually defined as 14:28–16:17) which fleshes out the sabbatical rhythm of the fourth commandment (5:12–15), whose concern with the economic domain[39] allows Deuteronomy's perspective on *TSL*'s primary concern—greater economic egalitarianism—to be considered.

5.3.1.   Deuteronomy 15:1–11

This text insists that all debts be cancelled in the seventh year. Lohfink is clear that Deuteronomy's determination to eradicate poverty by nipping it in the bud represents a more radical ideal even than the much admired Jubilee legislation of the Holiness Code (Leviticus 25). This seeks only *periodically to reverse* the downward spiral into poverty, and accepts the reality that some Israelites will experience poverty in the long 49/50 year period between jubilees.[40]

Whilst 15:11 maintains that "the poor will never cease out of the land", 15:4 insists "there shall [lit. "will"] be no poor among you." In this crux, the tension between these two apparently contradictory sentiments is best resolved as follows. Verses 4–6 portray an ideal situation; in a virtuous and mutually reinforcing cycle, Israel responds positively to Yahweh's gifts by fully obeying Yahweh's law, resulting in the eradication of poverty through an acute sense of economic solidarity which requires immense generosity. Conversely, vv. 7–11 reflect the wider Deuteronomic awareness that Israel would not, in fact, fully obey God in the economic domain. In reality, society would always include some experiencing poverty (v. 11). The exhortation of v. 4 is thus required to eradicate this poverty immediately.[41] Since, when the seventh year arrived, a debtor would be absolved from returning a loan to a lender (v. 8), Deuteronomy recognises that, as it approached, pragmatic self-interest would make wealthier Israelites ever more reluctant to lend to impoverished brother Israelites. But such reluctance is deemed a "mean thought" (v. 9) which should not be entertained. That way leads to the proliferation of poverty (v. 11). Rather, the loan should be granted in order "to meet the need" (15:8) and, moreover, be granted "liberally and ungrudgingly" (15:10), in pursuit of the societal goal of v. 4; "There shall be no poor among you."

Deuteronomy's interest in motivation is important here. The "stick" approach to motivating the wealthier to generosity (vv. 7–9) threatens that when, in response to a fellow Israelite's failure to respond generously to his need, the poorer brother appealed to God (lit. "cry"—qr', v. 9), this would place the parsimonious brother in a state of het', a sin which can only be expiated by the death of the sinner.[42] The divine response to the qr' of the *individual* of 15:9 against unfair treatment by a fellow Israelite echoes Yahweh's response to the *national* appeal to him (also qr') in Deut 4:7[43] (part of PIN) against unfair treatment from without. Lohfink also links 15:1–11 to 4:8 (also part of PIN) in observing, "It seems that the Deuteronomists saw the difference between their society and all other societies in the world not only in the justice in their laws but even more in this strong and divinely sanctioned defence against the first beginnings of progressive poverty."[44] If PIN, which initiates Deuteronomy's theme of Israel's witness to the nations, is capable of missiological interpretation,[45] these initial links between PIN and 15:1–11 offer an early indication that 15:1–11 is intrinsic to a missiological reading of the book.

TSL maintains that in order to motivate the wealthier to transform society, one must go beyond "coaxing or scaring the better off into adopting a more altruistic attitude to the poor", and rather convince them that "[t] he transformation of society is a project in which we all have a shared interest".[46] Significantly then, Deuteronomy offers its characteristic "carrot" as well as "stick" in the initial and complementary encouragement to embrace the alternative yet desired virtuous circle envisaged in vv. 4–6, 10 described above. A positive response to the divine command to practise generosity to needy individuals could, rather, generate divine blessing in the form of material prosperity for the entire nation. This resonates more closely with *TSL*'s positive approach.

These twin yet contrasting motivations, and their related outcomes, are reflected in the more general blessings and curses of chapters 27–28. In a political reading of Deuteronomy, these correspond to the positive motivations for observing ancient Near East treaties, and the sanctions for not doing so, imposed by the superior power (here Yahweh) on the lesser power (here Israel).

Here, again, Deuteronomy resonates with *TSL*'s notion that societies which practise economic solidarity function better, and that unequal societies are, rather, dysfunctional. Financial superiority at the national level (28:12–13) stands among the promises of material blessings for covenantal fidelity, directly repeating phrases and sentiments from 15:6. Blessings for fidelity to Yahweh's treaty are thus directly dependent on the prior practice of economic solidarity, the desired outcome in 15:1–11.

Moreover, chapters 27 and 28 pick up on the theme of Israel's witness to the nations by describing Israel's visibility before the nations, and their perception of Israel's potential functionality or dysfunctionality. The covenantal fidelity of economic solidarity is potentially instrumental in generating blessings which would cause "all the peoples of the earth" to honour (lit. "fear") Israel (28:10). Alternatively, covenantal *infidelity* is potentially instrumental in generating curses on Israel which would cause them to "become a thing of horror to all the kingdoms on earth" (28:25, cf. v. 37). Thus, once again, Israel's conduct in the economic domain (15:1–11) is tied to its witness to the nations.

How then does this relate to human health? The outcomes noted are for *corporate* human health, and are most explicitly presented in negative terms. Israel's negative international reputation (28:25, 37), *explicitly* visible through ill-health (28:22, 27–29, 61), results from a covenantal *infidelity* which *implicitly* includes the *failure* to practise economic solidarity (cf. 15:6; 28:12–13). Nevertheless, the positive corollary of this (economic solidarity brings good health to the nation—which is the big idea of *TSL*), can be implicitly deduced, since the blessings for fidelity and curses for *in*fidelity function antithetically. Israel's positive international reputation (28:10), *implicitly* indicated by good health, is *explicitly* visible through their financial superiority at the national level, which *explicitly* results from a covenantal fidelity expressed in their practice of economic solidarity (15:6; 28:12–13).

With regard specifically to human health therefore, Deuteronomy seems most readily to resonate with *TSL*'s identification of nations which act as negative, "dysfunctional" exemplars. "At the opposite end, suffering high rates of most of the health and social problems are usually the USA, Portugal, and the UK."[47] Nevertheless, implicitly, Deuteronomy resonates with *TSL*'s view that economic solidarity holds positive outcomes for human health nationally.

5.3.2. Deuteronomy 17:14–20: The King Law (KL)

Deuteronomy's King Law is set within the Constitutional Proposal (16:18–18:22) which, in the Deuteronomic Code, occupies the significant central position which, in ancient Near East treaty documents, is normally occupied by kings alone, a placement designed to emphazise royal authority and power. Conversely, Deuteronomy's central placement of the Constitutional Proposal achieves precisely the opposite effect. The king has to share authority with a further three office holders, and, furthermore, has the least power of all four. Moreover, the central placement of this arrangement serves to enshrine within the very structure of the book the radical nature of its vision of political authority. Rather than advocating royal despotism, these features serve to democratize the power and authority of the king.

Deuteronomy advocates the democratization of kingship and the corresponding monarchization of the entire nation.[48] PIN focuses pointedly on one aspect of this. "Wisdom and understanding" is a combination of characteristics normally ascribed to kings.[49] Thus, when PIN anticipates that, on account of Israel's diligent practise of *torah*, the nations will acknowledge Israel as a "wise and understanding people" (4:6), it accords the wisdom normally associated with kingship to the entire nation, thus complementing KL's democratization of kingship with a corresponding monarchization of the nation.

Within this democratized system, the king's authority is also to be exercised counter-culturally, in humility and exemplarity. This requires that he be persuaded to forego the accumulation of the accoutrements of power which normally accompany the office.[50] In vv. 16–17, via the thrice repeated phrase *welo' yrbh lo* ("and he shall not accumulate *for himself*" horses, wives, or silver and gold), wealth is one of three things he is forbidden to accumulate *for himself*. More positively, and echoing the negative threefold prohibition, he *is* to "write *for himself*" (v. 18)[51] a copy of the *torah* which curbs his power, and then, in an on-going educative process, read from it every day. This stipulation is required uniquely of him. The double mention of his heart (*lbb*) brings his motivation into clear focus. Ignoring KL and accumulating many wives would indicate that he had chosen to turn away (*sur*) his heart (*lbbo*, v. 17) just as considering himself better than (lit. "lift up his heart over"—*rom lbbo m* . . .) his brothers (fellow Israelites) would indicate he had turned (*sur*) from *torah* (v. 20). With the heart being the seat of the intellect, will, and intention,[52] the king's non-accumulation of wealth is also to be a deliberate decision. For Deuteronomy, brotherhood reflects an equality founded on Yahweh's redemption of all Israel, corporately from Egypt. This divine act renders all Israelites equal, and none superior, not even the king. The practical outworking of the social solidarity of the resultant "brotherhood" requires the king to practice self-restraint with regard to economic self-aggrandizement.

This resonates to some extent with *TSL*, which is also concerned that wealth ought not to be accumulated in the hands of an elite at the expense of the good of wider society, and recognizes that the rich need to be persuaded voluntarily to refrain from the accumulation of wealth if economic solidarity is to be realized.[53]

For Deuteronomy, from a negative perspective, the furthest reaching national effects of the abuse of power are potentially concentrated in the kingly office,[54] yet from the positive, the king is potentially the model Israelite, an exemplar to the nation for its benefit.[55] Miller affirms:

Finally, the law of the king places upon that figure the obligations incumbent upon every Israelite. In that sense, Deuteronomy's primary concern was that the king be *the model Israelite* ... The fundamental task of the leader of the people, therefore, *is to exemplify and demonstrate true obedience to the Lord* for the sake of the well-being of both the dynasty and the kingdom.[56]

The king's exemplarity specifically includes economic exemplarity. Elsewhere, through a number of links between the King Law and PIN, including the key elements of kingship and exemplarity mentioned here, I have demonstrated that Deuteronomy envisages that the king act as exemplar of diligent *torah* observance before the nation so that the nation might act as exemplar to the nations.[57] The king's exemplarity, which stands as a distinctively counter-cultural symbolism to the despotism to which the office of kingship in the ancient Near East was all too prone, is thus instrumental in transforming the nations' unjust practices, which is the *telos* of PIN. One implication at the economic level is this: inspired by the king's exemplary economic self-restraint (17:14–20), the economic solidarity of all Israelites (15:1–11) is to issue in the entire nation bearing witness before the nations (15:6; 28:12–13) and so to manifest, at the economic level, the outworking of PIN. PIN intends that the nations first admire and then imitate Israel's example. In Deuteronomy's presentation, the resulting international transformation towards greater economic egalitarianism represents the *telos* of God.

5.4.   MISSIOLOGICAL IMPLICATIONS

For Wright, this divine *telos* for the international community in PIN assumes missiological significance.[58] This rests partly on PIN's relationship with preceding texts in the Pentateuch deemed missiologically significant. PIN's notion that, by becoming a "great nation" (a phrase repeated three times in vv. 6, 8), Israel will bring benefit to the international community, stands firmly in narrative continuity with Genesis 12:1–3, which Wright considers "one of the most important places in a missiological reading of the Bible".[59] The purposeful syntax of this foundational missiological text envisages Abram becoming a "great nation" as a result of which "every kinship group on earth shall find blessing through [him]". Moreover, Genesis 18:18–19, the next in a series of five promises of international blessing in Genesis, indicates that the Abrahamic community's practice of social justice (righteousness [*tsedeqah*] and justice [*mishpat*])—the very demonstration of what it means to walk in the ways of YHWH[60]—will be instrumental in realizing this international blessing, a notion clearly echoed in Deuteronomy's PIN. For these reasons, Deuteronomy 4:6–8 might be considered not only Deuteronomy's Proposed *International* Narrative but also its Proposed *Missiological* Narrative (PMN).

The "great nation" of PIN re-defines greatness in terms of the religious and ethical greatness of Israel,[61] specifically the quality of social justice embodied in Israel's constitution and law.[62] Thus, Israel's exemplarity before the international community, grounded in the quality of social justice which the community demonstrates, assumes *missiological* significance. Wright observes:

> This seems to be a deliberate linking of Israel's role among the nations to the socio-ethical structure of their corporate life: mission and ethics combined. The mission of Israel was to be a model to the nations. Mission was not a matter of going but of being; to be what they were, to live as the people of the God Yahweh in the sight of the nations.[63]

Through this notion of national ethical exemplarity, Wright keeps the missiological and political readings of Deuteronomy closely bound together. Not unsurprisingly, the theme of Israel's witness before the nations, initiated in 4:5–8, and developed elsewhere such as in chapters 15, 27, and 28 as demonstrated above, also contributes to this missiological reading of Deuteronomy. With Israel's mission being to be a model to the nations, the balance of idealism and harsh realities recorded in Deuteronomy, as illustrated in 15:1–11, is both characteristic of the attempt to act as a national exemplar [64] and consistent with McBride's view of Deuteronomy as a constitution.[65]

A further point is important here. Just as Deuteronomy presents the ideal of economic solidarity in 15:4 as intrinsic to the realisation of the *missio dei*, so Acts too not only ties that same ideal to the *missio dei*, but, moreover, articulates it precisely by echoing Deuteronomy 15:4.[66] In Acts 4:34, Luke attests that, within the new community of Christ now living in the eschatological era of the Spirit, "there *were* no needy persons among them", thus virtually quoting the Greek Septuagint translation of Deuteronomy 15:4, "there *shall be* no needy person among you". Grammatical aspect is the principal difference between these texts. In this way, Luke presents the early Church in Acts as having fulfilled the sabbatical vision of Deuteronomy 15.[67] Bosch recognises that, in contributing to the prominent theology of economic solidarity which pervades Luke-Acts, Acts 4:34 is intrinsic to the Lukan missionary paradigm.[68] He observes:

> Luke wishes his readers to know that there is hope for the rich, insofar as they act and serve in solidarity with the poor and oppressed. In their being converted to God, rich and poor are converted toward each other. The main emphasis, ultimately, is on sharing in community. At various points in Acts, Luke highlights this "communism of love" (cf. Acts 2:44f; 4:32, 36f).[69]

Thus, in echoing Deuteronomy 15:4 in word and spirit, Luke 4:34 stands in continuity across the Testaments with a theology of economic solidarity in the service of God's mission—the benefit and blessing of the international community.

5.5.   CONCLUSION

How then does Deuteronomy's presentation of the mission of God, and in particular its economic aspect, relate to *TSL* and its big idea?

Methodologically speaking, like *TSL*, Deuteronomy 4:5–8 (PIN/ PMN) focuses on a comparison of the most advanced societies at the time. Practically, the twin and complementary elements of international comparison and exemplarity—the core of PMN's strategy to realize the divine missiological purpose—resonate deeply with the methodological assumptions underpinning *TSL*. For Deuteronomy, the *missio dei* reaches its economic goal in the international community's admiration and subsequent imitation of Israel's example of economic solidarity. Likewise, *TSL* holds up the more egalitarian nations as attractive exemplars to be imitated.

Deuteronomy envisages related outcomes for human health. The material flourishing resulting from economic solidarity could bear positive witness to the nations, whereas the failure to flourish, implicitly tied to a lack of economic solidarity and resulting in failing human health, could, conversely, act as a negative witness to the nations. These antithetical outcomes represent respectively the realization or the non-realization of the *missio dei* in Deuteronomy's presentation. *TSL* operates on a very similar premise. Economically egalitarian nations are held up as attractive exemplars to be imitated precisely because they enjoy better corporate health than nations which do not practise economic solidarity, which thus act as dysfunctional antitypes, negative exemplars.

These deep resonances of *TSL*'s thesis with the outworking of the PMN in Deuteronomy suggest that those contemporary nations which are presently experiencing a correspondence between economic egalitarianism and better human health stand in recognisable continuity with the outworking of the *missio dei* of Deuteronomy's presentation. Moreover, the nations thus held up by *TSL* as positive exemplars in this respect might be considered to be playing a role analogous to that which the PMN envisaged Israel would play in bringing benefit and blessing to the international community.

5.5.1.   Human perceptivity and the *missio dei*: The recognition of wisdom

According to Deuteronomy's PMN, the human ability to perceive the superior wisdom in a fairer system over a less just one is intrinsic to the realisation of mission.[70] Levinson maintains, "Deuteronomy 4:5–8 views observance of the commandments as the fruit of both faith and reason, of Israel's unparalleled *Heilsgeschichte* and universal human perceptivity. *Torah* is the intersection and consummation of the particular and the universal."[71] Contemporary scholars who recognize that the *torah* system's notion of social justice outstripped that of other social systems of the ancient Near East (ANE) demonstrate the same human perceptivity as that which PMN asks Israel and the nations to demonstrate. Similarly, the recorded ability of modern-day readers of *TSL* to perceive wisdom in the egalitarian practices of the contemporary nations which it holds up as exemplary—and so to perceive the wisdom in its thesis—resonates with the anticipated ability of nations to perceive wisdom in Israel's practice of the *torah* system.

The response to *TSL* has been so uniformly appreciative that Pickett and Wilkinson "have sensed there is an intellectual vacuum, a hunger for the evidence we present—as if under the surface the world was full of closet egalitarians".[72] One of three things they consider has contributed to this response is:

> [O]ur analysis seems to confirm people's intuition that inequality is divisive and socially corrosive. Again and again, people tell us they feel they have gained from the book a picture of the world which is both quite new to them and yet somehow also immediately recognisable, a picture they feel they have been waiting for and which changes how they see what is going on around them.[73]

Through what Levinson calls "universal human perceptivity", the connections between Deuteronomy's PMN and *TSL*'s thesis are easily made. This perceptivity contributes to a missiological reading of Deuteronomy, and allows it to offer to the discipline of Missiology an appropriate framework and approach which yields fruitful missiological reflection on the big idea of *TSL* and the issues it raises.

What might be some of the early indicators of this missiological reflection? In including the UK amongst countries deemed negative, "dysfunctional" exemplars, *TSL*'s analysis of the present situation in the UK resonates most deeply with Deuteronomy's depiction of Israel's *failure* to live out its exemplary missiological calling. Moreover, the explorations here might now inform further missiological reflection on the related question of a gospel for the North. An initial observation might be this. Economic inequality may operate not only on a North-South axis as Rooms argues, but also at a more local level within our northern cities,[74] in whose richest suburbs people can live nineteen years longer than those in the poorest neighbourhoods.[75] But, whatever the level at which it operates, the presentation of Deuteronomy (and its echoes in Acts) is that such a state of affairs is not congruent with the outworking of the mission of God.

NOTES

1. The conference, "Searching for the Angel of the North", was held at Bishopthorpe Palace, York, on 24 October 2013.
2. K. Pickett and R. Wilkinson, *The Spirit Level: Why Equality is Better for Everyone* (London: Penguin, 2010), published with revisions and postscript.
3. See the Introduction to this volume.
4. Pickett and Wilkinson, *The Spirit Level*, p. 81.
5. Editor's Choice, "The Big Idea", *British Medical Journal* (1996) 312 (7037): 0, quoted in Pickett and Wilkinson, *The Spirit Level*, p. 81.
6. Mika Vahakangas, "The International Association for Mission Studies—Globally in the Service of the Discipline(s)", in *Swedish Missiological Themes*, Vol. 113, (Uppsala: Svenska institutet for missionsforskning, 2014), p. 69.
7. See, for example, the chapter entitled "Luke-Acts: Practising Forgiveness and Solidarity with the Poor" in D. J. Bosch, *Transforming Mission: Paradigm Shifts in Theology of Mission* (Maryknoll: Orbis, 1992), pp. 84–122, and

"The mission perspective of Luke-Acts" in D. Senior and C. Stuhlmueller, *The Biblical Foundations of Mission* (Orbis: Maryknoll, 1983), pp. 255–279.

8. The biblical section of Bosch's *Transforming Mission* is entirely focused on the New Testament. See, however, his section entitled "Mission in the Old Testament"; Bosch, *Transforming Mission*, pp. 16–20. Space precludes a rehearsal of the imperatives for and benefits of grounding mission in the Old Testament. For this, see, for example, D. Senior and C. Stuhlmueller, *The Biblical Foundations for Mission* (Maryknoll: Orbis, 1983), and C. J. H. Wright, *The Mission of God: Unlocking the Bible's Grand Narrative* (Downers Grove: IVP, 2006). For critical appraisals of this latter, and Wright's response, see the various articles in *Anvil*, vol. 24:4 (2007).

9. C. J. H. Wright, *Deuteronomy* (NIBC. Peabody MA: Hendrickson, 1996), especially pp. 8–17.

10. All biblical references in this essay are taken from the Biblia Hebraica Stutgartensia; all translations are by the author.

11. Pickett and Wilkinson, *The Spirit Level*, p. 197.

12. G. Braulik, "Wisdom, Divine Presence and Law: Reflections on the Kerygma of Deut 4:5–8", in G. Braulik, *The Theology of Deuteronomy: Collected Essays* (N. Richland Hills TX: Bibal Press, 1994), p. 9.

13. Wright, *Deuteronomy*, p. 47. Emphasis added.

14. See, for example, Pickett and Wilkinson, *The Spirit Level*, pp. xv–xvii.

15. Braulik, "Wisdom", p. 9.

16. Wright, *Deuteronomy*, pp. 12–13.

17. Pickett and Wilkinson, *The Spirit Level*, p. 174.

18. For accessible introductions to the political interpretation of Deuteronomy and surrounding issues, see, for example, P. D. Miller, "Constitution or Instruction: The Purpose of Deuteronomy", in P. D. Miller, *The Way of the Lord: Essays in Old Testament Theology* (Grand Rapids: Eerdmans, 2007), pp. 253–268, and chapter 5, "A Political Nation: Deuteronomy", pp. 74–98 in J. G. McConville, *God and Earthly Power: An Old Testament Political Theology; Genesis-Kings*, Library of Hebrew Bible/Old Testament Studies 454 (formerly JSOT Sup; London: T&T Clark, 2006).

19. S. D. McBride, "Polity of the Covenant People", *Interpretation* 41 (1987), p. 243.

20. Ibid., p. 237.

21. Ibid., p. 234, n. 14.

22. Miller, "Constitution", p. 261.

23. Wright, *Deuteronomy*, p. 203.
24. R. D. Nelson, *Deuteronomy*, Old Testament Library (Westminster John Knox: London, 2002), pp. 210–236.
25. Ibid., p. 223.
26. B. M. Levinson, "The Reconceptualisation of Kingship in Deuteronomy and the Deuteronomistic History's Transformation of Torah", *Vetus Testamentum*, 51:4 (2001) p. 532.
27. McBride, "Polity", p. 243.
28. Pickett and Wilkinson, *The Spirit Level*, p. 197.
29. Wright, *Deuteronomy*, p. 48.
30. M. Weinfeld, *Deuteronomy and the Deuteronomic School* (Oxford: Oxford University Press), pp. 150ff.
31. Weinfeld, *Deuteronomic School*, pp. 282–297; N.F. Lohfink, "Poverty in the Laws of the Ancient Near East and the Bible", *Theological Studies* 52:1 (1991) 34–50, pp. 44–45; Wright, *Deuteronomy*, p. 48.
32. McBride, "Polity", p. 230.
33. Ibid.
34. Wright, *Deuteronomy*, p. 48. Emphasis added.
35. Cyril Rodd has critiqued Wright's approach from this perspective. C. Rodd, *Glimpses of a Strange Land: Studies in Old Testament Ethics,* (Edinburgh: T&T Clark, 2001). Wright replies in his *Old Testament Ethics for the People of God*, (Nottingham: IVP, 2004). See especially pp. 439–440 and 452–3.
36. Pickett and Wilkinson, *Spirit Level*, pp. 49–169.
37. See, for example, L. Stulman, "Encroachment in Deuteronomy: An Analysis of the Social World of the D Code", *JBL* 109:4 (1990), pp. 613–632.
38. McConville, "Political Nation", pp. 78–79.
39. Wright, *Old Testament Ethics*, pp. 296–297.
40. Lohfink, "Poverty", p. 49. Compare to W. Brueggemann, *Theology of the Old Testament: Testimony, Dispute, Advocacy* (Minneapolis: Fortress, 1997), p. 190; and Wright, *Old Testament Ethics*, pp. 198–205.
41. Lohfink, "Poverty", p. 47; Wright, *Deuteronomy*, p. 189.
42. Lohfink, "Poverty", p. 46.
43. Ibid., p. 49.
44. Ibid.
45. See below, "Missiological implications", pp. 83–85.
46. Pickett and Wilkinson, *The Spirit Level*, p. 237.

47. Ibid., p. 174.

48. P. D. Miller, "Kingship, Torah Obedience, and Prayer", pp. 279–297, in P. D. Miller, *Israelite Religion and Biblical Theology: Collected Essays,* JSOTSup 267 (Sheffield: Sheffield Academic Press, 2000), p. 283.

49. Braulik, "Wisdom", p. 11.

50. Wright, *Deuteronomy,* p. 209.

51. J.-P. Sonnet, *The Book Within the Book: Writing in Deuteronomy.* BIS Vol. 14 (Leiden: Brill, 1997). p. 72, n. 72.

52. F. Stolz, "*lēb* heart", in E. Jenni and C. Westermann (eds.), *Theological Lexicon of the Old Testament,* trans. by M. E. Biddle (Hendrickson, 1997), vol. 2, p. 639; Wright, *Deuteronomy,* pp. 98–99.

53. Pickett and Wilkinson, *The Spirit Level,* p. 237.

54. J. Grant, *The King as Exemplar: The Function of Deuteronomy's Kingship Law in the Shaping of the Book of Psalms* (Academia Biblia 17; Leiden: Brill, 2004), p. 194.

55. Compare to the title of Grant's 2004 monograph. See also Wright, *Deuteronomy,* p. 209.

56. Patrick Miller, *Deuteronomy* (Louisville: John Knox, 1990), pp. 148–149.

57. J. Wigfield, *Deuteronomy and David in Dialogue: Evoking a Conversation Between Two Conflicting Theologies and Configurations of Kingship in the Joint Introduction to the Psalter* (Unpublished MPhil dissertation, University of Nottingham, 2013), pp. 115–150 (Chapter 6, "The Role of the Deuteronomic King in the International Arena: Links Between the King Law (17:14–20) and the Proposed International Narrative (4:5–8)").

58. Wright, *Deuteronomy,* p. 12.

59. Wright, *Mission of God,* p. 199. For an alternative view, see R. W. L. Moberly, 'Gen 12:1–3: A Key to Interpreting the Old Testament?' in R. W. L. Moberly, *The Theology of the Book of Genesis* (Cambridge: Cambridge University Press, 2009), pp. 141–161.

60. Wright, *Deuteronomy,* pp. 11–12; Wright, *Mission of God,* pp. 362–369.

61. Braulik, "Wisdom", p. 13.

62. Wright, *Mission of God,* p. 379, n. 21.

63. Wright, *Deuteronomy,* pp. 12–13.

64. A consideration of the scholarly dispute over the apparent utopianism of legislation (such as 15:1–11 and the King Law in Deuteronomy, and its interaction with *TSL*) is instructive, but lies beyond the scope of this article.

65. Wright, *Deuteronomy*, p. 19, n. 28.
66. Wright, *Mission of God*, pp. 302–303.
67. Lohfink, "Poverty", p. 50.
68. Bosch, *Transforming Mission*, p. 104 and p. 118.
69. Ibid., p. 104.
70. Wright, *Deuteronomy*, pp. 47–48.
71. J. D. Levinson, "The Theologies of Commandment in Biblical Times", *Harvard Theological Review* 73 (1980), p. 26.
72. Pickett and Wilkinson, *The Spirit Level*, p. ibid., p. 274.
73. M. Slack, "Report on inequality shows city 'divided' by poverty", *Yorkshire Post*, 30 January 2013, p. 7.
74. As stated by Professor Daniel Dorling in a programme on Social Epidemiology in the BBC Radio 4 *Analysis* series; "Sick Society?", broadcast 24 September 2012 <http://www.bbc.co.uk/programmes/b01mw15s> (accessed 16 December 2015).

6. FRIENDSHIP IN FRAGILITY: A GOSPEL FOR THE NORTH?

John B. Thomson

6.1. INTRODUCTION

Since being ordained in 1985, my public ministry in England has been in the Northern Province of the Church of England in the Dioceses of Sheffield and York. My wife's parents served in the Dioceses of Newcastle and Carlisle and my mother's family live in the Diocese of Manchester. My observation is that fragility is a common reality in the North. In congregational terms, fragility is evident in attendance figures, apart from some middle class suburban and city centre churches as the recent *Anecdote to Evidence Report* shows.[1] In economic terms, much of the North is still reacting to the decline of industry and the domination of the South East in the service and financial sectors. In political terms, the North is less influential than the more affluent South East. In psychological terms, significant sectors of the post-industrial North remain locked in a bereavement narrative fed by memories of its impressive industrial past which has gone with little to replace it. In educational terms, much of the North is marked by a preference for practical learning in the light of its industrial and rural heritage rather than academic learning. Apart from a few pockets of congregational and economic affluence, the North represents Guy Standing's "precariat society": according to Standing, the precariat are an emerging and expansive group characterized by economic and social insecurity at all levels consequent upon the impact of globalisation on inherited forms of employment and society.[2] Whilst his focus does not include religious bodies, the metaphor is equally applicable to most of the Church of England in the North. Congregational attendance is precarious and the sustainability of vicarious religion, noted by sociologist Grace Davie, is increasingly vulnerable as the chain of memory upon which this depends becomes more fragile as well.[3]

6.2.   PRECARIAT AND PRAYER

Standing describes responses to the emergence of a precariat society as a politics of inferno characterised by increased surveillance, invasion of privacy, centrally controlled education policies, hiring and firing, paternalism, distraction, and demonization.[4] It is not difficult to see analogous temptations in religious institutions as understandable anxiety about survival informs more centralist and standardized organisational strategies and congregational decline is perceived by local church leaders and their congregations as due to their failures. Yet the key to responding to a precarious situation lies in the very word itself, which is derived from the Latin adjective *precarius*, "obtained by prayer, request", from the noun *prex*, meaning "prayer, request". Prayer, which represents conscious attention to God, suggests a different politics, a politics of trust and hope rooted in the faithfulness of God witnessed in covenant and the commitment of the risen Christ to be with and ahead of his people in the "Galilee mission" context (Matthew 28:20). Such a politics of trust and hope resists the logic of self-preoccupied survivalism in favour of faithful witness or presence, which is about engagement, commitment, and incarnationally informed improvisation rooted in worship.[5] It recognizes that much of the recent decline in congregational belonging is not necessarily the immediate fault of local congregations so much as the long term social effects of modernity reinforced by overzealous religious reform in the past.[6] It is aware of history and the way English Christianity has predominantly been about occasional conformity rather than intense participation since, as Percy says, "England has never been an outwardly religious country if church

attendance is anything to go by."[7] Yet, as conflict surrounding the closure
of church buildings and a renewal in tourism pilgrimage display, loyalty
to the symbols of faith and place remains remarkably strong.[8] Perhaps
this reflects the fact that, even today, "local churches have a long-term
future because for most people everyday life remains local".[9]

6.3.   FRAGILITY AND GOSPEL IN
BIBLE AND TRADITION

The Church of England represents the legacy of the fourth-century
Constantinian Settlement which integrated political and religious life
within one polity. The Settlement looks increasingly fragile even if it
remains a reality, particularly in more conservative rural areas in the North.
Yet this fragility is not necessarily alien to the Gospel of God's saving love
or friendship for creation. The Old Testament represents a story of divine
engagement with Israel in ways which are both fragile and surprising.
The Patriarch narratives mediate the story through an unexpected birth,
atypical succession, and dysfunctional family relationships. The Exodus
is rooted in racial oppression and flight, combined with precarious
survival in hostile environmental and social conditions. Israel's politics
in the Promised Land are predominantly a failure critiqued by prophets
and judged through military defeats, exiles, and colonization. Indeed the
genealogy of Jesus in the first chapter of Matthew's Gospel pivots around
four surprising and subversive women, Tamar, Ruth, Bathsheba, and Mary,
each of whom represent the Messiah's lineage through ambiguous stories
or rape, seduction, and unexpected pregnancy, and one of whom is not
even named but defined in the euphemism "Uriah's wife" to indicate the
sensitivity of her place in the story.

    The Church proclaims a Gospel whose central figure is the kenotic
Christ, God incarnate whose mission strategy involved self-emptying and
working with a dysfunctional group of disciples in ways which exposed
them as signs of his Kingdom to the judgement of their peers. For example,
the mission charges of Matthew 10 and Luke 9 and 10 suggest that Jesus'

community share in a similar kenotic mission to his own whereby the faith of those they live amongst is indicated by the reaction these people have towards them as ambassadors of Christ.[10] A similar theme is evident in the famous Parable of the Sheep and the Goats in Matthew 25. Here a close reading of the text indicates that the sheep and goats are identified by how they respond to the least of Jesus' brethren, his disciples, who, in Matthew's time, are hungry, thirsty, and in prison. The disciples are a fragile community inhabiting a world in which they cannot control the outcome of their mission but in which their faithfulness acts as a catalyst for others' conversion. In the Gospels, Christ always blesses the crowds despite their limited response to his call whereas the disciples are tested and often found wanting as fragile exemplars of his way. Such fragility is also evident in the Luke-Acts narrative which uses witness or martyrdom as a key mission category as Christians, such as Paul and Barnabas, travel across the Mediterranean region establishing or building up churches whose fragility is evident in the many problems and issues which Paul's letters in particular highlight. Indeed, Paul himself speaks of his own fragility in his Galatians and Corinthian correspondence when faced with internal dissent about his Gospel. Furthermore, Luke-Acts symmetrically patterns the journeys and passion of Paul on the same precarious pattern of Jesus' passion, the latter exhibiting ironic victory in Jerusalem, the capital of the Jewish world, whereas the former exhibits such a witness in Rome, the capital of the Gentile world of the day. Furthermore, the post-Constantine desert tradition further denotes friendship in fragility in its quest for white martyrdom through the stripping and breaking process of self-discipline (*ascesis*).[11]

Such a tradition of witness, biblical and post-biblical, is not passive romanticism but grounds itself in the faithfulness of God, the achievement of Christ's passion, and the call to faithful discipleship or holiness. Christ now reigns as the crucified, risen, and glorified Son of Man and, crucially, is witnessed to by *faithful* followers living out holiness. Consequently, the Church does not need to achieve victory for its cause since this victory is already achieved. Confident, hopeful, and faithful witness, rather than anxious survivalism, is therefore the Christian vocation and ensures that fragile congregational "Gospel gestures" can be faithful improvisations. Within the "Big Story" of salvation established in Christ's victory, these diverse micro-communities are positioned and contribute to the way this story of kenotic grace is told.[12] However, such friendship in fragility tests trust and involves the deepening and clarifying of desires and vision in order to make space for God to work and be revealed in ecclesial, meaningful flesh.[13] It divests disciples of fantasies and self-deception in order that their confidence in the presence of divine love is intensified. It invites attention to the luminal areas of society where fragility and trust have to exist together.[14] It reinforces the Anglican tradition of being a Church in the ordinary rather than in the spectacular.

6.4.   RECOVERING ANGLICAN CONFIDENCE IN A GOSPEL FOR THE NORTH

Stanley Hauerwas, the American theological ethicist, argues that the first responsibility of the Church is to be itself since "the truthfulness of Jesus creates and is known by the kind of community his story should form".[15] Hauerwas argues that churches need to be aware of their distinctive Christian identity if they are faithfully to fulfil their calling and mission. For Anglicans, this means that who Anglicans are as a Gospel sign is prior to what they do, since what they do will flow from who they are. Indeed, identity is itself a crucial witness of the Church since, as the body of Christ, the Church is an embodied apologetic of the Gospel.[16] Anglican Christianity is a material and political faith expressed in embodiment and context related improvising mission. As an incarnational faith emulating the contextuality of the four Gospels, it is attentive to its diverse contexts in order to converse with them about the Gospel of divine love for the estranged in forms of life which engage those distinctive contexts. As a Church whose theology is formed and embedded in worship, it is a practical holiness movement rooted in the soil of the contexts it witnesses within. Such witness is first about faithful, tangible Gospel presence out of which emerges appropriate rhetorical Gospel voice.

Given the fragility of the North and its predominantly practical learning tradition, a fragile and practically focused Anglican witness committed to remaining with these communities coheres with biblical, cultural, and missional realities. Ironically, the very fragility of its congregational life in many urban and rural areas in the North invites the Church to trust more upon its Lord and makes it less prey than where it is numerically strong to self-deception about its significance, the basis for its success, and uncritical cultural captivity to its host community. Suffering and struggle, therefore, act as reality checks on the sort of Gospel which is lived and proclaimed. They also mean that the Church engages in its mission from a situation akin to most of those it is reaching out to. As a result, the gathered community identifies with its context and, in this way, is challenged to deepen its discipleship in a manner that reflects trust and seeks the Spirit's improvisation for its contemporary mission.

The Church of England has identified three quinquennial goals in order to serve the Gospel in this country. First: to take forward the spiritual and numerical growth of the Church of England, including the growth of its capacity to serve the whole community of this country. Second: to re-shape or re-imagine the Church's ministry for the century coming, so as to make sure that there is a growing and sustainable Christian witness in every local community. Third: to focus our resources where there is both greatest need and greatest opportunity.[17] These goals cohere with the historic parochial commitment of the Church of England as an institution embodying God's saving friendship or love for English society rooted in the diverse fabric of English society and serving that society in the name of Christ.[18]

Yet, in the North, congregational and ministry fragility raise questions about capacity to realize such a vision unless we can imaginatively see a northern Gospel as a Gospel expressed in and improvised upon this very fragility. So, instead of dispensing with the vision of parish and common worship, it means drilling down into this inheritance in ways which enable us to go forward in a sustainable and improvising fashion that coheres with our historic Anglican commitments shared through the witness and improvisation of faithful congregations. These commitments are mutually accountable and ordered worship, shared, ordered, and distributed ministry, embedded mission, and the sign of catholicity in the episcopate.[19] For example, although the parish was historically understood as a geographical reality for mission, it is fundamentally about an agreed context within which this mission is focused and accountable to the diocesan bishop. There is no reason, therefore, why "parish" cannot, on occasion, be imagined in other contextual or relational ways under episcopal authority without subverting the fundamental mission imperative of the Church of England where this is appropriate.[20] What matters for Anglican witness is that such "parishes", whether as inherited or fresh expressions of Church, are improvisations grounded in forms of discipleship rooted in mutually accountable worship, ordered community, deep engagement with the Christian story and its Scriptures, and outward facing mission.[21] In this way, temptations to resistance or relevance do not dissolve into forms of spiritual narcissism which collude unreflectively with ambiguous culture.[22] Such an approach represents friendship for English society rooted in the missional character of the Church of England's parochial structure, a structure premised on embodying the divine friendship for those as yet estranged from God.[23] This is the sort of friendship which Jesus lived in the society of his day and which subverted classical views of friendship as loving the other as another self or like liking like because they are like each other.[24] The mission of Jesus, which Anglican witness seeks to follow, is therefore not determined by its effectiveness but by its character as love devoted to the well-being of the stranger.

6.5. FRIENDSHIP IN FRAGILITY: A GOSPEL FOR THE RURAL NORTH

As the Bishop of Selby, I have been given the role of Ambassador for Rural Life and Faith charged with developing a diocesan-wide vision and strategy for the re-invigorating of the rural Church in the light of the Diocesan Vision. This vision is of "Generous Churches Making and Nurturing Disciples" in rural contexts whose marks we expect to be registered in the growth of Christlikeness, commitment, partnership, influence, and numbers. In short, this is about enabling existing rural parishes and emerging Fresh Expressions of Church to embody the Good News of divine friendship amongst all the regions of this northern diocese in appropriate ways which cohere with the historic commitments of the Church of England's mission. Yet rural life in this part of England, as elsewhere, faces many challenges and is increasingly complex. Nationally, 65 per cent of church buildings are in rural areas, many of which are listed and expensive to maintain. Rural life is changing rapidly with net immigration of 54,000 per annum, mainly in the early middle-aged and third-age sectors, with 70 per cent of rural residents now being first generation residents.[25] Such net immigration from urban areas easily colonizes rural areas with an urban view of life reinforcing a theme park vision of the rural unaware of the challenges of rural poverty and isolation, emigrating young people in search of work, fragile and relatively expensive services, and broadband deserts.

A particular challenge for the Church of England is that rural ministry is also more expensive to sustain than urban ministry, harder to recruit to, and, due to cost and stipendiary clergy decline, involves more complex and extensive livings comprising of many small, often aging congregations and ancient expensive buildings with limited capacity to generate local support ministers. In rural contexts such as ours, therefore, the temptation is to conflate congregations, close buildings, and withdraw to more secure urban contexts. Yet this would undermine the historic Anglican calling, witness, and mission as described above. In addition, rural areas in particular still have a deep attachment to place and the memories place evokes, and, proportionately, members of micro-congregations are more involved in their local community than is the case in urban areas.[26] To undermine this legacy not only generates significant and time consuming conflict but further urbanizes the rural and disembeds local Christians from their immediate neighbourhoods. It would, therefore, not represent a Gospel for all the North but rather a retrenchment to those areas which are more statistically successful, the suburbs and university city centres; a Church for some but not for all.

The critical task, therefore, is to ensure faithful presence, witness, and engagement, particularly in fragile contexts as improvising exhibitions of the Gospel of divine friendship for the changing rural North. Certainly this will involve some refocusing of resources and a review of how church buildings are used relative to demographic, attendance, and financial data. More attention will need to be given to the ways in which contemporary people gather and travel to see whether adaptations to past practices which were appropriate to more static communities are needed to engage people, particularly younger, time-poor families. The Eucharistic-focused legacy of the "Parish and People Movement" will need to be reviewed given its dependency on clergy and more scope will need to be given to lay-led worship, appropriately supported by the wider Church often in local ecumenical partnerships. Stipendiary clergy in rural areas will need to be selected intentionally for this ministry environment which will require them to become episcopal vicars facilitating and developing local teams of people who can own the parish, benefice, or Fresh Expression mission on the ground and forming mission partnerships with deanery and possibly ecumenical colleagues to take forward the Christian agenda in the community. Such partnerships will enable fragile congregations to combine their resources without losing either identity or distinctiveness. In addition, such clergy will need much more bespoke ministerial development, such as the Arthur Rank Germinate Leadership Course, attuned to the challenges of an increasingly complex rural reality rather than generic leadership programmes which tend to privilege urban and particularly suburban understandings of church ministry and mission.

Since, in the North, historic church buildings remain significant foci of pilgrimage and community loyalty, ways of keeping these stories in stone active and open will need to be found. Festival churches, ecumenical sharing, and Community Hubs will need to be part of this mix and local communities beyond the congregations will need to be engaged in using and funding these buildings. Web facilities, mobile apps, and other communicative and educational aids which can tell the building's story and its witness will need to be explored, preferably privileging the favoured kinaesthetic learning styles of the majority community. The apparent hunger for places of retreat and spiritual renewal also invites the use of open church buildings as prayer stations within which refreshments and devotional aids can be available for visitors. Chaplaincy to schools and other local facilities also cohere with this vision. As in some other parts of England, with declining stipendiary ministry projections and the norm of multi-parish benefices in the North of England, there is a need to re-focus this ministry in a more episcopal way with oversight becoming the predominant responsibility of such ministers together with a shared, collegial approach to ministry which encourages and welcomes self-supporting local lay and ordained leadership, team-working, and congregational agency. This will require a clear sense of the call and purpose, the vision and strategy of each benefice, parish, and congregation, and a reflective and reflexive approach to ongoing development. Central to this agenda will be catechesis since renewing confidence in the Gospel entails deepening the discipleship of the committed but in a way that fosters outward engagement rather than sectarianism. The challenge is to re-engage the wider community in the light of the Anglican vocation and the terroir of that community with a Gospel attuned to the realities of the North.

6.6.   CONCLUSION

David Ford's work on the wisdom cries in Luke-Acts, John, Job, and Paul reveals the voices of those seeking to discern God's action in the most trying contingencies of life. Job and Jesus in particular exhibit the fragility of being stripped of all power in order to learn to love God for nothing and, in Jesus' case, to live and die for God's sake.[27] Contemporary Anglicans in the North similarly cry out to God for wisdom as they seek to improvise faithfully upon the Gospel of divine friendship for the estranged in analogous ways. Such wisdom is not technique or theory but the practically grounded insight which expresses a fruitful conversation between tradition and the changed present. It resists blueprints and abstract solutions, preferring instead to pray the terroir and to see in fragility opportunities for deepening trust and imaginative improvisation which better witness to the victorious grace of God for the very diverse precariat communities of this part of England. In this faithful improvisation is a Gospel for the North.

NOTES

1. *From Anecdote to Evidence: Finds From the Church Growth Research Programme, 2011-2013*, <http://www.churchgrowthresearch.org.uk/UserFiles/File/Reports/FromAnecdoteToEvidence1.0.pdf>, p. 10. The "solutions" to the challenges this report presents have merit but need to be tempered by local realities particularly in rural areas.

2. Guy Standing, *The Precariat: The New Dangerous Class* (Bloomsbury Academic, 2011).

3. Grace Davie, *Religion in Modern Europe: A Memory Mutates* (OUP, 2000), pp. 30-61.

4. Standing, *The Precariat*, pp. 132-47.

5. James Davison Hunter, *To Change the World: The Irony, Tragedy and Possibility of Christianity in the Late Modern World* (OUP, 2010), pp. 273-86. See also John B. Thomson, *DOXA: A Discipleship Course* (DLT, 2007) which uses the liturgy for formative catechesis.

6. Charles Taylor, *A Secular Age* (Belknap Press, 2007), pp. 25-51 and pp. 62-89.

7. Martin Percy, *Shaping the Church: The Promise of Implicit Theology* (Ashgate, 2010), p. 39 and p. 56.

8. See John Inge, *A Christian Theology of Place* (Ashgate, 2003), pp. 101-14.

9. Michael Moynagh with Philip Harrold, *A Church for Every Context: An Introduction to Theology and Practice* (SCM, 2012), p. 91.

10. See W. H. Vanstone, *Love's Endeavour, Love's Expense: The Response of Being and the Love of God* (DLT, 1977), pp. 55-74 in which he explores this kenotic theme.

11. André Louf, *Tuning In To Grace: The Quest for God* (Cistercian Publications, 1992), pp. 59-77.

12. See the Christ Hymn in Philippians 2:5-11.

13. Rowan Williams, *Anglican Identities* (DLT, 2004), p. 90.

14. John B. Thomson, *Church on Edge? Practising Christian Ministry Today* (DLT, 2004), pp. 100-101.

15. Stanley Hauerwas, *A Community of Character* (University of Notre Dame Press, 1981), p. 37. See also John B. Thomson, *Living Holiness: Stanley Hauerwas and the Church* (Epworth, 2010).

16. Brad Kallenberg, *Ethics as Grammar: Changing the Postmodern Subject* (University of Notre Dame Press, 2001), p. 156.

17. *General Synod GS MISC 1025: Pursuing the Three Quinquennium Goals—Report to the Synod on GS 1815 and GS Misc 995*, <https://www.churchofengland. org/media/1482516/gs%20misc%201025%20pursuing%20the%20three%20 quinquennium%20goals.pdf> (accessed 05 January 2015).

18. Martyn Percy, *The Ecclesial Canopy: Faith, Hope, Charity* (Ashgate, 2012), pp. 161–66.

19. Martyn Percy, *Clergy: Origin of Species* (Continuum, 2006), p. 75.

20. Moynagh, *A Church for Every Context*, pp. 126–31. For worked examples of this which are fruitful for both inherited and Fresh Expressions of Church see ibid., pp. 197–422.

21. For a richer engagement with this theme see John B. Thomson, *Sharing Friendship: Exploring Anglican Character, Vocation, Witness and Mission* (Ashgate, 2015).

22. For this criticism of Fresh Expressions of Church which, ironically, can also be levelled at many inherited modes of Church see *Andrew Davison and Alison Milbank, For the Parish: A Critique of Fresh Expressions* (SCM, 2010).

23. The Greek word *paroikos* can be translated as "stranger".

24. Liz Carmichael, *Friendship: Interpreting Christian Love* (T & T Clark, 2004), p. 7.

25. Jill Hopkinson, "Rural Multi-Church Ministry in the 21st century. A review of mission, ministry, fresh expressions, evangelism, growth, governance and structures within rural multi-church groups" (unpublished paper, 2014), 1.10.

26. Inge, *A Christian Theology of Place*, especially pp. 102–14.

27. David Ford, *Christian Wisdom: Desiring God and Learning Love* (CUP, 2007), pp. 43–62.

7. FAITH IN RECONCILIATION: A PERSONAL REFLECTION ON THE GOSPEL IN THE NORTH

James Newcome

For about eight hundred years, Rose Castle was home to the Bishops of Carlisle. Situated in the so-called "disputed lands" near the border between England and Scotland it was constantly fought over in its early days. Indeed, its medieval bishops were (together with the Bishops of Durham) agents of the king, with their own private army of about forty men. From time to time they would ride out at the head of that little army to confront marauding Scots, in particular the "Reivers" who stole sheep and other chattels from English homes. Indeed one bishop was noted more for his prowess in the saddle than in the pulpit; and Rose was frequently attacked, not least by Robert the Bruce who burnt part of it down. The present building is, as a result, about half its original size, but it remains a formidable (and rather beautiful) monument to a turbulent time in the history of the North West.

In 2009, with a change of diocesan bishop the Church Commissioners finally decided that the moment had come for Rose Castle no longer to be the "See House". For some sixty years they had been searching—fruitlessly—for a suitable alternative. Now, at last, Holy Name House in Keswick became available: an old vicarage which had served as a convent for the Community of the Holy Name for thirty years. This provided an ideal solution to a long-running problem. But it also raised the fascinating and highly contentious question of what should happen to Rose Castle itself.

After a flurry of rather acrimonious meetings and somewhat vitriolic articles in the local and national press, a group calling itself "The Friends of Rose Castle" was established in an attempt to purchase Rose and preserve it as a visitor attraction, or perhaps turn it into five flats with the current bishop living in one of them. When it became apparent that neither of these options was going to work, the Friends began to explore other alternatives. At exactly this moment I met a dynamic young theologian called Sarah Snyder who was then working with the Regius professor of Divinity (David Ford) in Cambridge. She suggested that perhaps some of the inter-faith reconciliation work with which she was closely involved could take place at Rose Castle. And so the "Rose Castle Foundation" was born, centred initially around a group of three people: Sarah, myself and an entrepreneur friend from Kendal called Christopher Townsend. The Foundation gradually took over from the Friends, and for the last two years has been trying to find sponsors who will enable us to buy, refurbish and endow Rose Castle as an International Christian Centre for Reconciliation.

Reconciliation is the key message at the very heart of the Christian Gospel. Jesus died on the cross so that we could be reconciled with God, and as St Paul observes, we ourselves are called to be agents or ambassadors of God's reconciling work. So what could be a more appropriate use for Rose than a ministry of reconciliation which would turn that early history of conflict on its head? We felt that the idea itself had been given at a *kairos* moment. And as the project has developed, again and again we have seen God's hand at work.

For a start, we have been provided with an extraordinary network of well-wishers, trustees and supporters, including the person who (we hope) will be buying the castle from the Church Commissioners and allowing us to use it. Everywhere we have turned doors have opened and it has become apparent that reconciliation is one of the chief needs in society today. It was the theme of the Queens's Christmas message at the end of 2014, and governments of all persuasions are desperate to see it happen. So we now find ourselves in a sort of partnership with seven major universities, the Foreign Office, more than one foreign government, and charities such as A Rocha, as well as other centres for reconciliation (e.g. in Coventry, London, Ireland, and South Africa.) Reconciliation is one of the current Archbishop of Canterbury's three main emphases, and the Archbishop of York (as Primate of the Northern Province) is our patron. One of the Anglican clergy in Carlisle Diocese has now also resigned his post in order to serve as full-time CEO of the Foundation.

What is more, a group of religious leaders in the Middle East have formed a "Ring of Faith" which is devoted to making peace, and the intention is that their efforts should be centred around Rose Castle. With its (soon to be upgraded) accommodation and large "state" rooms, it is an ideal location for this sort of work.

The reconciliation that we plan to see happening at Rose falls into four main categories. First, there is reconciliation between Christians, Muslims, and Jews through "Scriptural Reasoning", which leads not to some sort of watered down syncretism but a mutual understanding of difference. Second will be reconciliation between national leaders from around the world who will be able to engage in peaceful talks at Rose of a kind that currently take place only in the South. Third will be reconciliation between the Church and society as we promote "Religious Literacy" for employees in journalism, the NHS, the armed forces, the diplomatic service and so on. Finally, we propose reconciliation with the environment through sustainable agriculture on the "Home Farm" and the development of a six–acre garden as well as rehabilitation work with ex-offenders and others on the "care farm" principle.

There is a long way still to go with this project (which is currently in its early stages), but we believe that it has the potential to have a major impact on promoting the Gospel of Reconciliation in the North West of England, and demonstrating just how vital the Christian faith is for this essential work. At the time of writing, offers for Rose Castle made by the Foundation have been rejected by the Church Commissioners. We still hope that one day Rose Castle might be the base for our work: but even if it is not, that work will continue at an alternative location in the Lake District, and we remain absolutely committed to the task of mission it represents in the North West.

8. THE CONTRIBUTION OF THE NORTH TO THE NATIONAL CHURCH: A CASE STUDY IN WILLIAM TEMPLE'S LIFE AND THOUGHT[1]

Stephen Spencer

William Temple (1881–1944) is widely regarded as the most influential archbishop of Canterbury of the twentieth century. Among other reasons, this is because of his influence on British public opinion during the Second World War, especially in winning over the middle classes to the idea of a welfare state (which their taxes would pay for after the war). Temple also had a key role in securing the passage of the 1944 Education Act, and in laying the foundations for the creation of the World Council of Churches in 1948. His books were read widely, and two of them, *Readings in St John's Gospel* (1938–40) and *Christianity and Social Order* (1942), remained in print for decades after his death.[2]

What is not always appreciated is that much of the leg work behind these achievements took place not when he was at Canterbury, which occupied only the last two and a half years of his life, but during the long period when he was first Bishop of Manchester (1921–1928) and then Archbishop of York (1928–1942). Indeed, the years at York were especially important. The historian Adrian Hastings commented that:

The archbishopric of York may have been the one entirely suitable position he occupied in life. The trouble of the pre-1921 years had been the number of quite different jobs he had accepted and abandoned. York was right for him. Here was a *cathedra* for teaching, national, even international, rather than for formal ecclesiastical administration and political involvement.[3]

It was, in other words, the North of England that provided him with the setting and the stimulus to achieve many of the things that he did. This chapter tells the story of his life and work bringing to the fore this dimension in a way that has not been done before.

The first thing to grasp about Temple is that he was, in many ways, quintessentially a southerner! He was born in the Bishop's Palace at Exeter. His father, Frederick Temple, was the bishop of that diocese and would go on to be Bishop of London and Archbishop of Canterbury (1897 to 1902) (William would become the only son of an archbishop of Canterbury to follow his father in that office). Frederick was a very accomplished self-made man, attending university on a scholarship and then working his way to the top. William was close to his father but also probably in awe of him. He assisted his father as a page boy when Frederick crowned Edward VII as king in Westminster Abbey in 1902. His mother was from an aristocratic family, brought up in London as well as country estates, and had mixed with many leading Victorian statesman.

8.1.   EARLY YEARS

William had a very privileged upbringing, growing up in bishop's palaces, attending Rugby School, and then winning a scholarship to Balliol College, Oxford, where he studied Classics (Greek and Latin literature and philosophy). His education gave him a fluency and a precision with words, leading him to begin his career as a lecturer in philosophy. He had a gift of being able to communicate what he had learned with a calm and infectious enthusiasm. Even as a young lecturer he was being invited to speak around the country and his first book, *The Faith and Modern Thought* of 1910,[4] showed his logical yet fluent style almost fully formed. At this time he also developed a large waistline, having a lifelong passion for strawberry jam and ices. He had what seemed an everlasting good humour and a distinctive high-pitched laugh. His manner was relaxed, friendly, and "with no vestige of pomposity".[5]

But in 1905, while still at Oxford, he was recruited into the Worker's Educational Association, which brought together workers with university teachers in co-operative education. He later said this work, and especially his contact with Albert Mansbridge, the founder of the WEA, was one of the most formative experiences of his life.[6] Mansbridge was the son of a carpenter and had to leave school at 14 because his father could not afford school fees. He was self-taught and, after moving to London, was accepted into evening classes at King's College. He believed passionately in opening up education to ordinary people and founded a number of associations in Britain and around the world to enable this. For Temple, the young philosophy don from Oxford, Mansbridge was a revelation, providing a door into the vivid world of the self-improving working classes in the hard years before the founding of the welfare state. Temple would later comment of Mansbridge that "As a personal matter . . . he invented *me*."[7] Temple, in turn, was welcomed into the WEA by Mansbridge and its members. He was elected its president continuously between 1908 and 1924.

In terms of his day job, however, he followed a more conventional path. He became the headmaster of Repton School, following in the footsteps of his father who had been a distinguished headmaster of Rugby. But this role did not really suit him (he was no disciplinarian) and four years later he moved to be Rector of St James' Church, Piccadilly. Here he continued to work on philosophy, and in 1917 published a philosophical volume, *Mens Creatrix* (Creative Mind).[8] This and later books drew on his philosophical studies of Plato as well as German and British Idealist philosophy, his love of literature, especially Robert Browning's poetry, and biblical theology, especially the Fourth Gospel. He would later publish a companion volume, *Christus Veritas* (Christ the Truth) in 1924.[9] This was more theological in approach.

In 1916 Temple married Frances Anson, who also shared a commitment to social reform and to publishing. They did not have children and Temple was frequently away from home, but surviving letters show the couple enjoyed a supportive and loving partnership throughout their married life.

Temple became preoccupied with Church reform and, after three years, left St James' to work for the Life and Liberty movement, which campaigned to get Parliament to give the Church of England greater powers of self-government. The Enabling act of 1919 was its outcome, an act which created the Church Assembly and the setting up of parochial church councils with electoral roles. Davidson then moved him to become a canon of Westminster Abbey, where his preaching and teaching ministry gained national prominence. Some of his sermons were published in the volume *Fellowship with God*.[10] The journalist Harold Begbie has provided a portrait of Temple at this point in his life:

> Picture to yourself the youngest-looking middle-aged man you ever encountered, of a full countenance, and a body inclined to heaviness, with as much hair on his head as when he was twenty (in a condition a little untidy, like a boy's of fourteen), spectacles in front of bright and extremely steady eyes, a meeting of the brows at the centre in a line of concentration.[11]

8.2.   TO THE NORTH

Then in 1921, at the age of 40, after this succession of different jobs that "he had accepted and abandoned",[12] he was called north to become Bishop of Manchester, then the most populous diocese outside London with 3.5 million residents. Here he combined pastoral duties around the diocese with writing and speaking up and down the country. He would spend part of each summer at week-long missions in Blackpool, sometimes on the beach and sometimes in St John's Church, expounding the New Testament, including Revelation, to the holidaymakers. Something unexpected happened: the build-up of a rapport between this donnish cleric and the Bradford millworkers on holiday on the Lancashire coast. This is seen in the following description, written by one of the other missioners after learning that Temple was going to expound the book of Revelation to the holiday makers:

> Lunch-hour talks! In church! During August Bank Holiday week! In Blackpool! On the Revelation! Most of us felt that he was batting on a sticky wicket, and despite extensive postering not more that 40 or 50 turned up. The next day there were over 200, and for the remaining days the church was packed, a queue outside stretching almost down to the Front, waiting to get in—a wonderful example of his judgment and an amazing testimony to his power of exposition![13]

Temple himself was surprised. He wrote to his wife:

> Just back from my 3 sermons. Over 1,200 folk at each, and I think they went well. Everyone is commenting on the greater number of men at these functions, which is rather encouraging . . . This evening there were 900–1,000 in the church for "The Sealed Book". It is very striking that they should want to attend a 50 minutes' lecture on a bit of the Bible like that.[14]

Temple, it seems, was making connections with an audience that stretched beyond the Church and educational circles he had been moving in up until now. His coming to Manchester and the North had propelled his ministry into a new phase.

Furthermore, as he travelled through Lancashire's industrial towns, he saw the acute social and economic hardships faced by the majority of the population. Those who worked in the mills faced harsh regimes, and those who were unemployed could not rely on unemployment benefit because there was none. Nor was there a national health service, nor education beyond the age of eleven except for a few. In William Beveridge's famous

words, the scourges of want, disease, ignorance, squalor, and idleness
stalked the land. As Temple himself wrote:

> We see on the one side a considerable number of people
> enjoying a great many of the good things of life with
> singularly little regard to the needs of others, and we see
> on the other side a vast amount of real want and destitution,
> and also a great amount of vice which is largely due to
> poverty. That is a state of affairs with which the Christian
> cannot rest content.[15]

Temple did not rest content. He was determined to galvanize opinion
within the churches to build up pressure for change. So he convened and
chaired the ecumenical Conference on Politics, Economics, and Citizenship
(COPEC) which met in Birmingham in 1924 with 1400 delegates from
different churches. Hastings says of COPEC that its

> immediate consequences were small. Its importance
> lay within a longer process of adult education whereby
> the leadership, clerical and lay, of the Church was being
> weaned from high Tory attitudes to an acceptance of
> the Christian case for massive social reform and the
> development of a welfare state. In this it and its like were
> almost over-successful.[16]

Importantly, Temple himself coined the term "welfare state" in some
lectures of 1928. He contrasted the "power state" of the pre-First World
War Austrian and Prussian nations, in which the state coerced its citizens
for its own ends, with a "welfare state", which exists to serve the welfare of
all its people and which, he argued, was needed in contemporary society
(as, indeed, it is needed now).[17]

8.3.   LEADERSHIP FROM YORK

In 1929 Temple became Archbishop of York and, as Hastings pointed out above, this was an ideal post for him because, without a large urban diocese to run, he had more time for preaching and lecturing at national and international level. This he did with renewed gusto, giving university mission addresses in Cambridge, Dublin, and Oxford, the last of which became one of his most popular books, *Christian Faith and Life* of 1931.[18] He was also invited to give the prestigious Gifford lectures on natural theology in Glasgow, which were then published as *Nature, Man and God* in 1934.[19] These were his most extensive and mature essays in philosophical theology. Through all of this his main concerns were to communicate a vision of the whole of life—religious, personal, economic, political— with Christ at the centre as the one who makes sense of the whole and illuminates it with his truth. Temple also became more and more involved with the ecumenical movement, giving the opening sermon at the Faith and Order conference in Edinburgh in 1937 and being instrumental in the drawing up of plans for the forming of a World Council of Churches. He was the most senior Church leader to be involved in this movement and, in some fine addresses to the clergy of York Diocese, he provided careful and extensive mapping of how the Church of England should relate to this movement.[20] He also took a lead in encouraging the growth of the ecumenical movement at national level, preaching at the launch of the British Council of Churches in 1942.

But the 1930s were a time of gathering storms, with the rise of the Nazis in Germany and the Fascists in Italy calling into question the optimistic view of life that Temple had cherished. To his credit he began to revise the tone and content of his speaking, recognising that the world as it then stood did not make sense but was in need of redemption (a view which remains true in the modern day). In one of his best known books, the *Readings in St John's Gospel*,[21] he compared the world to a dark night in which only one light was visible, like a single but powerful ray from a lighthouse on a headland. For Temple, that ray of light was Christ, shining through the darkness of the world, 'cleaving it but neither dispelling it nor quenched by it'.[22]

When war with Germany was declared in October 1939, after Hitler's invasion of Poland, Temple rose to the occasion. In a BBC radio broadcast to the nation, he avoided the kind of jingoism that many churchmen had preached at the start of the First World War and, as became clear afterwards, he perfectly captured the mood of many in the country. The public mind, he said:

> is completely void of excitement. There is a deep determination, accompanied by no sort of exhilaration, but by a profound sadness. Men are taking up a hateful duty; the very fact that they hate it throws into greater relief their conviction that it is a duty. It is a duty first to Poland; but that is rather the focus than the real essence of our obligation for our purpose is to check aggression, and to bring to an end the perpetual insecurity and menace which hang over Europe, spoiling the life of millions, as a result of the Nazi tyranny in Germany.[23]

This broadcast turned Temple into a national leader. There was now little doubt that after the retirement of Cosmo Gordon Lang, the Archbishop of Canterbury, Temple would replace him.

Meanwhile, the social and economic needs of the population were very much in Temple's mind, and he was asking what kind of society Britain should become once the fighting was over. In 1942 he published a slim Penguin Special, *Christianity and Social Order*, which quickly became a best seller, with 139,000 copies eventually being sold.[24] With a radical clarity he set out the fundamental Christian principles that should govern the way a society organizes its life, and drew out some of the practical implications of these principles. In writing the book he received advice from William Beveridge, the academic and civil servant who wrote the *Beveridge Report* that set out extensive proposals for social security and post-war reconstruction, and the pre-eminent economist John Maynard Keynes, among others, and its popularity and influence has resulted in Temple being described as one of the architects of the welfare state created by Clement Attlee's Labour Government.[25]

1942 was also the year Temple was called to move south to become Archbishop of Canterbury. Before recounting what he did in this post, during the last and brief two and a half years of his life, it is worth quoting a note Temple sent to all his friends as he prepared to leave York for London. It sums up much of what he gained from living in the North over so many years:

> So many letters have reached us that is impossible to express our thanks to those who have written except in this way. It is unnecessary to say that the kindness of our friends is a very great help and encouragement as we look forward to new and largely unknown work. These are fearful times in which to take up so great a responsibility. May God give us His guidance and strength to meet it.
>
> The departure from our many friends in Yorkshire and from the beauty both of Bishopthorpe and of so many parts of the Diocese will be a terrible sorrow. We have become so attached to the Diocese of York and to the Northern Province as to feel that we belong to them and cannot be separated from them without very great pain. That is the price to be paid for the blessings of friendships like those which we have made here. But though we shall not meet our friends so often, the friendships themselves will not be broken.
>
> At whatever home we are able to establish either in what remains undamaged of Lambeth or in Canterbury there will always be a warm welcome for the friends we are leaving in the North as well as for those whom we hope to make as we take up work in the South. Please do not forget this or hesitate to act upon it.
>
> Many of the letters which have come refer to the anxieties which are unavoidable when we think about the future of our country and of the world. The difficulties and opportunities will both be very great. The only hope of meeting these in such a way as to bring the world nearer to what we know

must be God's purpose for it is to be found in a strong faith
in God and His upholding power.[26]

8.4.   ARCHBISHOP OF CANTERBURY

Temple and his wife moved into Lambeth Palace in London, living on
the ground floor because the rest of the house was bomb-damaged (Lang
had preferred to live at the Athenaeum Club). He was seen catching the
bus across Westminster Bridge and fulfilled his duties while putting up
with flying bombs by day and air raids by night. His continual travelling
took place on crowded buses and trains in the black-out.

He did not forget his social reform agenda developed while at York.
In late 1942 and early 1943, in the Albert Hall in London, he made some
widely publicized remarks on the banking system, suggesting that the
government should put curbs on profits and should place restrictions
on the issuing of credit by banks. The remarks were heavily criticized by
financiers in the City of London, but they again showed Temple challenging
the current order in favour of a new and fairer post-war world.[27]

In 1942, when it became clear how badly the Jewish peoples of Eastern
Europe were being treated by the Nazis, in public meetings and in the House
of Lords, Temple called for immediate action to provide help and asylum
for those Jews able to escape from Hitler's domains.[28] He had already been a
co-founder of the Council for Christians and Jews in 1942 and had built up
good relations with Jewish leaders. When he died the Jewish community in
Britain paid a special heart-felt tribute to him for these and other efforts.[29]

He gave crucial backing to R. A. Butler's education act in 1944, which,
for the first time, set up a national system that would include both state
and Church schools, and raised the school leaving age to 15. The act led
to the surrender of some Church schools to the state in some parts of
the country, because the churches could not afford their upkeep, and was
controversial. Temple backed the act because he saw raising the school
leaving age to be more important for the whole population than the
Church retaining control of some of its schools.

He continued to be a keen ecumenicist, involved not only internationally but at home: for example, he shared a platform with Cardinal Hinsley, the leader of the Roman Catholic Church in England and Wales, and encouraged joint prayers. If he had survived the war it is extremely likely that he would have been the first president of the World Council of Churches when it was inaugurated.

But he did not survive the war. After a prolonged attack of gout (from which he suffered all his life but which was now exacerbated by over-work), he died of a heart attack on 26 October 1944. As already mentioned, this was just two and a half years after becoming Archbishop of Canterbury. He was not to see Allied victory in the war, nor was he to assist with the social and economic reconstruction of the country in the post-war years. It was a huge loss. As Hastings has written:

> It is not true, as [the Bishop of Durham, Herbert Hensley] Henson claimed, that if he had lived he would have found that he had outlasted his eminence: on the contrary. The post-war world would have suited him admirably and his role in it as the great presider and spokesman of the enlightened consensus in matters religious not only for Britain but for the United State [which he had visited several times], Europe and the World Council of Churches would, undoubtedly, have been outstanding—a role no one person after his death could ever fill.[30]

8.5.   A NORTHERN ARCHBISHOP?

Overall, then, what kind of impact did Temple's living in the North have on this nationally and internationally important ministry? It is hard to answer such a question with any kind of precision, but his ongoing contact with northern working-class communities and their needs undoubtedly helped to form the leader he became. As the Birkenhead MP Frank Field has written:

[Temple] was as important as anyone in convincing the electorate both that it was safe to vote for radical change and that radical change was what the poor and the working class should demand. To the middle class he sold the idea of a continuing sacrifice, while for the working class and the poor he helped to convince them that their position of deference in British politics was coming to a close. Although William died in October 1944, his lasting influence was to be seen almost a year later as the ballot papers were strewn across the counting tables. Clement Attlee emerged with a record parliamentary majority, in no small measure thanks to the life of political campaigning by Frederick Temple's son William.[31]

Field adds a personal comment:

Those of us who are war-time babies, or who were born since, owe him a debt for helping to make our lives so different from the lives of those who grew up in the inter-war years. Temple raised people's hopes and encouraged them not to settle for another round of the 1930s.[32]

David Jenkins, himself formed by many years working in Leeds and then as Bishop of Durham, has drawn attention to the spiritual dimension of this impact:

As a teenager I attended the Albert Hall meeting which Temple addressed, along with others including Sir Stafford Cripps, and what I drew from this, as well as what I read of his utterances and writings, was a clear understanding that we should be deeply Christian and deeply concerned with current affairs. Christianity was neither a purely private religion nor a merely spiritual religion. This was so because of the nature and purposes of the God to whom Christianity was a response. Temple was, surely, a powerful devout man, and the demands which he put before one were clearly religious, devotional and godly. But godliness required concern for the affairs of society because men and women were so socially shaped, and often socially distorted, and because the transcendent God was committed to worldly particularities for the furthering of his purposes and the sharing of his love.[33]

George Bell, Temple's contemporary as Bishop of Chichester, summed him up in a different but striking way. Temple, he wrote, "had all the vividness and swiftness of a flame; he communicated warmth and light to all who saw or heard him".[34] Part of the warmth of that flame undoubtedly came from his long term contact with the northern communities which he served as a bishop and archbishop.

NOTES

1. A revised and expanded version of my "Introduction: William Temple's Life and Publications" in Stephen Spencer, *Christ in All Things: William Temple's Writings* (Canterbury Press 2015), pp. xi-xx.

2. William Temple, *Readings in St. John's Gospel*, 2 vols. (Macmillan, 1939–40; complete edition, 1945; and paperback edition, 1961); *idem, Christianity and Social Order* (Penguin Special, 1942; SCM, 1950; and SPCK, 1976).

3. "William Temple" in Adrian Hastings, *The Shaping of Prophecy* (Geoffrey Chapman, 1995), p. 61.

4. William Temple, *The Faith and Modern Thought* (Macmillan & Co., 1910).

5. F. A. Iremonger, *William Temple: Archbishop of Canterbury* (Oxford, 1948) p. 499.

6. Ibid., p. 77.

7. Ibid.

8. William Temple, *Mens Creatrix: An Essay* (Macmillan, 1917).

9. William Temple, *Christus Veritas: An Essay* (Macmillan, 1924).

10. William Temple, *Fellowship with God* (Macmillan, 1920).

11. Harold Begbie, "Religion and Politics: A Talk with Canon Temple", *The Daily Telegraph* (6 April, 1920).

12. Adrian Hastings, *The Shaping of Prophecy* (Geoffrey Chapman, 1995), p. 61.

13. In Iremonger, *William Temple, Archbishop of Canterbury*, p. 314.

14. Ibid., p. 315.

15. William Temple, *The Kingdom of God* (Macmillan, 1912), p. 74.

16. Adrian Hastings, *A History of English Christianity 1920-1985*, Fourth Edition (SCM Press, 2001), p. 179.

17. William Temple, *Christianity and the State* (Macmillan, 1928), p. 170.

18. William Temple, *Christian Faith and Life*, Oxford Mission addresses (SCM, 1931; reissued 1963; new edition, Susan Howatch (ed.), Mowbray, 1994).

19. William Temple, *Nature, Man and God*, Gifford Lectures (Macmillan, 1934).

20. William Temple, *Thoughts on Some Problems of the Day* (Macmillan, 1931).

21. William Temple, *Readings in St John's Gospel* (Macmillan & Co., 1939 and 1940)

22. Ibid., p. 7.

23. William Temple, "The Spirit and Aims of Britain in the War", in William Temple, *Thoughts in War-Time* (Macmillan, 1940), pp. 54-5.

24. William Temple, *Christianity and Social Order* (Penguin Books, 1942).

25. Frank Field, *Saints and Heroes: Inspiring Politics* (SPCK, 2010), pp. 34-5.

26. William Temple, *Some Lambeth Letters*, F. S. Temple (ed.) (Oxford University Press, 1963), pp. 7-8.

27. See Stephen Spencer, *William Temple: A Calling to Prophecy* (SPCK, 2001), pp. 101-4.

28. Ibid., pp. 105-7.

29. Iremonger, *William Temple, Archbishop of Canterbury*, p. 567.

30. "William Temple", in Adrian Hastings, *The Shaping of Prophecy* (Geoffrey Chapman, 1995), pp. 61-2.

31. Frank Field, *Saints and Heroes: Inspiring Politics* (SPCK, 2010), p. 35.

32. Ibid., p. 60. For a historian's perspective that, in general, supports this view of the influence of Temple and his colleagues see Matthew Grimley, *Citizenship, Community and the Church of England: Liberal Anglican Theories of the State Between the Wars* (Oxford University Press, 2004).

33. David Jenkins, "Christianity, Social Order and the Story of the World", *Theology*, (SPCK, 1981), pp. 321-322.

34. G. K. Bell, "Memoir", in A. E. Baker (ed.), *William Temple and His Message* (Penguin, 1946), p. 47.

9. LETTING THE POOR SPEAK: A STUDY OF CHURCH WORK IN MIDDLESBROUGH, AND WHAT IT MIGHT TEACH US ABOUT PENITENCE

Su Reid

9.1. CHURCH WORK IN MIDDLESBROUGH: LISTENING TO THE POOR

Together Middlesbrough and Cleveland, formerly Together Middlesbrough, is a co-operative venture between the Church Urban Fund and York Diocese. Managed by local people, it supports the voluntary work of Christians of different traditions addressing the needs of the poor in a very deprived area of the North of England. These include benefits claimants, struggling families with children, asylum seekers, food bank users, the homeless, the lonely, and many others whose very real needs can only be met by people willing to give regular personal support.[1]

On 3 October 2013, Together Middlesbrough hosted a conference entitled Bridges of Hope at which about 150 people came together to hear up-to-date accounts of the current causes of poverty in Middlesbrough, and to hear also about some of the work done by these church people.[2] I was among them. In this chapter I explain what I began to learn that day about how poor people's needs are often silenced, and about how these church people in Middlesbrough are enabling those voices to be heard. I also try to explain, later in the chapter, what I have begun to learn from this about the Church of England's languages of sin and penitence in formal worship.

Middlesbrough, with its surrounding urban area, is a stark example of northern English life. It grew with industrialization, though it is near much older towns and wildly beautiful countryside—the North York Moors National Park boundary is almost within its sprawl. The Stockton and Darlington Railway, opened in 1825 to link two old communities on the Tees, was extended downstream just five years later to reach deeper water for the export of coal, and a farm called "Middlesbrough" provided the land for what is still known as "Teesport", one of Britain's busiest ports (though, of course, all our ports are now much less busy than they used to be). The early coal-exporting business was overtaken when iron mining in the nearby Moors fed into huge steel-making and engineering enterprises. Middlesbrough's recorded population grew from 7,431 in 1851 to 91,302 in 1901.[3]

During the twentieth century, steel and engineering were joined by major petro-chemical installations. These huge plants are sited on otherwise empty land on the Tees estuary, which make Middlesbrough seem like an isolated industrial wilderness. Its wealthy industrialists were always there, and were later quickly joined by professional engineers, chemists, managers, doctors, and lawyers; they did not live locally, however, but just slightly further north in County Durham or on the rich farming land to the south, between York and the Tees. Their successors still live in these regions. The workers, in contrast, lived in terraced housing built near the river. Their descendants have only moved into large housing estates.

During the last quarter of the twentieth century major employers were bought out, often by foreign companies. Some plants closed, while others were mechanized and digitized so that far fewer people are employed now in these traditional industries. In a tour of Teesport in 2010 I was shown enormous warehouses where containerised goods imported for Sainsbury's and Marks and Spencer are redistributed by robots directed by one or two people. The descendants of the people who came to work in heavy industry are either moving away or are left hunting for work.

At Bridges of Hope we heard about ways in which both economic change and specific government policies have worsened the lives of people in Middlesbrough. We also heard about people's frequent sense of powerlessness. At the end of the conference, Dr Stephen Cherry (then a Residentiary Canon of Durham Cathedral and now Dean of King's College, Cambridge) gave us a "Theological Reflection" in which he asked this question: "What takes people's voices away from them?"[4]

This question was the most important thing I brought away from this conference. What makes poor people so unconfident, so powerless, so invisible to the prosperous? It has, however, a corollary: Bridges of Hope was attended both by people leading the Church's initiatives and by those benefiting from them—sometimes, indeed, beneficiaries had become leaders. The clearest thing I heard them say, both in formal sessions and over lunch, was that the work of the Church had enabled them, newly, to speak of their own lives, to be listened to and be heard rather than to be talked at. Sometimes, indeed, this meant they had gained confidence and had been able to find better employment at last. In other cases, though, the churches had simply provided listeners—coffee and biscuits in church rooms warmer than houses, and people happy to greet and hear others as people, not as "claimants" or "refugees". As Dr Cherry also said, dignity is taken from the poor; but the Church, by listening with real respect, can return it to them. This discovery is the start of my thinking in this chapter. How can the whole Church, like the people of Together Middlesbrough, better help people to speak about themselves? How might we all both hear and speak as both sinners and the sinned against?

9.2.   HOW THE POOR ARE SILENCED

Research among benefits claimants by sociologists in Middlesbrough's Teesside University has shown how self-respect is denied to people on welfare benefits. Their recent book, *Poverty and Insecurity: Life in Low-Pay, No-Pay Britain*,[5] demonstrates that claimants in Middlesbrough are seldom poor because of an unwillingness to work, but rather because the local economy only offers them short-term employment with rates of pay so low that they cannot build up enough savings to see them through the gaps between jobs. Their poverty is then worsened when they also lack full literacy or confidence with digital media, or when they simply feel intimidated by the benefits system and its slowness in processing claims. Instead of being offered support, many reported feeling "suffocated" or confused, or repeatedly being disbelieved by staff at Jobcentre Plus and welfare to work agencies.[6] A similar picture has been painted nationally in the recent study *Feeding Britain,*[7] funded by the Archbishop of Canterbury's Charitable Trust, which reports on an inquiry into food banks and their users. This report states, gently, that "the mechanism by which Jobcentre Plus captures and relays information does not always fit with the understanding and skills possessed by people in very difficult positions", and, writing less gently of benefits sanctions, also states that:

> Even if someone has applied for enough jobs to fulfil their requirements . . . they may be sanctioned for having filled in the forms incorrectly. This is particularly unfair on claimants who are barely literate.[8]

These conditions take people's voices away from them—they make it difficult for people to articulate their own needs and to make plans.

More insidiously, people who are themselves in poverty—people who cannot meet the basic costs of housing, utilities, and food—live within a culture in which they denounce themselves. *Poverty and Insecurity* cites "tabloid media portrayals" of people on benefits (who are actually often living without enough money) as "'scroungers', 'the workshy' and 'benefit cheats'".[9] It also shows, startlingly, that people who are themselves going without basics, such as a daily hot meal, share this view of "the poor".[10] Interviewees living on Job Seekers Allowance, and unable to buy quite basic household items, denied being "poor"—a term which they applied to "other people" who, they thought, spent money on drugs, alcohol or cigarettes.[11] They attributed poverty to personal failings, and often felt free, these Teesside researchers report, to hold "clear views on 'the undeserving poor' and . . . to castigate and blame them".[12] Even among neighbours in hardship, poverty is something "other people" are blamed for—not something which happens because of social conditions. This is, these researchers observe, an aspect of a wider social and political denial of poverty, a public discourse seeing poverty as non-existent or condemning it as "self-inflicted". It means that people who struggle daily to feed their families feel that poverty is something to be ashamed of; they therefore deny their own difficulties even to each other and to themselves, and claim to "manage".[13]

Some struggling people, moreover, feel blameworthy. This was demonstrated at Bridges of Hope by a brave live testimony from a young mother, Gemma (not her real name), who, encouraged by her children's school, had sought help from the local food bank. Gemma, whose testimony is still accessible online on the Together Middlesbrough website, says:

> I fell pregnant when I was eighteen and it was scary cos it's like you are still young yourself and it's like "how do you do it?" I didn't have much to spend on food after I'd paid my bills and stuff. Maybe ten pound? Kids would come home from school and it'd be like "you've got nothing in the fridge mam". I sat there and cried most days. It's horrible.[14]

The food bank provided support as well as food, so that Gemma, who lacked relevant skills and confidence, was helped to get a job which she has now held for over a year. "I can get what I want now", she says.

Alongside personal guilt about poverty, there is a characteristic of public political and moral debate which takes the people's voices away from them. The *Poverty and Insecurity* writers observe that, because their research method involved listening to individual claimants, it enabled them "to investigate subjective understandings of poverty" in ways which have not often been done: "the poor" have generally been *written about* by those who are not among them.[15]

This is demonstrably true of the 2010–2015 coalition government. Iain Duncan Smith, Secretary of State for Work and Pensions, gave a speech entitled "Getting Britain Working" in London on 11 August 2014 in which he said:

> There were . . . a series of apparent "generosities" in the welfare system, which were in fact quite the opposite. I have always believed that it was no kindness to park people on Incapacity Benefits, many of whom would never be seen again to establish whether there were any changes to their condition or any support we could give them to move into work. It was no kindness to put lone parents on Income Support for many years while their children were growing up without enough support and encouragement to move back to work allowing them to become detached from the labour market and making it much harder to make the move back into employment.[16]

This statement was self-righteously reproachful: the "welfare system" was reproached for having "parked" people without ongoing support; people on Incapacity Benefits were, implicitly, reproached for perhaps living with unreported changes in their circumstances; lone parents on Income Support were implicitly reproached for becoming "detached from the labour market" when left without "support and encouragement".[17] Later in the same speech Duncan Smith made claims about his introduction of a "benefit cap":

> The benefit cap [is] one of our most important changes in terms of its cultural impact and the message it sends out[:] the message that families on benefits must face the same choices about where they live and what they can afford as everyone else.[18]

This overt claim that families on benefits lack a basic notion of responsibility is strongly repudiated by the Middlesbrough study *Poverty and Insecurity*, not least in its revelations (already cited) that many people on benefits are proud to "manage" even where "managing" means going without food, and that they, alongside Duncan Smith, define their own rectitude by blaming nameless others.[19] The main point I want to make, however, concerns the contrast between this speech and the live testimony of the Middlesbrough woman called Gemma. Gemma has indeed been helped to find work. Her difficulty was not that she was content to live on benefits. Her difficulty was that she did not know what to do, and was emotionally undermined by the reproaches of her children. She did not need driving into work by being allocated even less money. She needed what the people working, voluntarily, with Together Middlesbrough through the Middlesbrough food bank gave her, and which *Feeding Britain*, as already cited, claims Jobcentre Plus and benefits staff do not:[20] individual attention and listening, basic respect, and help with the skills she needed to apply successfully for a job she could do. Gemma needed to be heard in her own voice, not represented within a third-person generalisation about other people. Together Middlesbrough made this possible for her, and they also make it possible for us to hear her.

9.3.   WHO DOES THE TALKING?

My concern is not just a political disagreement with the Secretary of State for Work and Pensions, but a simpler matter about who has a voice, and who is only talked about by public voices, and what they hear. It is a formal characteristic of public debate and policy-making, whether in a speech or in print, that a voice speaks about other people from a position of assumed power. The intention might be wholly honourable and generous, but those talked or written about go unheard, and are present only in the characteristics attributed to them by the speaker.

This is as true of public statements made by the Church as it is of politicians. It can be seen in major contributions by the Church to ideas of a just society made over the last century. Here are just three examples.

In 1942 William Temple, Archbishop of Canterbury, published *Christianity and Social Order*.[21] This short book contributed to debates informing the post-war Labour government and what we have become used to calling the "Welfare State". In it, Archbishop Temple acknowledged that much work "is done by Christian people fulfilling responsibilities and performing tasks" outside the "official system of the Church".[22] He cited work towards the abolition of slavery and reform of the penal system. Eighty years later we might similarly cite the work of Together Middlesbrough and, more widely, the food banks throughout the country. *Feeding Britain*, enabled by the present Archbishop of Canterbury, records that, while not all food banks are run by church people, nevertheless:

> In a country where the church is seen as being in long-term decline, it is the churches through their membership who have brought forward this most extraordinary welfare development.[23]

Temple also, however, asserted that:

> [The church] must supply [its members] with a systematic statement of principles . . . and this will carry with it a denunciation of customs or institutions . . . which offend against those principles.[24]

The final chapter of Archbishop Temple's book, "The Task Before Us",[25] set out a number of criticisms of current social institutions, and proposed new policies claiming to be based on such Christian principles. Temple wrote this, for example, about the provision of education for children and young people:

> If we are going to show a real respect for each individual as a child of God, we must see that from infancy to full maturity every child is set in such a social context as will best develop all the power which God has given him. To provide such an opportunity, not for a favoured few but for all children, is an urgent national duty. To fail here on the ground of the large expenditure required would be a national sin.[26]

This aspiration, based on a stated Christian principle, might well still command assent both from Church members and, broadly, from others. But its language, necessarily, speaks from a position of assumed power, not from that of the intended beneficiaries. These sentences certainly promise the children huge gifts, but they also enact those children as silent (girls doubly so when the child is called "him"). Readers can either align themselves with the speaker and consent (or not!) to the desirability of "giving" to children; or they can "listen" from the position of a child, but then there is only a silence. The children in these sentences are passive receivers—the recipients both of social contexts and of God-given "powers". In life, of course, both social context and individual "power" are inter-active.

Here is a second example: *Faith in the City* was a report from research, commissioned by the then Archbishop of Canterbury Robert Runcie, into the Church's roles in "Urban Priority Areas" (UPAs), or inner city areas in perceived economic and social decline.[27] It was published in 1985. The Church Urban Fund grew from *Faith in the City*, and its work today, as in Together Middlesbrough, focuses on participation within poor urban communities. It is not a top-down operation. At the time, however, it was more politically urgent for *Faith in the City* to speak from outside about the needs of identified Urban Priority Areas, and the role of the Church within them, than it was to articulate perspectives from inside. Here is a brief quotation from Chapter 4, "What Kind of Church?", which is explicitly addressed to Church members themselves:

> We have come to the conclusion that a local mission-centred Church must be a participating Church. It will participate by *collaborating* with the best expressions of local life and by *contributing* to the transformation of life in UPAs through God's sustaining power and purpose. By sharing in the life of God in the world more fully, the UPA Church can become a more responsive and confident Church.[28]

The "we" here are not speaking as members of a Priority Area community but on behalf of a national Church that is, as much as anything, seeking for itself to become "more responsive and confident". Where do "the best expressions of local life" exist here except as phenomena to be selected or defined, by someone unnamed, in due course? The people who actually do the "local life" are unheard. So are the members of the "local mission-centred Church". They are given a series of aspirations in generalised form—"participating", "collaborating", "contributing to the transformation of life", "sharing in the life of God in the world"; but these aspirations are abstracted instructions from the writers, not reflections of what such Church members might already be doing or hoping to do.

My third example is from *Feeding Britain* itself. *Feeding Britain*, like the work in Middlesbrough of the Teesside University sociologists published in *Poverty and Insecurity*, draws on many interviews with people engaged in the situations described. But when it states, heart-warmingly, that:

> The most widespread source and, in our view, one of the greatest strengths of the support available to people relying on emergency food assistance is the warmth, companionship and friendliness of the staff and volunteers. We encountered this from every food bank we visited during this Inquiry.[29]

Its readers, inevitably, hear the voice of the researchers, not that of either the food bank volunteers or their clients.

The point I have tried to make through these three examples is not any kind of complaint about the work behind these three reports. My point is just that when general principles or policies are proposed in relation to perceived social needs, the voices heard are the voices of the would-be reformers; and those voices assume they have some power over what can be done. These are not the voices of the people, the sinned-against perhaps, about whom the reformers are writing or speaking.

Feeding Britain's writers are aware of this, and their recommendations try to address the silence they have seen between national policy-makers and people most in need of help. They praise the food bank volunteers, again, because these volunteers do in fact hear the silenced voices:

> One of the fundamental reasons why we support the continuation of food banks . . . is that they have a proven ability to use food to reach "the hardest to reach" groups and engage them in a longer term process of overcoming hunger and in so doing offer them a fellowship that bureaucracy cannot.[30]

They also, courageously and idealistically, propose that "now is an appropriate time to move to a clearer contract-based welfare state".[31] In one of their closing recommendations they write, "We therefore recommend that the welfare contract be a genuine two-way contract between claimants and Jobcentre Plus."[32] Their proposal assumes that those with power—bureaucratic or political—and those in need of welfare support are *both* responsible parties, although with different needs and capabilities, and that the "contract" must be articulate for *all* parties: the requirements of both sides must be stated, which means all the rights and the forms of support provided for claimants must be explicitly stated and guaranteed.

I have some answers, then, to the question asked in Middlesbrough, "What takes people's voices away from them?" These answers involve bureaucratic insensitivity to people's needs and a culture in which poverty is a sign of personal failure and moral culpability; but they also identify a cultural structure in which public language silences individuals under generalized statements.

9.4.   WHEN CHURCH PEOPLE CONDEMN OTHERS

Some church people are addressing some problems. Church volunteers in Middlesbrough help people to get legitimate payments and, sometimes, to apply successfully for work. The "warmth, companionship and friendliness" that *Feeding Britain* reports, and the respect that participants described at Bridges of Hope, help people to talk about their needs and regain some self-respect. These are major gifts by church people to their neighbours.

These actions, however, contrast with other things church people do. Sometimes they judge others and even condemn them. There is some expectation among Church members, and in society at large, that "the Church" has specific views about matters of personal behaviour; and that those views have, over centuries, been influential across British society and, indeed, governance. A recent book has argued that changes in the law concerning personal behaviour in domestic and sexual contexts since the Second World War have meant that "the more or less Christian legislative framework for personal behaviour that had shaped the nation's morals for decades, and in some cases centuries, was swept aside".[33] An aspect of this is, it seems to me, the continuing belief among some members of the Church of England that they have the right to criticize others as "sinners" and to seek to marginalize or even exclude them in worship; and, by implication, to define themselves as more virtuous. The most obvious current examples concern people in same-sex relationships. I have also seen, however, a carefully written notice in a rural Yorkshire church where it is apparently necessary to plead with parishioners to accept that users of the food bank in a neighbouring town should not be condemned as idlers.

In the parable of the wedding banquet in Matthew 22, guests are called in from far and wide to take the places of invited guests who did not come. But one of these new guests is improperly dressed, and the host orders that he be thrown "into the outer darkness, where there will be wailing and gnashing of teeth" (Matthew 22:13). I wonder whether this part of this Gospel was written when Christians of Jewish origin rejected Gentile Christians who did not submit to circumcision, or even Jewish food practices. Be that as it may, the parable presents, on the one hand, an individual who does not conform and, on the other, a voice which claims authority and which judges and condemns the deviant. It calls to mind the judgements some church people make of their contemporaries. It opposes the work of Together Middlesbrough where people are accepted according to their needs.

9.5.   'SIN' IN ANGLICAN WORSHIP—WHAT IS IT?

This leads me, finally, to reflect on an aspect of the formal worship of the Church of England: the prominence given to penitence for worshippers' sins vaguely evoked, and the forgiveness that is offered through Christ but without the voices of the victims.

For readers who are unfamiliar with formal Church of England worship, here is a brief explanation. Current forms of approved public services are set out in *Common Worship*, a set of volumes published since 2000;[34] this accompanies the older *Book of Common Prayer*. *Common Worship* places Prayers of Penitence and Absolution near the start of almost all services, and only "authorized Prayers of Penitence" may ever be used.[35] *The Book of Common Prayer* includes a Confession and Absolution in its Order for Holy Communion, and a different "General Confession" near the start of both Morning Prayer and Evening Prayer—though the General Confession appears to have been added to the 1549 Morning Prayer only in 1559, and to Evening Prayer only at the 1662 re-publication.[36] In all these "Confessions" and "Prayers of Penitence" the congregation are required to declare that they have sinned, and to ask forgiveness *from God* (not from their victims). They are asked to characterize themselves as the (albeit repenting) sinners; those sinned against are left silent.

In daily life, surely, we are all failures, sinners, and also the sinned-against. The church volunteers in Middlesbrough enable conversations, dialogues, among people who are all both sinners and victims. But the formal worship of the Church of England structures thought away from such complexities and constructs its members only as doers of wrong to silent others, and asks us to apologize only to God. It articulates guilt but not responsibility.

Twenty-five years ago the theologian Daphne Hampson argued that a Protestant tradition in Christian theology advocates that the "self be broken", and the "person should learn to live from another who is God".[37] She rejected this on behalf of women who have already been taught, in Western civilization, to defer to men; she argued, instead, that women need "to come to themselves".[38] Without opening a debate here about gender difference, I find this idea helpful in thinking about the consciousness of Christians living in a society where wealth is distributed very unequally, and where, as in Middlesbrough, many people are victims of that unequal access to wealth. If the poor—Gemma, for example—come to a formal service using either *Common Worship* or *BCP*, and are faced almost at once with the requirement that they, as members of the congregation, declare themselves "sinners", it is at least possible that they will just find their own self-doubt increased. Meanwhile, in the other half of the congregation there will be people who have given long hours and much energy to listening to such people with respect, and to trying to find ways of helping them within society. Some of these, being habitual church attenders, will not deny that they are indeed "sinners"; but some might find accord with one who recently said to me that Evening Prayer had appalled him by insisting he was a "worthless worm". What is gained by articulating guilt but silencing social inequality?

With these concerns in mind, I look again at some familiar words of confession. I find that the ones we have used for centuries do not help us to think morally about our lives. Even within the theological structure of human sin redeemed by divine love and atonement, these prayers do not give us voices. The metaphor of sheep that have "erred and strayed from thy ways"[39] means little to those of us who do not work with hefted sheep, except a pleasantly rural picture. More generalized statements, like "we have left undone those things which we ought to have done", just provide an open space into which we might—or might not—simply unload, without debate or guidance, whatever we happen to be feeling guilty about just then.

Common Worship has gone some way towards offering clearer thinking about our own failures before God. Some of the seasonal Confessions, for example, do nudge us towards thinking about our lives, not as lone individuals with nameless bags of things "left undone", but as responsible members of a society within which we collectively fail. At Christmas, for example, we say:

> Your Son our Saviour
> was born in poverty in a manger.
> Forgive our greed and rejection of your ways.[40]

Who is speaking here? Not those who were born or now live "in poverty": they have no voice. Nevertheless, *Common Worship*'s widely used "Order One" for Holy Communion does offer a political standard beside which to voice our penitence. It quotes words recalling those of Christ to Pharisees in the days before his crucifixion, as given in Matthew 22:37–40:

> Our Lord Jesus Christ said:
> The first commandment is this:
> "Hear, O Israel, the Lord our God is the only Lord.

You shall love the Lord your God with all your heart,
with all your soul, with all your mind,
and with all your strength."
The second is this: "Love your neighbour as yourself."
There is no other commandment greater than these.
On these two commandments hang all
    the law and the prophets.
Amen. Lord, have mercy.[41]

The listing of these two major commandments is deeply familiar to those
of us who attend Church frequently; so familiar that we might not hear
their political import. In linking these two "commandments", however,
Jesus references Leviticus 19:17–18, which reads:

> You shall not hate in your heart anyone of your kin; you shall
> reprove your neighbour, or you will incur guilt yourself. You
> shall not take vengeance or bear a grudge against any of
> your people, but you shall love your neighbour as yourself:
> I am the LORD.

Leviticus is entirely about membership of a particular society, and its laws
and requirements. A "neighbour" in this passage is to be "loved", but this
means he (or she?) is also to be "reproved" if he does not observe the Law.
To "love" a neighbour, here, is to make sure he serves divine Law. The
Gospels, and the Christian Church over two millennia, have understood
Jesus to teach that "loving" one's neighbour is a personal demand. But
I suggest we must better recall that "love your neighbour" also had a
political and social dimension.

The conclusion I have come to, from thinking about the work of
Together Middlesbrough, is this. Formal worship in the Church of England
requires the expression of "penitence"; but that penitence, followed by
formal absolution, is often vaguely worded. Worshippers are not helped to
think about what their "sin" is, and what, apart from being broadly sorry,
they might do about it. Above all, the prayers do not ask worshippers, poor
or less poor, to think about "sin" as more than private personal behaviour,
or explicitly to confront their own wider roles within an unequal society

and to hear the needs of the poor. Together Middlesbrough's language—the talking and listening it supports—does both. Somehow we must learn to carry communal questions about what "sin" is into our formal worship, and to pray about "sin" as a matter of social and political responsibility, not just a matter concerning the private individual. If we do not do this we will continue to silence the poor.

NOTES

1. <http://www.cuf.org.uk/together-middlesbrough-and-cleveland> (accessed 8 April 2015).
2. For details, see <http://www.cuf.org.uk/blog/bridges-hope> (accessed 8 April 2015).
3. The classic account of Middlesbrough's early life, quoting Gladstone's view of it as "an infant Hercules", is "Middlesbrough: The Growth of a New Community", in Asa Briggs, *Victorian Cities* (Odhams Press, 1963; Penguin, 1968), pp. 241–276.
4. <http://www.cuf.org.uk/blog/bridges-hope> (accessed 8 April 2015).
5. Tracy Shildrick, Robert MacDonald, Colin Webster, and Kayleigh Garthwaite, *Poverty and Insecurity: Life in Low-Pay, No-Pay Britain* (The Policy Press, 2012).
6. Ibid., pp. 182–3.
7. *Feeding Britain: A Strategy for Zero Hunger in England, Wales, Scotland and Northern Ireland. The Report of the All-Party Parliamentary Inquiry into Hunger in the United Kingdom* (The Children's Society, December 2014), <https://foodpovertyinquiry.files.wordpress.com/2014/12/food-poverty-feeding-britain-final.pdf> (accessed 8 April 2015).
8. *Feeding Britain,* pp. 39–40.
9. Shildrick *et al, Poverty and Insecurity,* p. 173.
10. Ibid., p. 167.
11. Ibid., p. 168.
12. Ibid.
13. Ibid., pp. 167–9.

14. <http://www.cuf.org.uk/together-middlesbrough/about-us> (accessed 8 April 2015).

15. Shildrick *et al*, *Poverty and Insecurity*, p. 167.

16. Iain Duncan Smith, "Getting Britain Working": <http://www.gov.uk/government/speeches/jobs-and-welfare-reform-getting-britain-working> (accessed 12 August 2014; reported unavailable 8 April 2015). Reported in *The Guardian*: <http://www.theguardian.com/politics/2014/aug/11/iain-duncan-smith-more-reform-dysfunctional-welfare> accessed 8 April 2015>. Also referenced at <http://www.housemark.co.uk/newsletter.nsf/1/CC327D053E7DD82580257D32005235B7> (accessed 8 April 2015). The full text can be found at <http://ilegal.org.uk/thread/8731/idss-speech-before-gets-work>.

17. Duncan Smith, "Getting Britain Working".

18. Ibid.

19. Shildrick *et al*, *Poverty and Insecurity*, pp. 167–9.

20. *Feeding Britain*, pp. 39–40.

21. William Temple, *Christianity and Social Order* (Penguin Books, 1942).

22. Ibid, p. 17.

23. *Feeding Britain*, p. 19.

24. Temple, *Christianity and Social Order*, p. 21.

25. Ibid., pp. 62–74.

26. Ibid., p. 66.

27. *Faith in the City. A Call for Action by Church and Nation* (Church House Publishing, 1985).

28. Ibid., p. 77.

29. *Feeding Britain*, p. 19.

30. *Ibid.*, p. 20.

31. *Ibid.*, p. 42.

32. *Ibid.*, p. 53.

33. Nick Spencer, *Freedom and Order: History, Politics and the English Bible* (Hodder and Stoughton, 2011), p. 274.

34. *Common Worship: Services and Prayers for the Church of England* (Archbishops' Council, 2000–2008); <http://www.churchofengland.org/prayer-worship/worship>.

35. *Common Worship: Services and Prayers for the Church of England*, p. 26.

36. *The Book of Common Prayer: The Texts of 1549, 1559, and 1662*, Brian Cummings (ed.) (Oxford University Press, 2011), pp. 240–1, p. 251, and p. 399.

37. Daphne Hampson, "Luther on the Self: A Feminist Critique", in Ann Loades (ed.), *Feminist Theology: A Reader* (SPCK, 1990), p. 221.

38. Ibid., p. 221.

39. "A general Confession to be said of the whole Congregation after the Minister, all kneeling", in *The Book of Common Prayer*, pp. 240–251.

40. *Common Worship: Services and Prayers for the Church of England*, p. 123.

41. Ibid., p. 168.

10.   A BOOTLE GOSPEL

Claire Dawson

"Hello Brenda! Any luck?" I've bumped into Brenda coming out of the corner shop; she has a lottery scratch card in her hand.

"I'll need more than ******* luck if I am going to keep the loan sharks off!" Brenda's numbers did not come up and she went home to where most things had already been pawned; she would inevitably borrow from a neighbour to make the next payment.

The above encounter provides a window into life within our small community in Bootle, North Liverpool. Not everyone is in debt or has loan sharks banging at the door. However, there are deep-seated issues within our community and it is difficult sometimes to know how to respond as a church. The issues our community faces are similar to those faced by other deprived areas throughout the country. Like accents, however, there is definitely something very northern about the Gospel which emerges out of Bootle. It has its own uniqueness, which is born out of the northern context and will have a different tenor and resonance to a Gospel from south of the Watford Gap. The terroir of the Bootle Gospel is perhaps best described as resilience. It is something which has grown up within the cracks of life, like the buddleias in our community which always seem to flourish out of the smallest of cracks. The resilience is shaped by humour, a humour that is used to cope with the injustices of life, enabling a lightness to what would otherwise be suffocating and crushing circumstances. It is a Gospel that is unique to Bootle and is born out of people's lived experiences. What I offer here is a reflection on my own ministerial experience and what I have come to see as a Gospel for Bootle emerging out of the cracks of life.

When I first arrived in Bootle I sat in my car outside a redundant Welsh Presbyterian Church; the streets had an eerie feel to them. As I looked out from my car I realized that the majority of homes had their windows perspexed over. These were houses that were earmarked for demolition as part of the Housing Market Renewal Programme. Net curtains hung in the windows as a ghostly reminder of life that had been. The church building fared little better: trees were growing out of the gutter and the only visible notice stated "Danger Keep Out!" What was stirring within me was a prophetic desire to come and be part of this community, to get alongside. I felt I could "fix things", make a difference, "to stand in the gap on behalf of the land" (Ezekiel 22:30). It took about two years for me to realize that, in the end, I could fix very little and that, in fact, the community I had "come to heal" was actually healing me.

Over the past few years we have lived in a "no-mans land" as homes, schools, and churches have been demolished. There had been a promise to rebuild but this was short lived and curtailed by the economic crisis and government funding cuts. Gradually now the tide does seem to have turned and new homes are being built, but the promised community infrastructure will not be happening as the developers can only see profit margins in building houses. As a church too we have started to build again, quite literally. We bought an old United Reformed Church and are in the process of converting it into a community building. Church buildings are not always assets and there are many churches that would love to be free from the burden of buildings. But, in our community, buildings have become so significant that the building in itself is a sign. A sign of a promise of the kin-dom of God being amongst us, a sign of presence, that the community has not been forgotten, that they have not been abandoned.

The Psalmist laments being abandoned by God but then recounts the story of God's revelation amongst his people (Psalm 77). Within our urban community it is easy to become downcast and despairing that things will never change. We have found however, that if we remember and recount our own story we begin to have a sense of a God who is with us. Our circumstance may not have changed but we have an understanding of being the pilgrim people of God and being led into a promised land. As a church community, we have learnt that we are as much dependent upon our local community as we would like to think they are dependent upon us. Having no buildings of our own we have relied on the community's support and hospitality over the past four years. We now have a different understanding of what it means to be a local church. It is not about us "doing to" the community but about "working with"; together and alongside in friendship, partnership, and mutuality.

There have been moments when we have sensed the kin-dom of God amongst us. These have been times when we have quite literally gathered the community together: at the annual lighting of the Christmas tree or the inaugural summer fair with candy-floss and donkey rides. The church, not on its own but working with others within the community, has enabled or is enabling "regeneration", new life. Not perhaps on the scale that John Prescott promised but in a very small tangible and real way.

When the bulldozers demolished our community there was something that remained: a resilience to life. This resilience is there in Brenda's life, something that does not break in spite of the immense pressure and burden that life continues to churn up and throw at her. It is this resilience to life which forms part of the Gospel for Bootle: that even in the most inhospitable climate space can be created for life, for tears, and for laughter.

> The buddleias grow everywhere . . .
> Where there is no life there are
> Buddleias—where there are just
> Cracks left the buddleia takes hold.
> Now, at the heart of summer,
> She blooms purple-headed flowers
> That scream out life.
> Life from the rooftops,
> The window frames,
> Life from the derelict walls:
> All is life!
> In the midst of death and decay,
> Now sprouting is life.
> Life speaks out of the paving slabs

Like the desert coming to bloom.
What is this?
A reminder of life that was
Or a sign of life to come?
Or is She merely making her
Presence felt now?
Life . . . I am here,
I am present,
Have been,
Always will be . . .

11. CONSIDERING NORTHERN ENGLAND AND BIBLICAL SAMARIA: A MEDITATION ON COMPETING CLAIMS TO TRUTH AND POWER

Su Reid

This chapter considers two histories: Church history in the North of England and the Bible's accounts of Samaria. It sees both communities—northern English and Samaritans—as occupying borderlands sandwiched between more powerfully represented neighbours: northern England between London and Scotland, and Samaria, by the time the Gospels were being written, between Jerusalem and Galilee. It tells how I, living in North East England, have come to perceive a sequence of economically and politically powerful incomers imposing a succession of different Christian institutions and hierarchies onto northern English places. It then shows that biblical accounts of events in Samaria are also narrated from the point of view of outsiders (Judeans and then Christians), and it suggests how Gospel accounts of Samaritans can be newly interpreted if we read them from a different perspective. Finally, it argues that our understanding of the Christian faith is always enriched if we see that teachings claiming authority are only parts in a dialogue; the voices of the politically or intellectually powerful must be challenged by those over whom they claim power.

11.1.   CHURCH HISTORY IN NORTHERN ENGLAND

Northern England first. I was brought up in the Midlands, studied in the South (well, Oxford), and then lived in Aberdeen before moving south (yes, 300 miles south) to North Yorkshire. Nigel Rooms, in this volume, has mentioned disagreements about where "the North" is. I know that North Yorkshire is physically in the southern half of the British Isles. I think that the distinctive social geography of northern England—of the Northern Province of the Church of England—is a borderland geography, not an extremity. The people who like living here are unsure who else they belong with. During the 2014 Scottish Referendum campaign I commonly heard local people say that they "don't want to be governed by Westminster either", so could they "join" Scotland? In 2009 *The Guardian* reported that, while Ofcom upheld Channel 4's right to identify Middlesbrough as "the worst place to live" during a poorly-researched programme of mere "entertainment", some southerners did choose to live here, rejecting "the congestion, the overloaded infrastructure, the crowded countryside and the hectic pace of life" of Surrey;[1] but, in 2013, *The Economist*'s opinion of choices like that was, on monetary grounds, that "Middlesbrough, Burnley, Hartlepool, Hull, and many others were in trouble even before the financial crisis", and should be left to "fail" and their inhabitants helped to move to work elsewhere, instead of being "propped up on piles of public money".[2] I perceive that a Northern English identity today is almost that of a colony disputed by the English and the Scots.

I see something similar going on in our Church history through centuries. Because I live in North East England, I am surrounded by places where significant things have happened. Here is a rapid tour of some of them (which will feel hectic, because it is). Outside York Minster a statue commemorates the imperial proclamation, here, of Constantine, who became the first Christian Roman Emperor. There are still Roman stones in the churchyard at Lastingham, within the North York Moors National Park. A new monastery was founded on that site at Lastingham in the seventh century by monks from Lindisfarne led by Cedd; Cedd died there, according to Bede.[3] The Irish-influenced forms of worship Cedd practised were challenged and largely defeated, just before his death, by advocates of Rome, at the Synod of Whitby in 664.[4] Soon afterwards the Vikings destroyed Cedd's Lastingham, but it was refounded after the Norman Conquest by monks from Whitby Abbey, who then moved on to join to St Mary's Benedictine Abbey in York.[5] The Lastingham church building now joins nineteenth century vaults onto a Norman monastic church over a crypt with Anglo-Saxon stones.

Let us pause here briefly. Already we are confronted with how, within just part of North East England, the Romans brought Christianity but withdrew as their empire failed; how the pagan Anglo-Saxons who invaded the land were introduced to Christianity from opposite directions in the seventh century: from Ireland and Scotland via Lindisfarne and by partisans of Rome's teachings. Then, from the eighth century onwards, Viking raiders destroyed monastic communities across the whole of northern England and put their inhabitants to flight, being joined in this sometimes by Anglo-Saxon landowners.[6] After them came the Norman conquerors who ravaged much of the North at the end of the eleventh century and then, in alliance with Scottish power, settled the land with new religious communities, including the Benedictines in a rebuilt Durham Cathedral and, soon, the economically powerful Cistercians.[7]

To continue our tour: Fountains Abbey, now a World Heritage Site and a ruined Cistercian Monastery near Ripon—also once a Roman settlement—was founded by monks from York soon after the Lastingham monks joined them.[8] Not far away, near Helmsley, are the ruins of the other great Cistercian Monastery of the same period: Rievaulx. It was there, in the twelfth century, that Aelred was appointed abbot after leaving the service of King David of Scotland, and where he wrote both spiritual treatises and histories. In *The Battle of the Standard* he dramatically describes a fight in 1138 in which forces raised by the Archbishop of York, Thurston, defeated a larger army of less disciplined Scots.[9] These were led by King David himself, but Aelred's monkish loyalty and admiration in this piece is now with the Archbishop; Aelred had become a monk at Rievaulx just four years before the battle.[10]

To pause again: the twelfth century was a time of turmoil throughout England, but especially in the North. The civil war between supporters of rival claimants to the throne, Stephen (whom Thurston supported) and Matilda, was rendered more complex by the interventions of King David of Scotland who sought to impose economic stability in northern

England.[11] The monument to the Battle of the Standard, which stands just north of Northallerton in Yorkshire, shows how far south invasions from the Scots came as they tried to claim lands laid waste, and communities devastated, by the ravages of the Normans. Some local people think that the effects of the brutality of the Normans can still be seen in the relative sparseness of the population of northern England. Durham Cathedral, magnificent and beautifully decorated as it is inside with carved pillars and fine glass, proclaims the power of the Normans who built it to replace the cathedral they found already there. It stands like a fortress above a bend in the River Wear.

To resume our tour: behind Durham Cathedral's high altar at its east end is a shrine to St Cuthbert, Bishop of Lindisfarne—the monastery founded c.634 by Aidan, a monk dispatched from Iona.[12] Cuthbert died in 687 but his body was found, nine years later, to be undecayed.[13] Miracles were increasingly attributed to Cuthbert,[14] and when, in 875, Vikings drove the monks from Lindisfarne, they took his body to Melrose in Scotland, to Chester-le-Street near the Wear, to Ripon, and, finally, to Durham where their successors built the cathedral that the Normans destroyed. The Normans did, however, retain a shrine to Cuthbert. At the west end of Durham Cathedral, in the Galilee Chapel, is the tomb of Bede. Bede, who lived until 735, was a monk at Wearmouth-Jarrow, a twin-site Benedictine monastery founded shortly after Lindisfarne on the principles of the Church governed from Rome, rather than those of the Church on Iona.[15] Bede greatly admired Cuthbert, writing two accounts of his life.[16] His bones were moved next to Cuthbert's shrine in the new Anglo-Saxon cathedral at Durham early in the eleventh century, and then given their present place within the Norman cathedral later.[17] Nevertheless, Bede's greatest work, his *Ecclesiastical History of the English People*, completed shortly before his death, can be read, at times, as a critical account of the practices of the Lindisfarne community, and as an advocacy, instead, of national adoption of the ways of the Roman Church. His long account of the Synod of Whitby is the best-known example,[18] but in many slighter details also, Bede distances himself from Lindisfarne practices. His account of Cedd at Lastingham, for example, reads dismissively: Cedd determined to fast on the site for forty days before beginning building, and Bede reports that "'he explained that this was a custom of those from whom he had learned the discipline of a Rule"; but Cedd abandoned his fast when summoned by the king—asking his brother to take over.[19] It has been suggested that Bede, the first historian of England, was primarily concerned to "chart how the English became part of the universal Church and to establish their particular role in the economy of salvation".[20] Bede's *History*, in other words, is perhaps both a partisan account of Church politics in the seventh and eighth centuries and an early attempt to define one, unified "England". As I have suggested however, in the following centuries, the Church communities and institutions in the North of England repeatedly faced invasions and conquests.

11.2.   CHRISTIAN LIVING IN NORTHERN ENGLAND

I am tasked, with my local vicar, with providing whole-school assemblies several times a term for our local village primary school. This is not a Church school and some of its children's parents are quite fiercely opposed to religious education for their children. We are made welcome, nevertheless, and we have decided to try to interest all the children by talking to them about the Church history visible around them. We select sites they can visit, or perhaps have visited, with their parents. We choose one aspect at a time of the Christian life lived at each place. So we have talked of the making of the Lindisfarne Gospels; of the writing of Church history by Bede at Jarrow and, much later, by Aelred at Rievaulx. We have described regimes of prayer at our nearby Carthusian monastery of Mount Grace, and those of Cistercians at Rievaulx. We have also talked of Rievaulx and Fountains as centres of farming and trade, and so as stabilizing communities in an impoverished and war-torn land; and as places of hospitality for travellers. We have talked of Durham and York cathedrals as always-changing centres of public worship. We move forward, too, to discuss the gradual conversion of closed monasteries, after their Dissolution, into a parish church and a museum at Jarrow, or into landscape gardens of outstanding beauty at Rievaulx Terrace and at Studley Royal (which incorporates Fountains Abbey). We have also told the children about the twentieth-century writer Herbert Read whose early childhood, before the First World War, was spent on a farm near Helmsley. He recalls Sundays at the local church of St Gregory, five miles away, at Kirkdale. This church was built before the Norman Conquest and still displays a Anglo-Saxon sundial, and two Anglo-Saxon tomb slabs, and Anglo-Saxon wall benches.[21] Read writes:

> Our Church was still where the monks who first built it twelve centuries ago had wanted it to be, in a wild valley, near a running beck, gray like a wild hawk nesting in a shelter of dark trees.[22]

I have learned, from living here, from visiting these places repeatedly, and from talking to the children about them, that Christian living is about getting on with it; about doing things, many things, in particular places at particular times and under many different kinds of poverty or prosperity. It is about studying, and praying, in different languages. It is about loving God and loving one's neighbour in many different ways. We tell the children, and each other, about things that have happened, and been done, in this liminal place between the Scots and the South. We love its beauty. At the same time, we take weekly collections of food, donated by many people in the village, to the Middlesbrough food bank, to meet some of the desperate needs of people in that town. We know that people and places vary, and offer different needs and different joys. We have learned that no one way of teaching, or of worshipping, is "right".

I also know that being a Christian is not a matter of being obedient to a written text, as if such a thing ever has one meaning or can lead to constant understandings. I studied and taught English Language and Literature for over thirty years in three different universities. As a literary critic I know that different readers at different times construct parallel or alternative readings of written texts, plausibly and with conviction. I also know that this is true of readers of the Bible, which is a collection of written texts. With this experience, together with my knowledge that Christian communities in the North of England have found their own ways of living in faith among opposing hierarchies, I now propose to consider possible ways of thinking about New Testament accounts of the Samaritans.

11.3.   BIBLICAL WRITING ABOUT SAMARIA, AND ITS RELEVANCE TO NORTHERN ENGLAND

Samaria lies between Judah, with its capital Jerusalem, to the south and Galilee to the north; it is mostly now within the occupied West Bank. Biblical Samaritans, like the people of both Judah and Galilee, traced their descent from Abraham, and from the Children of Israel led by Moses from slavery in Egypt to the Promised Land. The Books of Kings in the Hebrew Bible tell how, after the death of King Solomon, they seceded from Judah, following their own kings in what is referred to as "The Northern Kingdom" or "Israel". They set up their own sites of worship, instead of Jerusalem, and made new idols (1 Kings 12). Through much of 1 Kings we read of skirmishes between Israel and Judah, and of visits to Israel by prophets represented, in these Judean narrations, as being messengers from the true God—the most prominent being Elijah who persuades their king, temporarily, to acknowledge the Lord and to destroy shrines to pagan deities—with the result that, as promised by the Lord, a drought breaks and famine ends (1 Kings 17–18). Lapses from faithfulness to the Lord continue in both communities however, alongside battles with neighbouring communities from Egypt, Assyria, and then Babylon. Eventually the Northern Kingdom is defeated, invaded, and resettled, and its infrastructure destroyed, by the Assyrians (2 Kings 17). Sometime later Judah is also invaded, by the Babylonians, and its people, or at least its leaders, taken into exile; and, in due course, Jerusalem and its Temple are destroyed (2 Kings 24–25). Then the Book of Ezra describes how, after some decades, King Cyrus of Persia, who had overrun Babylon, allowed the exiles to return to Jerusalem and rebuild their Temple. It is fair to say that many of the subsequent Books of the Hebrew Bible recount the miseries of the people of Judah during and after the exile, their hope of full restitution through a Messiah, and the warnings of prophets against their continuing sporadic apostasy from the worship of the Lord. The people of Samaria are generally present in these books only as problematic neighbours who have certainly fallen from loyalty to the Lord (Ezekiel 23; Hosea 8–10). Samaritan voices are seldom heard. Readers are not encouraged to imagine themselves among Samaritans.

On two occasions in the Gospels, however, the Samaritans appear more prominently: in the parable of the Good Samaritan in Luke 10:25–37, and the account of Jesus' meeting a Samaritan woman at a well in John 4:1–42.

If Luke's Gospel and the Acts of the Apostles did have the same author, he was aware of Samaritans as close neighbours who included followers of Christ. Early in Acts he indicates the existence of Samaritan Christian communities (Acts 8:4–25, 9:31). Perhaps Christian Samaritans were among his intended readership. What might we understand if, as we read Luke 10, we imagine ourselves reading in a Samaritan town? Immediately, I suggest, this otherwise rather fragmented chapter becomes more coherent. Its opening account of the mission of seventy disciples to "every town and place where [Jesus] himself intended to go" (Luke 10:1) confirms the mission which Acts 8 and 9 describe as having actually taken place later. The "Good Samaritan" in Luke 10 then becomes an image of someone from within this community, not an image of a near-foreigner. The dialogue with the lawyer and the parable together represent the way to "inherit eternal life" (Luke 10:25) as being through the values and the faith of the Christian Samaritan listener to the Gospel rather than through those of the Hebrew priest and Levite who were not Christians; and the chapter then climaxes with Jesus' praise of Mary, who listens to Jesus, over Martha who does not (Luke 10:41–42). Luke 10 becomes, in this "Samaritan" understanding, a consistent acclamation of those who accept Jesus as Christ, including Samaritans with a different history from the Jews, and a distancing from those, including Jews, who do not.

What has this understanding of part of Luke's Gospel got to do with Christianity in northern England? Just this: I have tried to show that faith among Christians in the North East of England is confronted by places of dispute. I think that these confrontations teach Christians that hierarchies inevitably change, and that while a simple commitment to loving God and one's neighbour persists, the ways in which that commitment is both described and acted out change with place and time. I am not offering this observation as a piece of "translation theology" on the Bevans model, which supposes in the phrase "a translation of meanings"[23] that the "meaning" exists somewhere else and is only framed in language. I prefer to explain myself by citing David Bosch who, in the context of encounters between Christianity and other religions, wrote that "both dialogue and mission manifest themselves in a meeting of hearts rather than of minds. We are dealing with a mystery", and that we must "accept the coexistence of different faiths and… do so not grudgingly but willingly", and must "[take] time for the essentially dialogical nature of the Christian faith to sink in and take root".[24] I think we neither know nor understand everything, and that faith comes nearer when we read even the Bible with a level of humility towards other ways of thinking.

11.4.   THE SAMARITAN WOMAN AT THE WELL

I will try to explain this further now by discussing the other significant Samaritan in the New Testament, the woman at the well in John 4. Put as simply as possible, the place and events here are as follows: Jesus travels through Samaria from Jerusalem in the south towards Galilee in the north and sits, alone and thirsty in a generally hostile land, on "Jacob's well"; he is joined there by "a Samaritan woman" (John 4:1–8). This well is a real landmark, which still exists.[25] Although its historical connection with Jacob is uncertain,[26] this account specifically locates it near a "Samaritan city called Sychar", and identifies it with land originally given by Jacob to Joseph (John 4:5–6). Later, the woman tells Jesus "our ancestors worshipped on this mountain, but you say that the place where people must worship is in Jerusalem" (John 4:20). A three-way connection is being suggested, therefore, in the telling of this story: in this place Jesus the Saviour meets a Samaritan; the Abrahamic ancestry shared by Jews and Samaritans was founded here; and on Mount Gerizim, not in Jerusalem, Joshua set up an altar, read the Law, and established the worship of the Lord within the Promised Land (Joshua 8:30–35). Mount Gerizim remained the main site where Samaritans worshipped, in rivalry to Jerusalem, until it was

destroyed late in the second century BCE.[27] Recognizing all this about this
place, I must read in expectation of a story involving a confrontation—or
at least a meeting—between the Jesus of John's Gospel, who is defined as
divine from the start, and a Samaritan who rejects teachings emanating
from Judeans.

Next, Jesus asks the woman to draw water for him to drink, and at
once the narration moves further into a discourse invoking both Hebrew
history and Christian theology (John 4:7). The woman says, and the
narrator agrees, that Jews do not share a drink with Samaritans. Jesus
replies by talking of "living water" as the gift of God leading to "eternal
life", and confirms, in answer to her, that this "living water" (which is his)
replaces the water from Jacob's well (which her community venerates)
(John 4:9–10). She then asks where she can find "living water". At once,
clearly, we are being told of Jesus, identified as Son of God, offering the
new faith to this non-Jew; and Jesus tells her to fetch her husband (John
4:11–15).

Then, in the strangest part of the story, she says she has no husband
and Jesus agrees, telling her she has had five husbands and now lives with
a man to whom she is not married (John 4:16–18). She says he must be "a
prophet" but he comes from Jerusalem rather than from her Samaritan faith
represented by Mount Gerizim—she is doubtful of his power, therefore.
He tells her that soon the distinction between their communities will
vanish, and that all people, irrespective of place and therefore of religious
history, will worship the one God, "the Father", "in spirit and truth". He
also declares to her that he himself is the Messiah, speaking to her here
and now (John 4:19–26). Finally, Jesus' disciples join him, and express
amazement and concern both that he is talking to a Samaritan and that
he has not eaten. He assures them that, as with the "living water" he spoke
of to the woman, his real food, and theirs, will be the coming of eternal
life. Meanwhile the woman leaves her old water jar behind, goes to her
people, tells them she has met someone who might be the Messiah, and
brings many of them back to Jesus. They recognise him for themselves
as "the Saviour of the world" (John 4:27–42).

So much of this passage specifically refers to theological matters that
I think that ought to be any reader's focus. I find, however, that many
Christians, including biblical scholars, have failed to pay much attention

either to the theology or to the location of this story which, for a Samaritan, must carry religious significance. Such readers have been preoccupied instead with the supposed sexual sinfulness of the woman—a judgment for which there is no support in the words in John 4. I think that in doing this they prioritize a deep, timeless, and generalized stereotype of mistrust for women over proper attention to the specific place and time named in the story, and that doing this allows them to avoid discussion of the theology discussed in John. Bailey, for example, who explores many implications of his recent knowledge of the Middle East for readings in the New Testament, sees the woman's coming to the well only as confirmation that she is a "'bad woman'", and the whole episode, therefore, just as evidence of Jesus' forgiveness of her, and so of "the radical nature" of "changes in the attitudes towards women that Jesus introduced".[28] Archbishop William Temple, in his magisterial *Readings in St John's Gospel*, spent some paragraphs debating how her multiple marriages might have accorded, or not, with Mosaic law.[29] During my training as a Lay Reader, I was subjected to a video of an American actress, dressed in leathers, pretending to be the Samaritan woman. This was supposed to be an example of a lively sermon. The "Samaritan woman" told us how she had "sinned" with many men. (Were they "sinners" too, with her? This was not asked.) But Jesus had seen her soul and forgiven her, and she was now living in virtuous restraint, or words to that effect. More academically, and more concerned with textual sources for the Gospel, John Ashton suggests that, in its origins, this chapter superimposes an argument about salvation coming only from the Jews onto an earlier "simpler" tale of a mission to Samaritans,[30] but this reading still sees the woman as a sinner.

The *Oxford Bible Commentary*, however, does express unease with a "naturalistic" reading that sees the discussion of the woman's past only as showing Jesus' "prophetic knowledge" of her private life.[31] Rather tentatively, it suggests reading the Samaritan woman not as a character in a domestic story but as a symbolic representative of the Samaritan people, as Nicodemus in the previous chapter of John represented Judean leaders. It then, still tentatively, recalls Josephus describing the Samaritans as being "'composed of five nations'", each with a god. It suggests these might be indicated by the five previous husbands, and that the present non-husband "could be YHWH whom the Samaritans are only partly linked to, because they worship him at a different place from that of the Jews".[32] The *Commentary* remains tentative about this reading of the woman as representative of her community, however, and recalls that the `"five nations" actually had seven gods, citing 2 Kings 17: 24–34.[33] I, however, wish to suggest, much more confidently, that this 2 Kings passage, which is part of an account of the overthrow of the Northern Kingdom of Israel by Assyria, does indeed offer a major indicator for readers of John 4. 2 Kings 17:24 lists *five* peoples, tribes perhaps, that the king of Assyria brought into "the cities of Samaria" after the "people of Israel" had been driven into exile. These five are listed as "people from Babylon, Cuthah, Avva, Hamath, and Sepharvaim" (2 Kings 17:24). They brought with them their own pagan habits of worship but when things went ill among them the king of Assyria sent back a native priest "to teach them the law of the land" (2 Kings 17:27). After that, the people "worshipped the Lord but also served their own gods" and "To this day they continue to practice their former customs" (2 Kings 17:33–34). This does indicate, to me, that the remaining indigenous people and their *five* groups of planted invaders are seen by the Judean narrator as having lived together and together worshipped various gods. This can feasibly be recalled by the "Samaritan woman's" five former husbands, if the reader is willing to understand her as a symbolic representative of her community rather than as some actual individual. Furthermore, in Jesus' time, Samaritans' worship of the One God was unacceptable to the Judeans because it rejected their Temple in Jerusalem, and this can be understood to be indicated by Jesus' remark that "the one you have now is not your husband" (John 4:18).

Readers who consent to understanding the woman as a sign for Samaritans presented in a place with specific historical significance for Samaritans, must be able to focus less on the impropriety of her talking to Jesus and more on a narrative about Samaritans accepting a proclamation of faith in Jesus as Messiah. Such a reader might also observe, within the discussion of thirst at the well, an echo of a more ancient story: that of Elijah's mission to a Samaria overcome by drought and famine, where the end of the drought came only when King Ahab of Samaria and his people had to recognize the true God, and destroy their shrines to Baal (1 Kings 18). If that is recognized, then we see that Jesus is indeed represented in John as the true Messiah, as he says— one greater than Elijah. The woman, meanwhile, foreshadows in John the other lone woman who first finds the risen Christ and brings the news to her companions: Mary Magdalene (John 20:1–18).

11.5.   CONCLUSION: WE MUST LIVE IN DIALOGUE, NOT CERTAINTY

The conclusion I want to draw is this: conventional critical discussions of both narrations seem, like the narratives themselves, automatically to accept that Samaritans are outsiders, people who fail to worship in the proper way. In the case of the "Good Samaritan", surprise that he behaves generously seems to be taken for granted. The case of the woman at the well is more complex because she is twice made problematic: as a Samaritan puzzled about accepting Jewish teaching, and as a woman. Women, of course, are often featured when a writer tries to represent an evil from which he wishes to distance himself or his characters. Ezekiel's representation in Chapter 23 of apostasies in both Judah and Israel as the behaviour of two "whores" is such a case—and is, to me, offensive. So, actually, is the assumption through the Christian centuries that Mary Magdalene, who first saw the risen Christ, had been, more than the rest, "a sinner"—possibly on the basis of Luke 8:2 which says of her "from whom seven demons had gone out". The relevant point here, though, is this: biblical commentators have followed uncritically the Gospel-writer's collusion with the traditional narrative use of women to represent that which is different and even reprehensible. By concentrating on this "problem" of the woman, commentators have managed to avoid discussing what seems to me to be a much greater complexity: the nature of the faith in Jesus as Son of God that is presented as overtaking the older beliefs of the Samaritans—offstage and quickly.

The Samaritan woman is, in this narration, really just a foil by means of which the claim that Jesus is the Son of God is set out. Jesus and his disciples have just left Judea because they are threatened by orthodox Pharisees (John 4:1–3). After this episode they move on to Galilee where

Jesus is now welcomed and acclaimed (John 4:43–53). In Samaria, the naïve people are converted to the belief also welcomed in Galilee. The Christology of John is, obviously, a huge and ongoing challenge to our understanding. Readers here, though, might consider how this chapter makes its claim about Jesus by prioritizing older Judean authority and a newly established Galilean enthusiasm over the beliefs and practices of the Samaritans. We might at the same time notice that no one in John Chapter 4 drinks or eats the water from the sacred Samaritan well or the food brought from the Samaritan town, and wonder if this Gospel account implies that the Christian Eucharist has emphatically replaced them?

I suggest, then, that if we try to image a Samaritan Christian reading this Gospel, as we imaged a Samaritan Christian reading the parable of the Good Samaritan, we will see Samaritans who have become followers of Christ. But we will also see that Samaritan history is still made to seem inferior to Judean history, even when both are overtaken by Christianity. Might an affinity with Samaritan history and practice have contributed to a different sense, perhaps now lost, of authority within Christian faith and practice?

Meanwhile I, a Christian in northern England, must recognize that different traditions do oppose each other while proclaiming a similar message of charity: Bede opposed Cedd; today, food banks have humanist supporters as well as Christian ones. In my other contribution to this book I have argued that simplistic notions of "sin", as something done by a "sinner" to victims, reinforce an idea that moral judgments are easy and that the righteous can condemn neighbours. I reject such assumptions on the grounds that such monolithic ideas conceal the complexities of people's lives within unequal societies. In this chapter I have argued, in parallel, that being aware of living within a culture overshadowed by the power of others might teach Christians that dogmatism, and moral over-confidence, probably result from assertions of organisational or rhetorical superiority. I suggest, like David Bosch, that none of us knows the whole truth, and that we must live and practice our faith in ongoing dialogue with others, including those who are not Christians—and not expect to find agreement about what is "right" or "true".

NOTES

1. <http://www.theguardian.com/money/2009/aug/05/middlesbrough-worst-place-to-live> (accessed 10 April 2015).

2. <http://www.economist.com/news/leaders/21587790-city-sicker> (accessed 10 April 2015).

3. Bede, *EH*, III 23.

4. Ibid., III 25.

5. <http://greatenglishchurches.co.uk/html/lastingham> (accessed 10 April 2015); Nikolaus Pevsner, *Yorkshire North Riding* (Penguin 1966, revised ed., 1999), pp. 224–6.

6. Robin Fleming, *Britain After Rome: The Fall and Rise 400–1070* (Penguin, 2011), pp. 318–321.

7. David Carpenter, *The Struggle for Mastery: Britain 1066–1284* (Penguin, 2003), pp. 77–8, 123, 140.

8. Pevsner, *Yorkshire West Riding*, pp. 203–5.

9. Marsha L. Dutton (ed.), *Aelred of Rievaulx: The Historical Works* (Cistercian Publications, 2005), pp. 245–269.

10. Ibid., p. 4.

11. Carpenter, *The Struggle for* Mastery, pp. 178–186.

12. *EH*, III 5.

13. Ibid., IV 30.

14. Ibid., IV 31 and 32.

15. Michelle P. Brown, "Bede's Life in Context" in Scott DeGregorio (ed.), *The Cambridge Companion to Bede* (Cambridge University Press, 2010), pp. 5–10.

16. Alan Thacker, "Bede and History" in DeGregorio, *The Cambridge Companion to Bede*, pp. 181–2.

17. <http://www.durhamworldheritagesite.com/history/bede> (accessed 10 April 2015).

18. *HE,* III 25.

19. Ibid., III 23.

20. Thacker, "Bede and History", p. 172.

21. Pevsner, *Yorkshire North Riding*, pp. 216–7.

22. Herbert Read, *The Innocent Eye* (Faber and Faber, 1933; Smith Settle Ltd, 1996), p. 53.

23. Stephen B. Bevans, *Models of Contextual Theology* (Orbis, 1992; second edition, 2002), p. 38.
24. David J. Bosch, *Transforming Mission: Paradigm Shifts in Theology of Mission* (Orbis, 2009), pp. 483–4.
25. Kenneth E. Bailey, *Jesus Through Middle Eastern Eyes: Cultural Studies in the Gospels* (SPCK, 2008), pp. 201–2.
26. J. Barton and J. Muddiman, *The Oxford Bible Commentary* (Oxford University Press, 2001, 2007), pp. 967–8.
27. *Ibid.*, p. 696.
28. Bailey, *Jesus Through Middle Eastern Eyes*, pp. 202–3.
29. William Temple, *Readings in St John's Gospel* (Macmillan, 1939, 1968), pp. 60–62.
30. John Ashton, *Understanding the Fourth Gospel*, second edition (Oxford University Press, 2007), pp. 97–99.
31. Barton, and Muddiman, *The Oxford Bible Commentary*, p. 968.
32. Ibid.
33. Ibid.

12. THE SECULARIZATION AND RESACRALIZATION OF THE NORTH: NEW CHURCHES IN THE NORTH EAST

David Goodhew

12.1. INTRODUCTION

How secular is the North of England? And is it becoming more secular, or is it possible for the North to be "resacralized"? The answers to these questions are fundamental to whether and how there can be "a gospel for the North". This chapter offers some answers to these questions, using the preliminary findings of a new research project, "New Churches in the North East",[1] which explores Christian congregations in the North East of England, formed in 1980. The answers it suggests offers both hope and challenge for northern churches.

Secularization is, arguably, the primary religious reality in contemporary Britain, including the North of England. Secularization, in one influential definition, has been defined as the decline of congregations, the decline of individual support for faith, and/or the decline of faith across an entire society. This paper focuses on secularization in terms of the decline of congregations, but is alert to its other aspects.[2] Over the last century, church congregations and religiosity in general have tended to decline.[3] Secularization, however, does not operate to the same degree in every part of Britain. It needs to be understood regionally. Indeed, it does not operate the same way in every part of every region. It is a rough rule of thumb that secularization has been more pronounced the further one gets from London. Thus Scotland has seen markedly greater church decline than any other part of the contemporary UK.[4] Whilst not secularizing as fast as contemporary Scotland, a range of studies suggest that the North of England has seen substantial secularization in recent decades. Bruce points to the drastic decline of Durham Methodism.[5] Gill sees rural Northumberland as embodying rural church decline.[6] Heelas and Woodhead use the Cumbrian market town of Kendal to illustrate their thesis that there is considerable interest in the spiritual, but that this is happening amidst ongoing church decline.[7] It is sometimes argued that, whilst congregational decline may have happened, communal attachment to the church via such things as occasional offices remains strong. However, a key study by Bruce on the North Yorkshire village of Staithes shows an area which did have small congregations and a high take-up of occasional offices in the 1970s suffering a dramatic decline in the take-up of occasional offices *as well* in the following decades.[8]

By contrast, the Anglican diocese of London has seen its membership rise by 70 per cent since the early 1990s. The recent London Church Census showed London's congregations grew by 17 per cent between 2005 and 2012.[9] But is such growth a "southern" phenomenon? Is London an outlier amidst more widespread secularization? In terms of secularization, is it still "grim up North"?

In a linked phenomenon, leading scholars assume not only that secularization is proceeding apace, but that any new congregations are of peripheral significance. Professor Steve Bruce, a leading sociologist of religion, comments:

> What matters for the secularization paradigm is the "net" numbers. If fifty people leave the Church of England and only ten people join the Blobbo Christian Fellowship, the second does not offset the first.[10]

For a range of scholars, any new churches are equivalent to "the Blobbo Christian Fellowship". However large or small their congregations, they are seen as a minor phenomenon compared to the scale of decline elsewhere.[11] But how true is this assumption?

12.2. NEW CHURCHES IN THE NORTH EAST: METHODOLOGY

A new research project, New Churches in the North East, began in 2014 with the aim of surveying new congregations founded in the North East of England since 1980 and conducting a simple survey of their activities. The project leaders will offer their reports after this volume goes to press, but initial findings provide new perspectives on the debate about secularization in the North.[12]

The project adopts a strict definition of what constitutes a "new church" in the North East. To qualify such entities must meet the following criteria:

- Be trinitarian
- Have been founded since 1980
- meet at least weekly
- consist of ten or more people
- be the primary form of worship for those who attend
- have a distinct identity that marks it out from other ecclesial bodies
- be either wholly new, or be an existing body which has seen such profound change as to be effectively a new entity—i.e., not just a "rebranding" of an existing ecclesial entity.

The use of 1980 as a cut-off point is an arbitrary, but necessary, limit. A number of churches which could be seen as "new" are excluded by the other aspects of the definition. The Ark, cited on the national "Fresh Expressions" website as a fresh expression of church at Crawcrook near Newcastle, is engaged with imaginative work with children and their carers, but does not meet for worship every week and is thus not included in this survey.[13] Victory Church at Horden near Peterlee changed to its current name six years ago, but the church was otherwise largely unchanged, and thus does not qualify as a "new church". St Columba, North Gosforth was built in 1982, but, as a merger of three other churches which were closing, it is not included since it is really a continuation of existing congregations on a new site.[14] The above definition of a "new church" is questionable on theological grounds as being too restrictive. There are wonderful churches which do not have ten members and/or do not meet weekly. But the definition has the virtue that if the data from New Churches in the North East can be questioned it is for being an undercount, not an overcount.

It should be noted that religious statistics are a mixed bag. This is illustrated by a recent official report by the Church of England which included a survey of 51 "greater churches". It found that the data of two-thirds of such churches was so poor as to be unusable. Yet such churches are better resourced administratively than the average parish, suggesting there is much "noise" in the data.[15] Consequently, data on new churches is being carefully checked in the current project. Data is being collected by questioning leaders of each congregation. It should be noted that historic denominations, such as the Anglican Church, rely on congregational leaders reporting their attendance figures. To test data from leaders and guard against exaggeration, it has been cross-checked with an independent advisory board and with other data sources. The lowest figure given is the figure used and, where a church has two Sunday services, 20 per cent of the attendance figure is discounted to allow for those who attend twice. The primary measure is the usual Sunday attendance. This does not measure the overall size of the worshipping community which, given that many congregation members do not come every week, is larger than the usual Sunday attendance. The resulting figures undercount the actual size of the church communities of the new churches.

12.3.   NCNE PROJECT: THE NUMBER AND SIZE OF THE NEW CHURCHES

How many new churches have been founded in the North East since 1980? A conservative estimate is 130, a number which is likely to rise once the project is complete. By comparison, this is greater than the combined number of United Reformed and Baptist churches in the North East (118 churches). The Anglican diocese of Newcastle alone has some 200 churches.

Churches are opening in the North East—but are many closing? In contrast to the 130 "new churches", around 150 churches have closed in the region since 1989.[16] In other words, whilst the overall number of congregations in the North East is declining, it is declining only to a small degree. Of the new churches opening, how fragile are they? A small number appear to be volatile, being subject to name changes, relocation, and/or closure. However, the bulk of the newly founded churches endure.[17] This chimes with evidence from Peter Brierley with regard to new churches in London, which suggests that, whilst some new churches do fold, the great majority (93 per cent) do not.[18]

What of the aggregate attendance? Detailed data is available for fifty new congregations which represent a range of sizes, vary in ecclesial traditions, and come from right across the North East. Based on such data, a conservative estimate of the total number of adults attending Sunday worship in new churches in the North East started since 1980 is 8,000 to 12,000 adults—the size of a small Anglican diocese.

It is sometimes suggested that "transfer" growth is the key to such new churches. This is inherently very hard to measure, but it is highly unlikely that such growth is largely the result of the shuffling of an existing "pack" of Christians. Church closures are predominantly happening in smaller, more rural communities; new churches are opening, primarily, in larger urban centres. The churches which are shrinking the most are ethnically mostly "white British" (in terms of census definitions), but new churches have a high proportion of people from ethnic minorities. This is not to say that "transfer growth'" is not part of the picture—but teasing out the part it plays requires careful work.

Other metrics offer a sense of new church vitality. In these 130 churches, 500 (or more) baptisms were conducted in the past year prior to the survey.

Large numbers of children, young people, and students are attending such churches. In Durham City, leaving aside Roman Catholic churches, four of the five churches with the largest number of students are "new".

12.4.   NCNE PROJECT: THE NATURE OF THE NEW CHURCHES

Ethnicity is crucial. There is a growing literature on black and minority ethnic churchgoing, which has seen startling growth in recent years.[19] The scale of such church growth has been noted by scholars such as Andrew Walls,[20] although there is also the question of how effective such churches will be in retaining second and third generation migrants. Study of the North East shows that this is a major development in recent years. Around 40 to 50 new churches have started in the North East since 1980 which are wholly or largely rooted in Black, Asian, and other minority ethnic communities. In addition, a significant number of new churches have major ethnic minority components—for example, Newcastle City Church has an Iranian congregation. Several new Durham City congregations have significant minorities of East Asian congregants. Of course, a number of historic congregations also have significant numbers of minority ethnic congregants. A sense of the overall impact is, for the moment, hazy, but it would be reasonable at this stage to suggest that, for around a third of all new congregations founded in the North East, ethnicity was a key factor.

As to the patterning of such ethnicity, the largest component appears to be African (roughly 50 per cent of ethnic minority congregations)—particularly West African. There are also significant numbers of Chinese congregations (5), plus a number of congregations which contain a minority of Chinese Christians. There are significant numbers of Eastern Europeans, spread across Orthodox (7), Roman Catholic, and independent churches. But ethnic minority churchgoing in the North East is highly diverse—evidenced by the presence of such entities as Eritrean and Congolese congregations.

The chronology of the ethnic aspect of new church formation in the North East requires much more work, but it should be noted that a handful of these churches have a lengthy history. The Orthodox churches, for example, were operating in Newcastle from the 1960s, and the Chinese "True Jesus Church" began its activities in Newcastle and Sunderland in the early 1970s. However, the bulk of the new churches are much younger and activity has markedly increased in the last decade.

The North East is amongst the more "white" regions of the UK and, indeed, of the North of England. Yet even the North East has seen distinct ethnic shifts in recent years, especially in the last decade. The overall population is static, but, within this, the proportion of those classified as "white British" is slowly shrinking, whilst the number of people from ethnic minorities doubled between 2001 and 2011. There is an additional age-weighting to such shifts. The population aged over 65 is overwhelmingly white; the population aged 18 or under is markedly more diverse. Within the Newcastle local authority, around 25 per cent of those aged 18 or under are from ethnic minorities.[21] Whilst the issue of migration is highly charged politically, it should be noted that substantial levels of migration show little sign of abating and that this is having a very positive impact on congregational life in the North East.

Geographically, new churches are concentrated in the major urban centres of Tyneside, Stockton/Middleborough, and Durham City. Sunderland has relatively few new churches, given its size. Most of rural Northumberland and rural County Durham are less touched by this phenomenon. However, new churches can be found across the region, springing up in rural towns such as Hexham and Barnard Castle. There are some intriguing geographical patterns. Hartlepool and Newton Aycliffe are broadly similar as largely white, economically poorer settlements in County Durham. Yet Hartlepool has one new church, despite having more than twice the population of Newton Aycliffe, which has five.

New churches correlate most closely with what may be called "trade routes": areas which are adjacent to major transportation routes, seeing population increase, and/or increasing ethnic diversity. Thus Newcastle and Durham—which sit astride the East Coast mainline railway and the A1 trunk road—have the highest concentration of new churches, followed by Teesside. "Trade routes" are areas of economic dynamism, but not necessarily areas of wealth. The wealthier suburbs of the North East and wealthier rural areas are not seeing high concentrations of new churches. "Trade routes" also correlate with student populations. Newcastle and Durham University students (and, to a lesser extent those of Sunderland, Northumbria, and Teesside Universities) are key constituencies for new churches. The evidence suggests that many new churches connect well with people towards the foot of society, especially ethnic minorities, but these generalizations need qualifying. African migrants starting churches in Sunderland and Far Eastern students in Durham's student churches are not necessarily in the same social bracket.

What do such new churches "do"? Do they have programmes of social action? Do they connect with the wider community, and, if so, in what ways? A small number of new churches appear to focus entirely on the congregation, with mission seen solely in terms of evangelism. However, the vast majority—over 90 per cent of those surveyed—see social action as a key part of their remit and are engaged in a wide range of forms of service to the wider community. These are far from being "holy huddles".

Some broad comments can be made with regard to the theological stance of new churches. Of the 130 the new churches, around 20 stand within the historic denominations. Of the historic denominations, the Baptists have been most active in starting new churches—but the Church of England, the Methodist Church, and the Salvation Army have also started new congregations in the North East since 1980. Aside from the Orthodox, the bulk of new churches stand outside the historic denominations (and the Orthodox are, in UK terms, arguably not an "historic denomination", since Orthodox congregations only began to proliferate from the 1960s onwards). Amongst the churches rooted in minority ethnic communities, most stand outside the historic denominations—with the small exception of Chinese Methodist congregations that have sprung up in Newcastle, Middlesbrough, and Durham.

In theology, the bulk of new churches can be described as "evangelical-charismatic", although there is much variety within that label. Around seven are from various strands of the Orthodox tradition. A handful of new churches can be characterized as liberal by tradition, such as Newcastle's Metropolitan Community Church and the Anglican "Celtic Springs" congregation in Bishop Auckland. What is striking is how few new churches describe themselves as an "emerging church". There is growing evidence that those owning the label "emerging church" are largely white and middle class, whereas the new churches of the North East are dramatically more diverse in terms of ethnicity and class.[22]

New churches have been starting across the North East with increasing frequency since 1980. The total number founded between 2000 and 2014 is larger than the number started between 1980 and 2000. This is especially the case for congregations rooted in ethnic minority communities. Approximately two thirds of such congregations came into being in the present century. A small but significant minority of new congregations are plants from other new congregations in the North East. There is no evidence that the phenomenon of new church start-ups is slowing down. Rather, evidence suggests that it is speeding up in the North East.

An exploration of the nature of the North East's new churches suggests that their proliferation since 1980 is caused by a wide range of factors. Amongst them one might include the energy of some new denominations, and the shifting patterns of economic activity within the region (such as the growth of a knowledge-based economy around Durham City and central Newcastle). But ethnicity is arguably the most significant single factor in the creation of new churches in the North East since 1980.

12.5.   CONCLUSION

The city of Durham gives some idea of the extent of new church activity in the North East. Thirteen new churches have started in Durham City since 1980:

- SS Cuthbert and Bede Orthodox Church, Durham
- King's Church
- Emmanuel Church
- Durham Presbyterian Church
- Durham Vineyard
- Christchurch Durham

- Apostolic Lighthouse Church, Durham
- Chinese Methodist Church
- Durham Community Church
- Redeemed Christian Church of God: Sanctuary of Power
- Redeemed Christian Church of God: Good Word Christian Ministries
- Redeemed Christian Church of God: Living Grace Church
- Bethshan, Durham

Some of Durham's new congregations are small, but Durham's thirteen new churches include Kings Church, which has nearly 400 adults at its Sunday services and attracts the largest number of students of any Durham church. Durham is not a place usually associated with ethnic diversity, but five of the thirteen new churches are predominantly ethnic minority congregations. Durham is not entirely typical of the North East, but neither is it wholly atypical. Ninety per cent of the North East's new churches have been founded outside of Durham City. The area with the most new churches is the area within three miles of central Newcastle. Durham City is thus not the exception, but an illustration of the extent and the diversity of new churches starting in the North East since 1980.

The number and size of the North East's new churches constitute a major counterweight to the secularization thesis. There is significant resacralization happening alongside secularization in the region. Almost as many churches have opened as have closed since 1980 and in some areas, such as Durham City and central Newcastle, more have opened than closed. The reality of church growth is increasingly recognized with regard to London, but it deserves to be recognized with regard to the North East of England. And if it is happening in the North East, it is likely to be happening in many other parts of the North of England—especially on the "trade routes".[23] Beyond this, the scale of new church formation, of whatever ethnic background, means dismissing new congregations as merely the "Blobbo Christian Fellowship" is not possible. The advent of 130 (or more) congregations in the North East with an aggregate attendance of around 8 to 12,000 adults constitutes a unit equivalent, roughly, to a new Anglican diocese. New churches in the North East show that religious change is not a one-way street. There has been marked secularization in the North East in recent decades, but there has been significant church growth too. The church in the North is certainly not doomed to secularity, but can grow—and in some areas and amongst some sections of the population it has been growing fast.

Within the evidence of new church vigour, the most important trend is the importance of ethnic minorities for such growth. Ethnic minority-based churches and congregations which contain significant numbers from ethnic minority communities have become now a major—and growing—component of Christianity in the North East. Neither the wider population nor the Christian churches in the North East are overwhelmingly white British any more. This is a crucial factor for the gospel within the North of England, given that much of the North West and Yorkshire are far more ethnically diverse than the North East. It could be argued that such dynamism is a temporary "blip" and that, in time, the new congregations will shrink. Two responses can be made. First, if it is a "blip", it is a large one. Second, to argue that such new congregations "must" decline eventually is to ignore those new congregations which have proved robust and to show a questionable fatalism about the "inevitability" of secularization. The influential Anglican "Tiller Report" assumed in the 1980s that the future would include a static UK population, the continuing decline of the church in London, blanket secularization across Britain, and no significant migration to the UK. These assertions proved to be entirely incorrect.[24]

The dynamism of the new churches is significant for the existing denominations. The advent of non-historic churches, especially those centered around minority ethnic communities, is increasingly recognized as significant in London and the South East, but they need to be recognized as significant in the North too. Historic churches can let go of any ecclesial fatalism and the assumption that churches are "bound" to decline. If new churches can be founded in such numbers even in the North East, the dominant secularization narrative can be subverted. Yet, whilst the existence of new churches in such numbers is an encouragement, it is also a challenge as to why they have proliferated when, often, historic churches have not.

The new churches are far from perfect, but observers from historic churches should beware the tendency to ignore or downplay such ecclesial bodies. Rather there are things to be learned from them:

- a recognition of the potential for starting new congregations, even in supposedly "depressed" areas such as the North East
- a recognition of the huge importance of working with minority ethnic populations, even in supposedly "white" regions, such as the North East
- A recognition of the importance of student Christianity
- A recognition of the currency that "church", Sunday, and standard Christian congregations continue to have. Almost all new churches meet on Sunday, are congregations, and readily use the word 'church' to describe themselves
- A readiness to identify and use "trade routes", big and small, for mission. One of the distinguishing marks of New Testament mission was its use of the trade routes of the ancient world.
- The vast majority of new churches are church plants or grafts. The North East offers little evidence to suggest that the more radical forms of "emerging church" have a particular purchase in the region.[25]
- New churches are impressive for missiology, but they contain significant weaknesses. Operating either outside of a wider framework, or with only loose oversight, they can be vulnerable to the failings of "one-man-bands" and institutions without a wider network of support. This suggests that there may be great value in a reinvented ecumenism and via networks such as the "Gather" network of leaders meeting for prayer, which can provide support, advice, and a wider platform from which to engage with wider society.

The North East has a long track record of innovative Christianity. Aidan and Cuthbert started monastic church planting from Lindisfarne. The early Methodists showed how to do mission in industrializing Weardale. Pentecostalism first stirred in Britain in Sunderland through the Anglican parish priest Alexander Boddy (1854–1930). A study of the churches started in the North East since 1980 shows that that tradition of innovation is alive and well—and should encourage all concerned for the spread of the gospel in the North of England.

NOTES

1. Details of this project can be found at: <http://community.dur.ac.uk/churchgrowth.research/research/new-churches-in-the-north-east>.

2. K. Dobbelaere, *Secularisation: an Analysis at Three Levels* (Frankfurt am Main: Peter Lang, 2002).

3. A wide range of scholarship charts secularization, but see, for example: G. Davie, *Religion in Britain Since 1945: Believing Without Belonging* (Blackwell, 1994); S. Bruce, *God is Dead: Secularisation in the West* (Blackwell, 2002); and C. Brown, *The Death of Christian Britain* (Routledge, 2001).

4. P. Brierley, *UK Church Statistics, 2: 2010–20*, (ADBC: Tonbridge 2014), 1.1.

5. S. Bruce, "Methodism and Mining in County Durham, 1881–1991", *Northern History*, vol. 48, no. 2 (2011).

6. R. Gill, *The Empty Church Revisited* (Ashgate, 2003), pp. 26-37.

7. P. Heelas and L. Woodhead, *The Spiritual Revolution: Why Religion is Giving Way to Spirituality* (Blackwell, 2005).

8. S. Bruce, "Secularisation, Church and Popular Religion". *Journal of Ecclesiastical History*, vol. 62, no. 3 (2011).

9. See, for example: P. Brierley, *Capital Growth: what the 2012 London Church Census Reveals* (ADBC, 2013).

10. S. Bruce, "Secularisation and Church Growth in the United Kingdom", *Journal of Religion in Europe*, vol. 6 (2013), p. 279—stated at greater length in Bruce, *God is Dead*, pp. 167–184.

11. Davie, *Religion in Britain*; Brown, *Death of Christian Britain*; and Heelas and Woodhead, *Spiritual Revolution*.

12. The project will report in the autumn of 2015 and its findings can be found at: <http://community.dur.ac.uk/churchgrowth.research/research/new-churches-in-the-north-east>.

13. See: <http://www.freshexpressions.org.uk/stories/arkcrawcrook/oct14> (accessed 1 July 2014).

14. <http://www.stcolumbaswideopen.co.uk/> (accessed 1 July 2014).

15. J. Holmes and B. Kautzer, *Cathedrals and Greater Churches* (Cranmer Hall: Durham 2014)—also available online via: <http://www.churchgrowthresearch.org.uk/findings>.

16. Brierley, *UK Church Statistics, 2*, 13.1.4.

17. The research team have been looking for examples of churches which have opened and then closed since 1980. They have found a handful of examples, such as Marske Baptist Church and a French-speaking congregation formerly based at St Silas Church, Newcastle. Some churches have shown a predilection for name changes: Whickham Community Church was, for example, Birtley Community Church. The current Bethshan congregations have had a variety of names.

18. Brierley, *Capital Growth*, p. 134.

19. See, for example, B. Adedibu, *Coat of Many Colours: the Origin, Growth, Distinctiveness and Contributions of Black Majority Churches to British Christianity* (Wisdom Summit, 2012); A. Adogame, *The African Christian Diaspora: New Currents and Emerging Trends in World Christianity* (Bloomsbury, 2013); and Brierley, *Capital Growth*.

20. A. Walls, *The Cross-Cultural Process in Christian History: Studies in the Transmission and Appropriation of Faith* (Orbis, 2002).

21. Gary Craig, Maggie O'Neill, Bankole Cole, Georgios A. Antonopoulos, Carol Devanney, and Sue Adamson with Paul Biddle and Louise Wattis, *Race, Crime and Justice: mapping Black Minority Ethnic (BME) and Refugee Groups and Communities in the NE Region,* a research project of the School of Applied Social Sciences, Durham University (Durham, 2009). For data on Newcastle, see <http://www.nomisweb.co.uk/census/2011/DC2101EW> (accessed 29 January 2015).

22. G. Marti and G. Ganiel, *The Deconstructed Church: Understanding Emerging Christianity* (OUP, 2014).

23. A similar process has been observed in the city of York. See D. Goodhew, "From the Margins to the Mainstream: New Churches in the City of York, 1980 to the Present", in D. Goodhew (ed.), *Church Growth in Britain, 1980 to the Present* (Ashgate, 2012), pp. 179–192.

24. J. Tiller, *A Strategy for the Church's Ministry* (CIO Publishing, 1983), pp. 11–17 and p. 164.

25. This stands at odds with other analyses of the church in the contemporary west: see, for example, Marti and Ganiel, *The Deconstructed Church*, p. 195.

13. PRAYING FOR GOD'S TRANSFORMATION OF THE NORTH

Matthew Porter

13.1. THE CALL

The gospel of Jesus Christ is good news for every community in every place in every age: the North of England is no exception.

This message of Christ first took root in the North during the Roman occupation, declining with the departure of the legions, only to be replanted in AD 625 when King Edwin of Northumbria (d. 633), influenced by his Christian wife Æthelburh (d. 647), brought the bishop Paulinus (d. 644) to Northumbria. Paulinus, a member of the last group of missionaries sent to Britain by Pope Gregory I (r. 590–604), built a wooden church in the old Roman legionary headquarters in York and baptized Edwin there. The present churches of York Minster and St Michael le Belfrey (where I am Vicar) stand in the exact location where Edwin, the first Christian king in northern England, replaced that first wooden church with a more permanent stone structure.

Since then the strength and vitality of Christian communities in the North has ebbed and flowed. Aided by gifted evangelists, caring pastors, and social reformers, the Church in the North has been revived on multiple occasions. Many followers of Christ in these early days of the twenty-first century sense a fresh awakening to pray for the North. For some it feels like a divine call.

I led a seminar in 2010 at a New Wine conference entitled "A Vision for Revival Coming in the North". I began by asking who had sensed God calling them to pray particularly for the North of England in recent months. I was surprised to see that of the 150 or so people present at least half raised their hand! That response reflected something of my journey of the previous two years.

When I had arrived in York to work at St Michael le Belfrey (having moved an hour's north from Sheffield) I spent considerable time seeking God for vision. I talked with people and listened and prayed. When The Belfrey's Church Council eventually met to clarify the church's vision, there was one thing that Roger Simpson and I were sure of, and one word we definitely wanted included in the church's vision statement. The word was "North".

Soon after this we began working more closely with St Thomas Crookes in Sheffield and St George's Leeds, and together we helped establish St Barnabas Theological Centre, a training institution with a vision "to provide excellent church leadership training, to put theology in the heart of the church and to see churches grown and planted in the North of England".[1] Roger Simpson now works more closely with John Sentamu, the Archbishop of York, as the Archbishop's Evangelist for the North. As the two of them have worked together they both have a growing sense of a call to the North, so much so that in 2014 the Archbishop called all the northern bishops together for a conference in Lindisfarne on the re-evangelization of the North!

For an increasing number of people it feels God wants to pour out his Spirit afresh on the North.

13.2.   THE CONTEXT

The people of the North of England are friendly and warm. In some areas community spirit is particularly strong. There are pockets where the Church is vibrant. However, many have little or no knowledge of Christ or of the Christian faith. Church-going tends to be below the national average and in some cities just 3 per cent attend church.[2] Census returns show a growth in allegiance to other religions and especially to "no religion". Social trends point to a move away from traditional Christian values with cohabitation being the norm before marriage and divorce rates being slightly higher than the present national average of 42 per cent.[3] The gospel of Christ is rarely presented in the media as intellectually credible, and the binge-drinking and soft drugs culture amongst many 18–30s indicate a hedonistic, dissatisfied people.

The North is a context ripe for an awakening of the Holy Spirit. It seems that a growing number of believers have an increasing desire for the spiritual and social transformation of the North and are responding by crying out to God in prayer.

13.3.   THE CRY

I am aware of a variety of prayer initiatives taking place *in* the North *for* the North—with people calling out to God in private prayer, church service intercessions, and prayer meetings. At The Belfrey over the last few years we have also been experimenting with extended times of prayer, such as half nights, 100 Hours, and 24/7 prayer weeks. But one of the most significant developments, I believe, is the growth of the House of Prayer (HOP) movement. I know of such Houses in Manchester, Warrington, Chester, Kendal, Newcastle, Sunderland, Durham, Sheffield, Chesterfield, Newchurch-in-Pendle, and York.

Opening in February 2014, St Cuthbert's House of Prayer (HOP) in York is an interesting example of such a prayer centre. It is part of St Michael le Belfrey in York and staffed by a core team of worshippers from The Belfrey, but, despite being just over a year old, is already used by a wide variety of other churches and para-church organisations in the city. The core team is made up mainly of people in their 20s who give at least two days per week to pray in the HOP. They have a passion for intercession and revival. There is a strong sense of community amongst the team, using a "new monastic"-type model with a daily rhythm of prayer and worship, and the centre is open every morning for people to drop in, pray, and receive prayer. The building is an ancient Anglo-Saxon church with a long heritage of prayer and worship. People often say it is an easy place to pray in. It is named after Cuthbert, the so-called "apostle to the North". The vision of St Cuthbert's HOP is simple, to be "seeking God and his transformation of the North". It will be interesting to see if similar prayer centres spring up in the North with a vision for the North.

13.4.   CONCLUSION

There are other signs of a growing prayer movement in the North, such as prayer conferences and occasional prayer blogs. A new website is presently being developed where prayers and prayer requests for the North are posted and updated. No doubt more initiatives will come. The question is, will the prayers lead to the revival for which so many are praying?

NOTES

1.   This is the summary vision of St Barnabas Theological Centre; see <http://stbarnabastraining.org> (accessed 25 July 2015).
2.   See <http://www.thinkinganglicans.org.uk/archives/005927.html>, <http://www.brin.ac.uk/news/2010/church-attendance-in-england/>, and <http://www.vexen.co.uk/UK/religion.html> (accessed 25 July 2015).
3.   See <http://www.relate.org.uk/files/relate/separation-divorce-factsheet-jan2014.pdf> (accessed 25 July 2015).

14. DURHAM: A NORTHERN CATHEDRAL

Michael Sadgrove

14.1. A NORTH EASTERN PLACE

When I was a boy growing up in London in the 1950s, I would spend many hours at weekends and in school holidays at King's Cross Station. Like all avid train spotters, I was armed with Ian Allan books that listed the steam locomotives that hauled trains up and down the East Coast Main Line. Not far from the platform end, the prosaically named Gasworks Tunnel closed off the view. You never knew what would emerge next from its black portal. As often as not, it was a modest tank engine pulling the stopping train from Cambridge. What we would wait for hours to see was one of the great Gresley Pacifics, and, best of all, the sleek lines of the streamlined A4 class, such as Mallard which still held the world steam speed record reached on that line in 1933.

But my memory was not only of steam locomotion. I found the atmosphere of a busy London terminus beguiling: arrivals and departures, greetings and farewells, people hurrying or lingering, or sitting still and solitary while the crowd swirled busily round. This liminal place seemed to encapsulate so much that felt important. I would gaze at the tracks disappearing into the tunnels and wonder what lay on the other side. I heard on the tannoy the litany of places to which these long and beautiful trains carried lucky passengers. Their names seemed like poetry: Darlington, Durham, Newcastle, Berwick-upon-Tweed, Dunbar, Edinburgh, Aberdeen.

I had heard of them, and had traced them on a map. But, to a southerner, they were another country entirely. They belonged to the mysterious North, the strange remote lands beyond Gasworks Tunnel. How I longed to make that journey myself. It would be many years before I did.

I had become seduced by the hyperborean myth, though I did not know that word at the time. The ancient Greeks believed in a people they called the *hyperboreoi* who lived beyond *Boreas*, the north wind. In my suburban habitat of neo-Tudor and privet hedges, I imagined it to be a wide, wild, grasping, exposed, little-populated place. Above all it was remote. I never knew about the stereotypically southern clichés of flat caps, whippets, industrial dereliction, brown ale, slums, and coal. My imagined "North" (and by this I mean the North of England) was paradisal, beautiful in its severity and starkness, a mythic landscape where any traveller's longings would be fulfilled.

I first made the longed-for train journey to the North in 1966. It was the first time I had ventured beyond the Midlands. By then, the East Coast Main Line was powered by diesels. I was a teenager applying to read Maths at Durham University. Like so many who have made the journey, I shall never forget my first sight of the Cathedral from the train as it emerged from the cutting and crossed the viaduct. It was a bleak November day, the Cathedral sitting darkly on its acropolis beneath a lowering gun-metal sky. In those days, Durham was a dour city, its sandstones blackened by coal deposits from the mines not far away. Yet to me, the prospect of Castle and Cathedral standing proud above the town huddled beneath seemed like an epiphany, a new Jerusalem. I did not know that in the eighteenth century one writer described Durham as England's Zion,[1] nor that the University's motto, taken from Psalm 87, "her foundation is upon the holy hills", referred to this memory. It more than fulfilled my romantic notions of "the North". I stepped out of the Edinburgh express on to a foreign yet delectable soil.

Later I found I was not alone in this. In a penetrating and beautiful book, Peter Davidson charts the magnetic appeal "North" has held for painters, poets, and writers in modern times. Entitled *The Idea of North* (a title with an intriguing cultural history of its own), it is a fascinating essay in the history of the human imagination.[2] "North", of course, is mostly a relative rather than an absolute concept: it means north of where

I am, though it is fed by the notion of an absolute north that lies beyond all these places:

> Everyone carries their own idea of north within them. In Britain, the shadow at noon points towards stone-walled slopes of Derbyshire, steep cities of West Yorkshire, limestone solitudes of Weardale and Allendale . . . To say "we leave for the north tonight" brings immediate thoughts of a harder place, a place of dearth: uplands, adverse weather, remoteness from cities. A voluntary journey northward implies a willingness to encounter the intractable elements of climate, topography and humanity.[3]

Among the English "norths" Davidson describes is the County and City of Durham:

> Durham City is not only islanded in the Wear, but is itself an island—a medieval and Georgian county town with miles of working villages and pit towns on either side. It is a place of dignity and stark beauty, but mired in sadness, weighed down by missed chances civic and academic, by the automatic nostalgia generated by the wooded canyon of the river Wear, the bulk of the Cathedral and the lights of the Cathedral Close. The night view from South Street across to the Cathedral is Victorian in yearning, a nineteenth-century imagination of a clerical ideal city. Time is passing; the Wear is flowing, moving the present away from the friendly past. The lit Gothic windows across such a gulf of darkness, trees and water seem hardly to be shining from the same century: they seem oil lamps and gas mantles in studies heated with coal fires. Time to draw the curtains, time to shut out the view of the Cathedral, to shut out the past before it infects the present and renders it unendurable.[4]

This elegiac "take" on Durham Cathedral's northernness is echoed by another writer with a flair for encapsulating the downbeat. Mark Hudson's great-grandfather and grandfather were pitmen at Horden Colliery on the Durham coast. As someone who was not himself a native of North East England, he was fascinated by the memories of Horden that were passed down the family, and decided to live there for a while to discover what had become of it since the miners' strike of 1984. He writes about the Durham Miners' Gala, and how the banners of collieries where men had died in the year's pit disasters would be lined with black crepe and processed into the Cathedral. He describes the links between the Cathedral and the mining communities: the Haswell banner in the south transept and the Miners' Memorial in the south aisle to those who had died in mining accidents. Here is his introduction to this aspect of Durham life:

> Anyone who wants to say that they have *seen* Durham Cathedral, should see it not only in summer, the three great towers rising hazy and visionlike through the balm of the great cloud of foliage, its interior bathed in golden light, the majestic columns dappled with the reflected hues of its stained glass, but also in the very dead of the year, when the last leaves have departed the elms that cling to the great rock, its gaunt winter face peering down through soot-encrusted eyelets into the black dank water of the Wear, when the light seems hardly to penetrate much of the interior, and the broad blank expanses of stone between the rows of upper and lower arches rising from the submarine dimness towards the feeble light from the upper windows have about them the clammy, irremediable chill of river mud.[5]

Hudson captures the inescapable northernness of Durham Cathedral: who would write about other riverside cathedrals such as Salisbury, Worcester, or York in that way?

But other writers—the vast majority—strike a less melancholy note. The praises of Durham Cathedral are sung across the world. Clichés from the travel-writer's lexicon abound: words like "iconic", "stunning", "amazing", and "award-winning". This last epithet is a reference to Durham's being consistently rated as one of Britain's best-loved buildings if not the favourite. Owen Chadwick is content with a less hackneyed, and altogether more theological, word when he describes it as "one of the glorious buildings of Christendom".[6] Who could dissent from that? This, together with its incomparable landscape setting and relationship with the Castle, is among the reasons that the core of the peninsula was designated a UNESCO World Heritage Site in 1986.

But what about its distinctive northern qualities? Among British authors on whom "north" exercised a powerful pull, Davidson singles out W. H. Auden for special attention. A Midlander, he fell in love as a young man with the tough lead-mining landscapes of the North Pennines. For him, the North of England was the "Never-Never Land of my dreams".[7] In one of the earliest pieces in the canon of his mature poems, he describes how he found his poetic voice in the Durham Dales. It happened in 1919 at a little place called Rookhope in a remote side-valley off Weardale, an archetypal County Durham lead-mining village with industrial archaeology all around. Auden recalls that he casually threw a pebble down a disused mine shaft on the fells above the village, and listened to it reverberate as it hit the bottom. He became aware "Of Self and Not-self, Death and Dread".[8] He has a lot more to say about the Pennines than about Durham Cathedral, but—in a dream at least—the apparition of an immense floodlit building was overwhelming and unforgettable. He says that it taught him how his standards up to that time were all, in his words, "second-rate".[9] Auden does not name the Cathedral, but he clearly means Durham. He would no doubt have approved of Pevsner's much quoted rhapsodic introduction to the long section on the city in the *County Durham* volume:

> Durham is one of the great experiences of Europe to the eyes of those who appreciate architecture, and to the minds of those who understand architecture. The group of cathedral, castle and monastery on the rock can only be compared to Avignon and Prague, and (a particularly lucky circumstance) the old town has hardly been spoilt and is to almost the same degree the visual foil to the monuments that it must have been two and five hundred years ago.[10]

Like Auden, Pevsner found nothing second-rate at Durham: "it is one of the most perfect and also historically most interesting buildings in

Europe".[11] He understood its *genius loci*, its unique sense of place in northern England.

I have tried elsewhere to find words that express what the "north-eastern" identity of Durham Cathedral means, at least to this Dean who has lived and worked in and around it for more than a decade.[12] It is a rich and complex aggregation of themes which the rest of this chapter will try to explore: historical, theological, and spiritual. But we must not forget the part that the building, the physical environment and the broader topography of County Durham play in this. Visitors sometimes comment on how the monumental sandstone buildings on the peninsula seem to grow out of the rock; indeed, from the path above the river gorge immediately below the Galilee Chapel, the edge of the bedrock is visible and we realise how precariously the Cathedral is perched on it. But that is precisely the paradox, because precariousness is precisely *not* the message conveyed by this building that is so anchored to its mooring, so stable and trustworthy. There is in Durham, to borrow a phrase from John Betjeman, a "gospel in stone" that is as much about its rootedness and "stability" (a good Benedictine word) as it is about the quality of its landscape setting and architecture.

Its northern sandstones apart; this quality is not perhaps unique. Much the same could be said about other great hilltop shrines: Lincoln or Laon or Vézelay, or indeed Pevsner's favourite citadel of Prague. But the geography of Durham plays an important part in defining its northernness. It sits astride the river Wear that, like its southern and northern companions the Tees and the Tyne, connects the Pennine uplands to the North Sea. This is partly a matter of physical, partly of social geography. The Wear seems to sum up the long and varied story of County Durham. The Pennine stretches are lead-mining country, abounding evidence of the early stirrings of the industrial revolution in the North. As the waters flow more sedately into the lowlands, they skirt Auckland Castle, the country residence of the so-called prince-bishops, a quintessentially northern institution.

Next, the Wear enters the landscape of the North East Coalfield where, once upon a time, the pitwheels and spoil heaps would have conveyed the indisputable message that coal is king. Downstream of Durham, where the river turns north, it passes by the spire of St Mary and St Cuthbert, Chester-le-Street, County Durham's mother church and its earliest cathedral where the Community of St Cuthbert settled for a century. Here, the river becomes tidal; at Wearmouth, where it finally succumbs to the North Sea, Sunderland's legendary ship-building industry once flourished. It has all disappeared now, but the Anglo-Saxon church of St Peter remains, where Bede once lived and prayed and studied, a movingly eloquent symbol of Anglo-Saxon Northumbria's Golden Age of scholarship, arts, and learning. Few rivers connect such a variety of landscape, and a heritage both ancient and modern, that are so characteristic of their "place". All these northern themes are, at least in the imagination, gathered up by the Cathedral's physical location on Durham's *presqu' ile*, this "almost-island" that is surrounded on three sides by a river so freighted with associations.

14.2. A NORTH EASTERN SAINT AND HIS STORY

In 1890, a book of sermons was published under the title *Leaders in the Northern Church*.[13] These addresses, given in a wide variety of places across North East England, celebrated the men (and one woman) who had given the Church in this region such impetus from Anglo-Saxon times to the eighteenth century. Joseph Barber Lightfoot was one of Durham's great scholarly bishops, a man who, perhaps more than any other bishop of his century, had a great "feel" for the distinctiveness of the Church's mission in this part of England. It begins with the mission of Iona to Northumbria, headed by Aidan and based at Lindisfarne, and covers with insight and reverence the best known of the Anglo-Saxon saints: Oswald, Hild, Cuthbert, and Bede. It goes on to explore Richard de Bury, a late medieval bishop, Bernard Gilpin, the sixteenth-century missioner who was dubbed "the Apostle of the North", John Cosin, Durham's seventeenth-century bishop who did so much to enhance the "beauty of holiness" in the Cathedral and many other churches in the region following the Civil War, and Joseph Butler, the great philosopher-bishop of the eighteenth century. It is a fascinating book for anyone who loves the North East.

But readers should not neglect the copious footnotes in which Lightfoot, always the impeccable scholar, documents his sources and raises his love of the northern Church from romantic ideal to a rigorously argued analysis. In this part of the chapter, I want to focus on just the earliest Anglo-Saxon period because it was formative for so much that followed it. It is vital for our understanding of northern Christianity that we grasp its significance, especially for the way we "read" Durham Cathedral as a place of lived Christian faith, life, and mission.

The story of the Cathedral is inextricably bound up with St Cuthbert. His shrine is the emotional and spiritual heart of the building. He is, together with the other "northern" saints (such as Oswald, Aidan, and Hild, and Bede, the scholar who told their stories in his marvellous *Ecclesiastical History*), as essential to the Cathedral's northern character as its physical geography. If the River Wear connects the Cathedral to its landscape setting, it is Cuthbert who connects it to its spiritual hinterland and helps us to understand why the Cathedral holds such symbolic significance for North East England.

What makes Cuthbert the patron saint of the North? There is Cuthbert the historical figure who was honoured and loved in his brief life, and then there is Cuthbert the focus of an even greater honour and love after his death. Both lie right at the heart of his story. There is not space here to do justice to either of these vital features that make Cuthbert what he is: a saint who is possibly unique in England's long history of holy men and women of God. But we should focus on what is distinctive about his connection with the North, and how this has shaped and coloured the Cathedral's identity as a northern shrine.

In a recent account, Sarah Foot draws attention to how essential Cuthbert was to the fortunes of the Anglo-Saxon kingdom of Northumbria.[14] It is much more than simply his origins in what we now call the Border Country around Melrose (we need to remember that in the seventh century, the Anglo-Saxon kingdom of Northumbria extended as far as the Firth of Forth where Edinburgh was its northernmost stronghold, the place whose name folk etymology incorrectly explained as King Edwin's Burg). To begin with, it is to do with the network of places across the North where it is known that he worked, preached, studied, prayed, or cared for the communities entrusted to him. Among these were Boisil's community at

Old Melrose, where Cuthbert learned the essentials of theology, biblical study, and monastic life; the monastery at Ripon, where he became guest master; Lindisfarne, where he became first prior and then bishop; Carlisle, where Bede tells us that he ministered and preached; and, finally, the island of the Inner Farne opposite the royal palace at Bamburgh, where he retreated to live as a hermit and where he died. He never ventured, as far as we know, further south than what we now call North Yorkshire, nor further north than the Forth where, in his day, Scotland proper began. Nevertheless, there are other places that, for centuries, have claimed an association with Cuthbert in his lifetime. But Durham as we know it was never one of those places.

The second part of this remarkable tale began with Cuthbert's death in 687. Barely more than a decade later, his body was taken out of its grave on Lindisfarne and found to have been miraculously preserved. This was all that was needed, in the Anglo-Saxon Church, to demonstrate his sainthood. His coffin was set up in a shrine in the monastic church, launching thirteen centuries and more of pilgrimage. However, the next century brought disaster to the *insula sacra* or Holy Island. That place, lying low on the exposed and vulnerable coast, was among the first to experience the ferocity of Viking sea-raiders in their long ships. That was in 793. The news spread far and wide and caused consternation across England. Alcuin, a native of the North though living at Charlemagne's court at the time of the attack, asked what had become of a world in which even St Cuthbert could not defend his own. Sarah Foot, in her recent account of Cuthbert, concludes that, by the end of the eighth century, he had come to assume the role of a patron saint not just of Lindisfarne but the whole kingdom of Northumbria.[15]

The subsequent history is complex and the sources take a lot of unravelling. But this much is clear: the "people of the saint", the *haliwervolk* as Cuthbert's island community was coming to be called, left Lindisfarne to find a safer refuge inland. They took with them their most precious possessions: the relics of their saints, including Cuthbert, together with the head of St Oswald, the king who had brought Christianity to Northumbria through Aidan's mission, and the gospel book that had been written in the scriptorium on Holy Island in Cuthbert's honour, the Lindisfarne Gospels. They visited many places across the entire extent of northern England, including Norham on the banks of the River Tweed, the coastlands of west Cumbria (probably planning to sail across to Ireland from where Columba and Aidan had come to bring the gospel to northern Britain), Crayke in Yorkshire, and, finally, Chester-le-Street. Here they settled for more than a century until, with the threat of further Viking raids inland, they migrated in their quest for ever greater security, travelling via Ripon and ending up on the peninsula of Durham. Wherever the community rested, be it for a few days or a century, a church would be established in memory of the saint who had rested there, often being dedicated to Our Lady and St Cuthbert.

All these churches were, strictly speaking, the consecutive "cathedrals" of the see of Lindisfarne because it was in each place that the bishop had his headquarters. It was a mobile missionary diocese. The church at Durham is not exceptional except in its size and permanence. Like Chester-le-Street, its first Anglo-Saxon church, of which nothing now remains, was the focus of the bishop and his community's mission in Northumbria. It is important to state it this way round: Durham has never been a cathedral that has a shrine in it, but a shrine that has a cathedral around it, as all its predecessors were.

But the northernness of this story has another dimension that it is important to notice. The long pilgrimage of Cuthbert's community may not have been as simple as merely fleeing from the Vikings and looking for a well defended home. Cuthbert had bequeathed many gifts to Lindisfarne, but not all of them turned out to be spiritual. Pilgrims brought offerings out of gratitude to the saint for his miracles, and these added greatly to the shrine's wealth. Rich land owners bequeathed their estates to the community to secure Cuthbert's goodwill and prayers. Because Cuthbert was a saint of the North, the estates were mostly located in the North as well. So we could see the community travelling round its own estates to secure their firm connection to Cuthbert and to find the best site from which to administer them.[16] The journey created what we can call a "sacred geography" of the North. It mapped not simply the physical or social facts of kingdoms defined by coastlands and roads and contours, or power and politics, but the spiritual reality of "place" as it becomes indelibly linked to a holy man, a holy gospel book, and a community that lived and prayed there.

This was most keenly felt in the lands to the east, Deira in the south and Bernicia in the north, which together made up the kingdom of Northumbria. This was the kingdom's golden age of intellectual, cultural, and artistic achievement. Of course this is not only due to Cuthbert, though he plays a part in it through the Lindisfarne Gospels, the climax of Northumbrian art, which were written in honour of "God and St Cuthbert". But I believe it is fair to suggest that the debt Christian Northumbria owed to its saints and the communities that jealously guarded their relics was incalculable. Because of this, the politics of the kingdom developed in an increasingly "sacralized" direction. Anglo-Saxon kings had to reckon with the power of their saints, the importance of gaining their favour and the hazards of displeasing them. This was true in the other English kingdoms, but Cuthbert's sway in the North East was uniquely potent. So when the Normans invaded and set about establishing themselves in the North against fierce resentment among the native Anglo-Saxons, there was no evading the question of St Cuthbert. In 1083, the Norman bishop William of Saint-Calais disbanded the Community of St Cuthbert whose rule of life had become lax by the continental monastic standards he knew. He replaced them with Benedictine monks.

Bishop William, however, knew better than to displace Cuthbert himself. So when the huge project of building the present Romanesque cathedral was inaugurated in 1093, it began with the creation of a great new shrine behind the high altar. The east end, shrine, sanctuary, and quire were complete by 1104 and hallowed. This turned out to be shrewd move: "Alive and dead, Cuthbert could act as a critical ally to those willing to espouse his cause, especially those whose support took the form of material gifts and moveable wealth."[17]

So Durham Cathedral is inescapably northern because of this remarkable story. Nothing like this happened on the same scale anywhere else in England. And there is one last element that we must not miss. In the united kingdom of "England" that the Normans conquered in 1066, it suited their monarchs to take advantage of the political identity and muscle of the North. For beyond lay England's implacable enemy: Scotland. Raiders could, and did for many centuries, sweep down across the "debateable lands" and wreak havoc in England. The solution was to draw on the experience of Northumbrian "sacral kingship" and create a palatinate, ruled by bishops, that could defend England from its foe. The so-called prince-bishops (or, as we should properly call them, counts palatine), ruled the territory between the Tees and the Tyne, together with detached portions further north in ancient Cuthbert estates around Lindisfarne, Norham, and Bedlington. This is what we used to know as County Durham before the boundary changes of 1974.

The counts palatine had powers unique among bishops in England. They could levy taxes, muster armies and lead them into battle, mint coins, and try cases at law. The "land of the prince-bishops" was a kind of theocracy that lasted until the Reformation in the sixteenth century. Indeed, vestigial powers remained for as long as three more centuries before they were reincorporated into the rights of the Sovereign. Today, the See of Durham owes its seniority as the fourth among English dioceses to this distinctive northern history. The bishops of Durham have a ducal coronet included in their arms, and are said to be appointed to their see "by divine providence", like archbishops, rather than "by divine permission", which is the normal style among other bishops. Northumbrian Christian history is still expressed in these small but symbolically significant ways.

Durham Cathedral famously houses a massive bishop's *cathedra* or seat, built by Bishop Hatfield in the fourteenth century (and incorporating his own tomb underneath). It reflected the almost absolute power held by bishops in the County Palatinate. It is in every sense a potentate's throne. In what it symbolises and the history it expresses, it is also very northern. When you hurry up or down the north-south roads that connect the North East to the south, the A1M, A19 or A68, you pass signs that announce "County Durham: Land of the Prince Bishops". Where else in these islands is geography defined in terms of the Church and, by implication, the story of faith it stands for?

But we need to have a sense of perspective. What this has this proud throne, popularly said to be the "highest throne in Christendom", got to do with the servant ministry of a bishop? Perhaps there is a clue in an unlikely place, the list of bishops at the back of *Crockford's Clerical Directory*. The Bishops of Durham begin not in 995 when the Anglo-Saxon community arrived on the peninsula, but much earlier. The name at the top, under the heading "Bishops of Lindisfarne", is Aidan's, the founder of the see. A little further down comes Cuthbert, and, after him, bishops of the first cathedral in County Durham at Chester-le-Street. It is an important reminder of mission on the move, a mobile cathedral that was a "fresh expression" wherever it settled. When a Bishop of Durham lays down office, the episcopal crozier is solemnly laid on Cuthbert's shrine during the farewell service as a symbolic handing back of the "spiritualities" of the Diocese which will be guarded by the Cathedral Chapter. Bishops have spoken of this moment as a powerful reminder of the long episcopal succession that goes back all the way to Cuthbert. Similarly a new Bishop receives the crozier from the shrine on being enthroned.

We may think, looking at Hatfield's throne, that Durham Cathedral has come a long way from those simple, saintly Anglo-Saxon beginnings, and the development is not necessarily for the better. Yet the shrine of Cuthbert, now stripped of its elaborate medieval accretions and consisting simply of a gaunt slab of Frosterley marble with the name CVTHBERTVS inscribed on it in crude letters, perhaps reflects the better reality, that all Durham's bishops are his successors, just as the Cathedral is always the shrine of a humble man who gave himself totally to God and to the life of the gospel of Jesus. In all the complexity of Durham's northern story, this is the one that matters most for the mission of its great cathedral today.

14.3. MISSION WITH A NORTH EAST ACCENT

There is a lot of geography and history in this chapter. I do not apologise for this: it is impossible to do justice to Durham Cathedral's place in the north-eastern scheme of things without it. But the question remains: what about the mission of the Cathedral today? In what sense does "the idea of north" continue to influence and even determine aspects of its life that are distinctive, not found in *quite* this way anywhere else?

When I was researching this chapter, I went back to two books I had read as a parish priest in North East England.[18] One was a theologian's account about how she had tried to help churches in the region reflect on how to "do" theology and ministry in the particular setting of the North East, and what difference context made to the account we give of how God is at work in the world. If God was incarnate in Jesus as a particular human being in a particular place at a particular time, does this not imply that all theology has to be "made flesh" in the particularities of our native geography, history, culture, and social existence? In France (this is my analogy, not hers), wine experts speak about the *terroir* that determines the quality of the grape and therefore the kind of wine it produces. Geology, soil, climate, agriculture, local tradition, and much else distinguishes a Burgundy from a Claret, and within Burgundy, marks out this *appellation* from that. Her question can be restated: what is the theological, historical, cultural, sociological, and spiritual *terroir* of North East England that is forming the churches and their members and giving their mission a distinctive regional accent?

The other book, slighter in scope, did not pretend to tackle this agenda but simply identified and described a number of local church and community projects across the region that seemed to speak about the presence of God's kingdom in that place. I looked in both books for inspiration: surely it was not possible to write about the Church in North East England without mentioning Durham Cathedral! But neither of them had anything to say about it. Others must make of that what they will. To my mind, it seemed like an unwelcome statement that the Cathedral had no part to play in contributing to a contemporary theology and mission praxis that was genuinely indigenized even if it was recognized as the most familiar symbol of the Christian north.

Let us start with the Cathedral's current mission aims. Most cathedrals have purpose statements that recognise similar priorities. While these are both excellent in themselves and vital to the contribution cathedrals make to the mission of the whole Church, my task here is to focus not on what is acknowledged everywhere, but on what is distinctively Northern. When we devised Durham's purpose statement a few years ago, we wanted to include language that explicitly referenced the North East. So the top-level description "Our Place", quoted on every Sunday service sheet, reads: "Durham Cathedral is a Christian Church of the Anglican Communion, the shrine of St Cuthbert, the seat of the Bishop of Durham and a focus of pilgrimage and spirituality in North East England." Next, "Our Purpose" defines our aim as being "to worship God, share the gospel of Jesus Christ, welcome all who come, celebrate and pass on our rich Christian heritage and discover our place in God's creation". Here, "heritage" includes, even if it is much more than, our prized northernness as I have tried to outline it in this chapter. And among the Six Pillars of the Cathedral's life (a reference to the six famous Norman drum piers that flank the nave), "Outreach and Engagement" is described as working "in active partnerships for the good of the Diocese and the communities of North East England and to contribute to Durham's flourishing and significance".

Let me suggest three ways in which Durham has tried to preserve its north-eastern "accent" while not sacrificing the universal dimension of catholic faith that every cathedral and church stands for.

In *liturgy*, there is a "Durham" use just as at York, Salisbury, or St Paul's. These uses interpret the Church of England's authorized services in ways that have come to suit each cathedral's liturgical spaces and worshipping communities. In one respect, however, we are distinctively north-eastern. This lies in the liturgical calendar followed by our Cathedral. As in some other cathedrals and churches, the principal holy men and women with whom there is a particular regional or local association are honoured with their own feasts. Here they are gathered up in *The Book of Durham Festivals*. Some already feature in the Church of England's calendar, such as Oswald, Aidan, Hild, Benedict Biscop, and Margaret of Scotland; in Durham they are elevated to "red letter days" with the full complement of services for the day. In particular, the feasts of Cuthbert and Bede are celebrated with much joyous solemnity, the former having two festivals of his own: one to commemorate his death on 20 March 687, the other to remember the translation of his relics into the present shrine on 4 September 1104.

Among the "lesser festivals", a number of distinguished leaders and servants of the Church, from Anglo-Saxon saints to modern bishops, are honoured: the abbess Aebbe, Cuthbert's friend; Edwin, Oswald's predecessor as king of Northumbria who was the first to embrace Christian faith; Godric, a world traveller and hermit at Finchale, downstream of Durham; Thomas Langley, founder of the Cathedral schools and Chancellor of England; Bernard Gilpin and Joseph Butler, whom I have already mentioned above; Granville Sharpe, the tireless slave abolitionist; Bishops Lightfoot and Westcott, both outstanding nineteenth-century biblical scholars, the latter of whom is also commemorated for his support for Durham miners during bitter strikes; and the two much-loved twentieth-century Bishops Ramsey, Michael and Ian—the list is a long one. All have their own collects and readings proper to the day together with short biographies. The calendar helps to earth the liturgy in the traditions and stories that are native to north-eastern Christianity and that have played an important part in shaping its spirituality. I doubt if any other Cathedral has a *sanctorale* as richly stocked as Durham's.

In *scholarship*, Durham Cathedral is the heir to possibly the longest history of continuous study and learning in a single place anywhere in England. The community of St Cuthbert brought its precious manuscripts to Durham where they formed the nucleus of the Priory's legendary library long before any recognisable university was founded in these islands. No fewer than three Oxford colleges have centuries-old associations with the Cathedral. It was this tradition that Oliver Cromwell intended to build on by founding a university for the North in Durham, a project that foundered because of objections from Oxford and Cambridge. When Durham University was eventually founded in 1832 as a result of huge benefactions by both Bishop Van Mildert and the Dean and Chapter of the Cathedral, the aim was the same: to create a university of the North. At first it was governed by the Chapter. Even today, the Dean remains an *ex officio* governor, just as the statutory Van Mildert Professor in Theology, the oldest statutory chair in the University, is by virtue of his or her office also an *ex officio* member of the Chapter.

Giving expression to this close relationship between Cathedral and University remains a priority at Durham, as at Christ Church Oxford which inspired the institutional model of a cathedral "embedded" in the academy (or is it the other way round?). From this history derive other aspects of a partnership in learning and scholarship that is essential to Durham's flourishing, not least in Christian adult education, heritage, and the arts. And by "learning", I mean not only academic biblical and theological research activity, vital though it is for the Church to continue to invest in scholarship that is engaged with the "confessional" concerns of the faith community. I also mean the task of building bridges between the academy and the Church that interprets the activity of biblical scholars and theologians for the benefit of laity and clergy who make up the community of faith. In Durham, for example, thanks to a bequest, the Chapter has been able to endow a new chair in Anglican Studies in the University. Named after Bishop Michael Ramsey, it is of course a research post in its own right, but with the explicit task also of helping the Church in the Diocese, and as part of it the Cathedral, become more aware about its Anglican identity and the value it adds ecumenically especially in the North East.

In its relationship to the *community*, the Cathedral seeks to engage, as all cathedrals do, with the issues that are particular to the region, city, or locality. One event brings out its north-easternness very strongly. The annual Durham Miners' Gala originated in the nineteenth century as a celebration of an emerging mining community with a clear identity. In its heyday, when coal was king in County Durham, it was said that a quarter of a million people from all over the County and beyond poured into the small city each July for a day of rallies, political speeches, and family partying. The numbers are smaller now (a mere 25,000), but the spirit is alive and well. One tenth of that number find their way into the Cathedral for the service at which that year's harvest of new banners are processed in with their colliery bands, to be blessed by the Bishop. Many linger at the Miners' Memorial in the south aisle where the names of those who have died in accidents and pit disasters are commemorated in a book of remembrance. The Haswell colliery banner in the south transept is another poignant focus.

Yet there is no deep mining left in County Durham. So what purpose does it serve today? Surprisingly (and this is marked difference from some of the other mining areas in England), the undaunted spirit of the pit villages lives on, not least among the young. Someone told me, when I arrived in Durham, that I would never understand the Cathedral until I had been to the miners' service. He was right. It is important not to romanticize this: the relationships between the Church and the mining communities was always complex, a mixture of mutual pride alongside reserve, even at times contempt. Part of the narrative recalls how "the 'Barchester' part of the Durham diocese had an awkward relationship with its working-class poor".[19] Another aspect has to do with the lingering anger at pit closures that have cast a long shadow over the North East, and no doubt also an understandable nostalgia for what has been lost. "Mining touched everyone's life in this county, and the Miners' Gala celebrates their history, which is why so many people in old pit villages have raised funds to get their colliery banners renewed or refurbished. It's all about pride in our heritage."[20]

When it comes to "heritage", there is always a difficult tension between conserving the past and embracing the future, whether we are speaking about the landscape, built or cultural environment. Yet the annual Miners' service does feel overwhelmingly to be an affirmation, as if the people of the region are claiming back the Cathedral as their own place, and the Cathedral in turn is honouring them as communities and their contribution to the social capital of the region. It is an important annual reminder to bishops, deans, and chapters that the sacred space belongs not to ecclesiastical dignitaries but to the ordinary people, the *laos* of this part of England. This helps to explain why the Cathedral is held in such huge affection by those who live in County Durham and the North East. This demotic, popularist, aspect is not always found in cathedrals. The miners' service is a real expression of a cherished sense of connection that is deeply felt by north-eastern people for Durham Cathedral, and by the Cathedral for its own native working communities. At this service you hear, literally, North Eastern accents in all their bewildering variety, from Teesside to Wearmouth, from the Durham Dales to Geordie Tyneside, from Northumberland to the border. But this is a metaphor of a deeper wish to speak with a local "accent", to try to practise mission in ways that are genuinely indigenous and not the spurious play-acting that sometimes passes for it.

And this of course needs to be true of the Cathedral, as it needs to be true of every church that takes the word "local" seriously. A central task of mission is to discern how to bear witness to the gospel that is good news for the whole world while also being able to proclaim good news for this distinctive part of it. Honouring the particular alongside the universal is precisely what it means to believe in incarnation, as the best evangelical and catholic theology have always insisted.

In this chapter, I have tried to hint (no more than that) at ways in which I see Durham Cathedral as rooted in the distinctiveness of North East England not as something that is merely incidental, but rather as an essential aspect of its Christian character and identity.[21] The idea of "north", which includes the idea of a Christian north, is perhaps an aspect of Durham Cathedral's unique contribution to the witness of the Church in England.

To put it simply, its northern landscape setting, its history and culture, its people and communities, and its relationship with locality and region, Durham Cathedral is perhaps able to affirm, in a highly public and visible way, that God cares about North East England as part of his care for the whole of creation. It can pose questions raised in the titles of the two books I mentioned earlier: what kind of God is it who is at work in the North to point to the kingdom of justice and peace? And what does it mean to talk about "the kingdom of God and North East England"? It can help to interpret difficult theological and spiritual questions as the life of this region poses them. It must make the most of its assets as a glorious edifice on its rocky Wear-girt acropolis to which so many are drawn. A Christian writer who has studied Durham's sense of place has coined the word "Durhamness" to describe the elusive quality that the city evokes. He says of the Cathedral:

> The existing Norman structure represents time locked-up, a gigantic pause in the temporal flow of history. At the same time . . . one is aware in Durham of the presence, as well as the pastness of the past, for the story is kept alive, celebrated, enacted daily, weekly, annually by its clerics along with citizens, scholars, miners and a host of other regional and diocesan groups as well as by modern pilgrims. In short, it is the incarnation of our existence.[22]

This is at the heart of what it means to be a northern cathedral. Its unique history and heritage can, and must, be put to work for the service of the gospel in the present and point to the future that God is creating. But the ancient story of Cuthbert and his community give us another, more primitive, model of mission to discover: learning once again to be a mobile cathedral, travelling light, moving out to the people of our time as God's love for the world always does, not only here in North East England but everywhere.

NOTES

1. R. B. Dobson, *Durham Priory 1400–1450* (Cambridge University Press, 1973), p. 11.
2. Peter Davidson, *The Idea of North* (Reaktion Books, 2005).

3. *Ibid.*, pp. 8–9.
4. *Ibid.*, pp. 225–6.
5. Mark Hudson, *Coming Back Brockens: A Tear in a Mining Village* (Jonathan Cape, 1994), p. 121.
6. Owen Chadwick, *Hensley Henson: A Study in the Friction Between Church and State* (Canterbury Press, 1983), p. 113.
7. W. H. Auden, "I Like it Cold", *House and Gardens* (1947); quoted in *Myers Literary Guide*, <http://www.sclews.me.uk/m-auden.html> (accessed 25 March 2015).
8. W. H. Auden, "New Year Letter" (1940), cited in Alan Myers and Robert Forsythe, *W. H. Auden: Pennine Poet* (North Pennines Heritage Trust, 1999), p. 24.
9. Alan Myers and Robert Forsythe, *W. H. Auden: Pennine Poet* (North Pennines Heritage Trust 1999), p. 14.
10. Nikolaus Pevsner, *The Buildings of England: County Durham,* 1st edition (Penguin 1953), p. 77.
11. *Ibid.*, p. 79.
12. Michael Sadgrove, *Landscapes of Faith* (Third Millennium, 2013), pp. 24–63.
13. Joseph Barber Lightfoot, *Leaders in the Northern Church: Sermons Preached in the Diocese of Durham* (MacMillan, 1890).
14. Sarah Foot, "Cuthbert and the Search for a Patron" in David Brown (ed.), *Durham Cathedral: History, Fabric, Culture* (Yale University Press, 2015), pp. 9ff.
15. *Ibid.*, p. 15.
16. *Ibid.*, p. 17.
17. *Ibid.*, p. 25.
18. Margaret Kane, *What Kind of God? Reflections on Working With People and Churches in North-East England* (SCM Press, 1986); James D. G. Dunn (ed.), *The Kingdom of God and North-East England* (SCM Press, 1986).
19. Robert Lee, *The Church of England and the Durham Coalfield, 1810–1926: Clergymen, Capitalists and Colliers* (Boydell Press, 2007), p. 26.
20. Peter Crookston, *The Pitmen's Requiem* (Northumbria Press, 2010), pp. 65ff.
21. Michael Sadgrove, "Identities Past and Present" in Brown, *Durham Cathedral,* pp. 505ff.
22. Douglas Pocock, *Durham: Essays on a Sense of Place* (City of Durham Trust, 1999), p. 61.

15. "MISSION: REGARDING THE OVERLOOKED ..."

Mark Tanner

The city of Durham, with its world-class university and internationally renowned cathedral, forms an oasis of privilege in the middle of one of our nation's most challenged counties, and yet also manages to serve as a focal point for many of those communities. Here you find little of the town/gown conflict I remember from my Oxford days, but instead experience a pragmatic co-existence arising from the heart of a scarred but resourceful people who often feel that they are overlooked and on their own. In the middle of this sits Cranmer Hall, a leading theological college with almost a hundred students comprising an intentionally formational Christian community.

Here, as we strive to be well shaped for a lifetime of service to the gospel, the Church, and our Lord, I often challenge the community with the truth that Durham ought to be the most evangelized city in the North. There are only 70,000 residents and we are 100 evangelists. "Join a club with 70 members and between us we have got 10 per cent of the city covered!" Moreover, the gospel-task does not stop at the city limits, and only gets more dynamic as students come alongside some of the country's most resourceful and loveable people in some of our most overlooked communities.

I love the way that this challenge is reflected throughout the community. In particular, the students do a "micro-mission" as part of Michael Volland's first year mission course. The idea is really simple: students are told that, four weeks into the course, one 2-hour lecture will be used by them as a small-scale mission. They are given complete freedom and a very small budget. Their task is to share the good news of the kingdom somewhere within reach of the College. In Michael's words, their brief is to "Go, and as you go proclaim the Kingdom!"

This has now been repeated a number of times, and we have witnessed some very ordinary extraordinary things. This year we saw a "sitting room" set up in the market square to enable shoppers to relax in a homely environment. The students reported:

> Highlights were speaking to a load of young people about God and what they believed, speaking to a pagan chap about early Christianity and the early Celtic Christians, like Patrick etc., and how they held an interest in the natural world and talking to an atheist who admitted he believed in God.

(This and other quotes are taken from <http://www.mikromission. wordpress.com> where you can view all of the micromission stories and pictures.)

Other students set up a question-board on one of the medieval bridges into the city. They report, "What was remarkable was the genuine inquisitiveness of people", and record how people would go away to think about what they would like to ask God. They go on to report:

> As with all these [micromissions], the best bit was simply talking to people. [One of us] had about an hour long chat and a pray with someone who said she would go away and read a Gospel . . . It was a fantastic moment when we prayed at the end and were all left a little blown away by how God had used us to witness to people.

Quite a lot of students offer to pray with people, some with a visual or creative approach such as coloured leaves that are written upon and hung on a prayer tree, others with a more "charismatic" approach, such as "treasure hunting". This latter method involves the team meeting before going out and asking God to reveal "treasures" that they will go and find. They listen prayerfully, asking the Lord to reveal the location of the treasure, people's names, particular needs, and any unusual things they will look for; then they go and look for them and talk to the people they find.

Some do practical things like cleaning shoes, others engage in a more unusual way. Two male students decided that they were simply going to buy open tickets and sit on a bus, and talk to whomever wished to talk to them.

This instinct to serve in practical ways and genuinely to give people attention is noticeable and important. The people of the North East generally and genuinely feel that they are overlooked, ignored, and abandoned. We are a long way from London and we are not Scotland. Outsiders do not care—and yet the micromissions proclaim that Christ does, and people respond.

I also notice how all of this is naturally "covered by prayer", and this unites our community around the activity of those who are engaged in the micro-missions. We are told to "pray to the Lord of the Harvest" to send workers: that this is His work not ours. It is interesting, though, that we pray more, and more together, when we are actually doing something!

Where possible, we follow up the fruit that we see from these micromissions, but what is remarkable is that the follow-up is all student-driven. When people get a taste for mission they want to keep going. From them we have seen a chaplaincy to the Market Place begun, as well as a weekly presence on one of the (other) bridges around Durham simply praying for people. All of this is natural and unforced, but it arises out of a passion which is birthed as people engage in this kind of activity.

This, I think, is the third thing I notice: mission is something that we simply need to do. We can feel paralysed when confronted by some of the challenges of our communities, particularly in places where employment and social cohesion has been decimated in a multi-generational way (for us, usually by the closure of coal-pits), but, when we go to where people are and reach out in small ways, people respond.

It does not need to be clever, well resourced, or practised. It does need to be where other people are comfortable rather than where we are, and it needs to be about Jesus. With that, we can see extraordinary things in very ordinary activities. It is really difficult to predict what is going to go well and what is simply going to be an afternoon's activity. Some students are excited, others a little less keen, but all can do it. You might expect that this should be true of trainee-vicars, but our experience is that it is true of all who take part in the courses. People come back encouraged, humbled, and wanting to do it again. It reminds me a little of the return of the 70 in Luke 10, where Jesus, too, had simply told them to go and proclaim the kingdom as they did.

16. VOCATION AND RESURRECTION: FACING THE CHALLENGES IN THE NORTH

Mark Powley

Christian ministry is never less than an exercise in resurrection. This is certainly the case for any consideration of vocation and deployment in the North of England. Statistics for the recruitment and retention of priests look bleak, as we shall explore. It is easy to speak of death. Yet we are bound by Easter faith to speak of new life. We must have hope. But hope for what? What is to be named as death, and what as life? How are we to distinguish between the morbidity of managed decline and the life-giving sacrifice of faithful risk? For the Church deals not in generalities of death and new life, as if resurrection were a universal law or statistical trend, but rather in particularities: this lifeless body in an borrowed tomb, this dwindling congregation with an unaffordable building, this seemingly impossible context for mission. We see Paul engage this task in 2 Corinthians, discerning the particular dynamics of resurrection in his context: affliction in us, consolation in you (1:6); death carried through apostolic sufferings, life made visible by the extraordinary sustenance of God (4:10); death in us, life in you (4:12). The same dangerous yet vital task of discerning death and life is needed here.

The present chapter examines some of the challenges for the Church of England in encouraging vocation and deployment of ordained ministers in the North. It will then consider potential avenues for response, in particular arguing in support of a cooperative and entrepreneurial approach. A particular model of engagement I will examine is that of contextual theological training, reflecting from my own experience in directing the work of St Barnabas Theological Centre since its launch in the autumn of 2013. Given the pioneering nature of this work, and the relatively recent development of this model of training in the Anglican Church, these comments will have an unavoidably provisional character. They are reflections from the road on a journey that is still unfolding.

16.1.   NAMING THE CHALLENGES

"Go Spread the Word of the Lord? Only Down South Says Choosy Church of England Clergy", so ran the story in *The Independent* in February 2014.[1] This followed a report from Madeleine Davies in the Church Times:

> In London, it takes, on average, 4.6 months to appoint to a vacancy. The average shortlist contains three applicants. In Guildford, it is five to six months, and a shortlist of four. In contrast, in York, the average is a year, with an average shortlist of two. In Wakefield, "shortlists are very rare". In Manchester, there is often only one candidate, occasionally two.[2]

The sense of both reports was that clergy deployment has become problematic in a significant number of northern areas compared to the South, especially the South East. Commentators have remarked on the unfair implication of the headlines, and the difficulty of forming an accurate picture.[3] The discussion, as it unfolded in the media and online, focussed on stipendiary clergy, which we must admit is only part of a much wider picture. However, it remains the case that, by 2022, the Northern Province is predicted to be over 600 full-time clergy short. This represents a shortfall of 40 per cent against desired levels and is a greater discrepancy than that forecasted for the South.[4] Northern Anglican dioceses are neither ordaining, nor able to attract from elsewhere, enough full-time ministers to meet their hopes. Importantly, according to the research, they have also been significantly overestimating the personnel they will have at their disposal. The issue is not simply one of unequal distribution but a leadership gap of disturbing proportions. Reflecting on the national scene, the Resourcing Ministerial Education task group recently stated, "At present, if we take no action, we face a significant net decline in the number of stipendiary ministers and alongside this further decline in congregations and hence our capacity to serve every community."[5]

In *The Shape of Living*, David Ford writes of the power of naming and describing that which threatens to overwhelm us: "Describing [our overwhelming] frees us from the wrong sort of guilt and from paralysing isolation. It also helps in countering the response of despair."[6] How, then, can we describe the challenges facing northern vocation? In what follows I identify six key factors, though such a list cannot be exhaustive. Obviously, the wider context of cultural marginalization of the Church of England and its institutional fragility impact its ability to recruit and fund clergy. Some have also questioned the spiritual health of the Church, if its leaders prefer wealthier and less challenging posts. But the focus of this chapter will be on strategic and practical issues relating to the separate but overlapping areas of recruiting clergy, retaining them in the region and attracting new clergy from elsewhere.

16.2.   SIX CHALLENGES

Firstly, there is the challenge of resources.[7] The historic North-South divide plays out in a variety of limiting factors, including the inability of significant numbers of northern churches to afford additional clergy posts and sometimes in reduced prospects for spouses to secure work. It has also played out in provision of training. For much of recent history Oxford alone has boasted as many Anglican residential theological colleges as the entire Northern Province. When I was working as a young teacher in Birmingham and felt called to ordained ministry, the options for training led not back to the North West where I grew up but largely to the South.

Having relocated to Oxford to train, a curacy in Croydon seemed a not unreasonable move, and this was followed by an associate role at a larger southern church. I had not given the drift South much thought, but the distribution of resources paved my way.

Secondly, there is the fact of relational ties. Blogging on this issue, Ian Paul relates: "When I was thinking about training and ordination, I was single and in my twenties, but even then was mindful of my responsibilities to ageing parents. They lived in Kent . . . So I drew a line two hours from Kent, which reached as far as Nottingham—and that's where I went."[8] With London significantly exceeding other dioceses in producing ordinands, a Southern bias is embedded into the system.

Third, there is the challenge of cultural distance between clerical life and local culture. This phenomenon works in both directions: clerical to cultural and cultural to clerical. The distance from clerical life to local culture is in evidence when southern vicars (or vicars from middle class northern backgrounds) find connecting with a northern parish unappealing in prospect, when considering a new post, or unachievable in reality. A gifted young minister I know moved to the North for the first time for his first incumbency and within eighteen months saw dramatic signs of growth in the church where he served. However, there were numerous issues of cultural transition for him and his family, for which he had received no prior training, and the pioneering aspects of his role received uneven support from the diocese. Shortly afterwards he returned to the South. Other ministers might take a northern parish but never truly "get" their local context (might it be possible to move on before even realizing this has been the case?). The reverse dynamic, the distance from local culture to clerical life, is experienced by local people who feel that, for a host of reasons related to culture, class, gender, and ethnicity, ordination does not happen to "people like me". Just one aspect of this is geographic mobility. In one instance, a potential ordinand was advised that she would struggle to be selected for stipendiary ministry so long as she felt called to serve only in her own immediate locality. But this insistence on mobility sits uneasily with the fact that around 60 per cent of the British population live within 20 miles of where they lived when they were 14 years old. In recent political analysis this statistic has sharpened the objection that Westminster career politicians are not representative of their constituencies.[9] But how many within this 60 per cent would also feel excluded from the representative role of priesthood, given its association with the geographic mobility of a clerical class? Alan Hirsch and Michael Frost have commented on the dangers of "homeless" leadership which "might at first look like just the kind of flexibility needed for missionary activity" but "can lead to the kind of spiritual Teflon coating that means they never actually stick anywhere".[10] A system that naturally promotes ministerial mobility and filters out candidates with a thoroughly local mind-set could be seen as a triumph of deployability or a failure to connect locally.

Fourth, there is the lack of lay discipleship and leadership development. As several recent Church of England reports have noted, a culture of discipleship and team leadership at a local level is not sufficiently in place to raise new vocations. Diocesan Directors of Ordinands testify to being overstretched in time and capacity, and the selection process itself is too risk averse. The system is not set up to effectively identify and release leaders, whether lay or ordained. Admittedly, some voices have questioned whether focussing on discipleship and leadership in the local church, as we do throughout this chapter, is too clerical and congregational an approach for Anglicanism.[11] The alternative view, however, is that the shallowness of our participation in Christ's character, and our inability to release others into his calling, is a deep weakness in the contemporary Church. If this is so, an approach to discipleship and leadership which is at once more demanding and more empowering is a vital necessity for the Church of England. One example of this is the case of church planting. A potential church planter needs, among other things, the opportunity to gather a team, a generous local support network, and a genuine sense of geographical connection. The classic model of residential training removes all these factors for 6–8 years, during which a candidate is expected to live in four consecutive locations: sending context, then initial training, then curacy, then incumbency. Planting a church in the 1–2 years before selection would be discouraged, in the 2–3 years of residential training it is barely possible, and normal patterns of curacy also provide little scope for it. An entire season of ministerial life has been made inhospitable to the act of church planting, ruling out its considerable formational potential for ministers in training, at the very time young leaders may be most suited to launching something new.

Fifth, there is the disconnect with youth. The northern Church has suffered a drastic diminution of its youth and young adult active membership. Yet many experience a call to ordained ministry in young adulthood, mid- to late-teens, or even earlier. Without young people, future vocations dry up. And without procedures for discernment that inspire and equip young people, what sense of calling there is may be lost. One young adult candidate I know of was told she was "too fun" and should come back in ten years. Another young candidate waited two years in the process before, faced with further delay, he concluded that his calling would not flourish in the Church of England and took an opportunity to pursue ministry overseas.

Sixth, absence of shared vision. When I took up a post in the Diocese of London, I was summoned to the diocesan office. On arrival I was greeted by a series of banners setting out the 2012 vision for the city and its churches. In the briefing that followed I was inducted into the diocesan strategy for growth in numbers and depth of discipleship, including proposals to review financial support for congregations which were failing to effectively serve in their context. When I later moved to the (now historic) Diocese of Ripon and Leeds and arrived for the first time at the diocesan office, I was met instead by a map of the diocese on which every Grade I listed church building was marked, pictured, and named. Shortly afterwards, at the first clergy conference I attended, the very notion of diocesan vision was questioned at the highest level in favour of the localism of a parish-led approach. Despite the warmth and hospitality of the welcome I received, the contrast with my previous experience was striking. London was the first diocese to buck the national decline in the Church of England; Leeds, like many others, is still seeking to reverse the trend. In *Hope for the Church*, Bob Jackson has drawn attention to the key role the diocese can play not just in permission-giving, but in actively fostering policies and strategies to support church growth.[12] Without any shared vision the worst kind of parochialism of strategy and action ensues. Without coherent vision and planning, training institutions themselves easily disconnect from meaningful strategic dialogue with churches. One high-level consultation at a theological institution understandably set itself the question, "What are the needs of the church?" However, when probed, it emerged that not one of the many participants was currently in parish incumbency. Vision, training, deployment, and practical missional reflection belong together.

16.3.   RESPONDING TO THE CHALLENGES

The question of what distinguishes a death that precedes resurrection from mere morbid decline is a profound one. No ultimate answer can be given except the sovereign creative work of God in Christ Jesus. But, as we have seen, Paul's approach was not to speak of resurrection only in general terms, but to identify in his own experience what it meant to "rely not on ourselves but on God who raises the dead" (2 Corinthians 1:9). In our own situation, too, our response to the challenges in raising vocation is critical, either constituting a creative act of life or a collusive act of death. In what follows we sketch out potential avenues of response and argue for the importance of a shared confrontation of the overwhelming challenges we face.

First, we need to acknowledge that stasis, or a set of responses that amount to stasis, remains an option. Despite the flurry of recent reports that recognize the challenges listed above, there will always be plausible justifications for the status quo. There is a natural concern to prepare candidates for the current realities of ministry, to emphasize breadth of exposure and the need to manage multi-parish life. Dioceses can become settled into rigid, centripetal patterns, and may lack the institutional energy to create a new narrative and the relationships to sustain it. The statistical analysis we have already discussed suggests just this kind of lack of capacity to strategically address the area of vocation and deployment.

And yet the urgent vitality of the gospel, not to mention the rapidity of present cultural change, suggests that this cannot be our default approach. The guidance of the Spirit must be sought for the present moment, privileged modes of operation must remain open to question. As Hans Küng wrote:

> A church which pitches its tents without constantly looking
> out for new horizons, which does not constantly strike
> camp, is being untrue to its calling . . . [we must] play
> down our longing for certainty, accept what is risky, live
> by improvisation and experiment.[13]

Bob Jackson comments:

> The Church is not a business operation . . . [b]ut it is not
> less than a business. . . . [I]t needs not less but more courage
> than a business to research its problems and opportunities
> and develop solutions to them. . . . Before it is too late, the
> culture of the Church needs to change to make research
> and development of its own life a priority.[14]

It remains the case that many northern contexts are not inimical to church growth or the release of vocation in fresh ways. In an inner urban parish in Leeds, for example, a deconsecrated Anglican Church building has been renovated by an independent congregation as a base for gathered worship and a community cafe. Another new church in the city currently has over 100 people enrolled on its informal theological training course, many of them young adults. Creative alternatives are available to the established Church in the window of opportunity that we have. Resurrection, we should bear in mind, is not a law to be taken for granted in decline; it is a promise to be received by faith in action.

A second possible option in the present climate is to avoid potentially overwhelming institutional challenges by circumventing them. Individual churches, or church networks, may pursue independent forms of training, or abandon formal training altogether. The Church of England still provides space for highly-traditioned groups to foster their distinctive culture through select sponsorship of certain colleges, mutual association, and patronage. Churches in these networks can be more successful at growing membership and recruiting leaders because they maintain the plausibility structures necessary to flourish in an uncertain culture, as Andrew Walker has noted.[15] The result can be an oasis of worship and discipleship in a hostile climate, and a powerful advertisement for Christianity. In such circles, centralized visions of training and deployment are often rejected in favour of pathways over which candidates and sponsoring churches have more control. Emerging leaders can be kept "in house" through internship and staffing schemes, or even if ordained may only serve within a particular network of churches. These networks, and larger churches especially, can function as independent micro-systems, insulated to some extent from the weaknesses of the wider institution by their greater resources.

How is such an approach to be evaluated? Any localized reversal of ecclesial fortunes is cause for rejoicing. But we need also to be aware of the larger dynamics at work. Writing in 2003, Tom Smail diagnosed in the UK Church a deepening sense of exile. In such a situation, there is a natural temptation to "immediate revivalistic escape".[16] His target is charismatic revivalism, but his words apply to any strategy for return to health and influence based on a straightforward avoidance of the Church's institutional malaise, whether through a new technique, the correct theological affiliation, or well-resourced networks:

> [T]he negative of judgement and the positive of renewal live in very uneasy relationship with each other; there is no easy or prescribed path from one to the other, no ten easily treadable steps from failure to success . . . [T]hat the "Yes" of renewal should follow the "No" of rejection is never a foregone or indeed calculable conclusion, but always a creative and sovereign act of God.[17]

We could add that the mark of genuine kingdom life is that it is life-giving. It does not simply cheat death, still less survive by monopolizing much-needed resources. The challenge, therefore, for such networks of power as we currently have, is to reverse the flow of Christians to the oasis. Or, better, to utilize this flow as a means of galvanizing, equipping, and then enlisting Christians for courageous mission. The church planting strategy of Holy Trinity Brompton is a prime example of this approach, at its best when at its most generous. So far as any new initiative exists in tightly-branded isolation, it will tend to be culturally monochrome and less catholic in ethos. It is theologically, not to mention sociologically, impossible for fullness of life to flourish in these silos. Our approach must be more holistic. The miracle of new life in Christ does not occur limb by limb, but as the resurrection of the body. The locus of the revitalizing power of the Spirit is the body of Christ in the giftedness of its diversity, not just a privileged or isolated part of it.

If the first two options correspond to the evolutionary instincts of "freeze" and "flight", the last option is to "fight", understood as shared confrontation of the overwhelmings we face. This third approach detects in the responses above something of the hopelessness once diagnosed by Moltmann: the activist presumption of radicalism on one hand, and the barren despair of stasis on the other: "Both forms of hopelessness, by anticipating the fulfillment or by giving up hope, cancel the wayfaring character of hope. They rebel against the patience in which hope trusts in the God of the promise. They demand impatiently either fulfillment 'now already' or 'absolutely no' hope."[18] Arguably, neither take seriously enough the radical judgement of the cross on our corporate ego or the power of the resurrection to create not just new statistics but new relations within the Church.

Our argument here is not that only one response is required. There is a place for strategies of faithful perseverance on the one hand and of (equally, but differently, faithful) innovation on the other. But it is essential to confront the challenges of vocation and deployment directly and cooperatively, refusing to sacrifice either our commitment to the wider Church or our obligation to the gospel. Our lead here can be taken from the earliest Church. As the narrative of Acts unfolds, it is clear that the Jerusalem Church safeguarded the traditions and permissions handed to them by Jesus. Increasingly, though, Paul comes to represent the undeniable but unsettling prospect of a new kind of mission dawning in the name of Jesus ("Is he still trying to kill us?", they feared, and not just literally). But the bold procession of the Word of God was not via clunky centralization of the new missional possibilities in Cyprus, Antioch, and beyond; nor was it via independent and isolated ministry on the part of Paul. It was, instead, through a Spirit-empowered partnership, built on the bridge-like generosity of Barnabas. Risky for the Church, and sometimes fractious for Paul, it entailed a practice of surrender which led to life. As a result, unchartered territory opened up for the gospel, while in the process the institution was recalled to the treasure in its keeping. Established tradition and radical mission can cooperate, indeed they must, and the Church of England is well placed, even now, to pioneer this approach.

What does such an approach mean in practice? A thoroughgoing engagement with the issues we face, and experimentation marked by cooperation and risk. It is being willing not just to tinker with the details of an unchanged regnant paradigm but to rethink training from the ground up, being much more creative about partnerships, particularly where traditions have become siloed or power relations frozen. It requires the courage to ask direct questions. This is just what the recent "Green Report" on senior leadership proposed:

> Organisations which have come late to the rigorous management of risk can easily read across from management to aversion. . . . We are advocating the embrace of credible risk as an integral part of our adventure in Christ. We are proposing a radical step change in our development of leaders who can shape and articulate a compelling vision and who are skilled and robust enough to create spaces of safe uncertainty in which the Kingdom grows.[19]

If this prospect causes us to feel fear (and speaking as one involved in the process, it certainly does) we might reflect on the prospect that a more authentic faith, with all its uncertainties and costs, may be called forth by just such an adventure. Hirsch and Frost speak of the liminality experienced in risk as the only way for the Church to recover its own vocation:

> On the whole, churches seek to conserve the past, and particularly in the historic denominations their primary orientation is often backward to an idealised past rather than forward to a new vision of the future . . . Hence the mainline denominations are leading the decline of the church in the West, due almost entirely to the fact that they are closed systems built on an institutional systems story. But when liminality, either deliberate or otherwise, is allowed to impact and inform the church, we are propelled outward toward the edge of chaos where [the church] has

to constantly adapt to the missional challenges it faces. It
becomes the highly responsive learning organisation that
it should be.[20]

When this logic is applied to ministerial recruitment, training, and
deployment, we might ask: what would be the marks of solutions that
address the six regional challenges we named earlier? Rather than being
hampered by the challenge of resources, they will be marked by resource
creativity, including investment into the North from central funds but
also financial creativity at a regional level. They will work with the
grain of relational ties, for instance, by raising vocation locally, in close
partnership with individual congregations. They will be marked by cultural
embeddedness and connectivity, focusing not so much on a mobile clerical
class but on commitment to locality and fostering representative diversity.
Deployability, in these terms, is not measured so much by geographical
mobility as by the ability to truly reach people where you are. This is, in
fact, a corollary of Anglicanism's commitment to outworking the gospel in
every place. They will be part of an empowering shift towards developing
discipleship and leadership. The emphasis will not be on clergy being
sent, but on leaders raised up in context. This is related to a theology of
priesthood as inclusive rather than exclusive representation, whereby the
ordained minister releases the priesthood of all.[21] To be ordained is not
to signify what God's people are not, but to enable who they are. It will
involve serious engagement with youth. As Bob Jackson suggests, "The
leaders of a new church plant aimed at people in their twenties should be
that age themselves . . . The Church that has the courage to support the
young wherever they lead is the Church that will conquer the future."[22]
Lastly, it will be marked by shared vision and strategy that calls forth
sacrifice. This requires a new, and redeemed, entrepreneurialism as well
as new kinds of relationships between dioceses, churches, and training
institutions.

16.4.   THE PROMISE OF CONTEXTUAL TRAINING

It remains to reflect on this proposed approach in the light of a specific instance which seeks to address some of the challenges to vocation, namely contextual theological training. Without laying out a full justification here, my aim is to highlight some key features of contextual training and the rationale that underpins it.

There are several current models of contextual training, some initiated by traditional theological colleges and courses, others emerging from new partnerships. Inspired by the logic of the previous section, St Barnabas Theological Centre (SBTC) arose out of cooperation between several larger churches (St George's, Leeds; St Thomas, Crookes; and The Belfrey, York) and regional training institutions (including the Yorkshire Ministry Course for Anglican ordinands and Northern Baptist College for Baptist ministers in training). We launched in September 2013 to provide ordination training, an independent leadership track, and wider theological resource hosted at the Crookes Campus in Sheffield. Our model is based on ordinands serving roughly half-time in a missional context, with weekly gathered training in term time and, for Anglican ordinands, regular experience of residential community as part of the Yorkshire Ministry Course at the Mirfield Centre, home of the Community of the Resurrection.

The aim of SBTC is to provide rigorous academic study alongside practical missional engagement. This represents an important shift from the study-focused model of a residential college, or a part-time approach where church commitments may have to be significantly pared back, to a model that blends theology and practice. This shift can be illustrated rather bluntly with a couple of illustrations based on my own experience. When I was at college, training for preaching meant preaching to a small group of ordinands in a tutors' office. Once, when studying the topic of baptism, a toy doll was passed down the rows of students so that we could practice holding a baby. By contrast, just recently one of our contextual ordinands preached at his church's largest Christmas service. This was only natural as, because he is training by this route, he is a full member of the church's leadership team. He was also able to invite many local friends with whom he had built up relationship over several years. The following week he led a service of adult baptism, involving several people who had come to faith in the previous months. And yet alongside this, perhaps even because of it, he is making excellent progress in his academic studies.

Models of training which aim to form reflective practitioners through apprenticeship in tandem with formal study are by no means restricted to the arena of theological education; they are widespread in medicine, education, social work, and business. But there are also substantial biblical and theological grounds for this approach. In *Reenvisioning Theological Education*, Robert Banks has produced an excellent theological manifesto for practical missional training. Firstly, this pattern can be clearly seen in the practice of biblical figures, especially Jesus and Paul. In the case of Jesus and his apostles, "it was not preparation of the twelve for mission that was uppermost in his mind, but engagement of the twelve in mission".[23] Likewise, Paul's practice hinged on the creation of localized yet dynamic missionary groups. Banks concludes:

> The purpose of these groups was not increase in knowledge of their basic traditions, progress in moral or spiritual formation, or the development of skills associated with ministry or leadership. It was active service or mission in furthering the kingdom. . . . Within that framework, however, spiritual development and practical development, as well as substantial learning, also took place. Such learning was often in-service and nonformal in character; at other times it was more extensive and systematic.[24]

This kind of active learning is a crucial context for the development of virtue (as in Philippians 4:9, "Keep on doing the things that you have learned and received and heard and seen in me, and the God of peace will be with you"). But this should be understood not principally in classic terms as paideia (with its emphasis on cultivation of character) or even theologia (with its emphasis on reflective wisdom) but as missiologia (the life-engaging practice of mission).[25] Since the launch of SBTC, I have been asked more than once how contextual ordinands experience the "formation in community" normally associated with fully residential training. My reply is that the principal context for Christlike formation is the local body of Christ on mission. Unusual conclusions would follow if we were to propose otherwise. More importantly still, ministerial formation as formation-in-mission is deeply rooted in the missional nature of God himself. He cannot express his love for (and ministry to) the world without sending and being sent, proclaiming and demonstrating love in action. It is partly because of this that truth itself can never be words alone, no matter how finely studied. "Little children, let us love not in word or speech, but in truth and action" (1 John 3:18). Word and flesh must be properly joined in Christian formation.

There is precedent for this form of training in the North already. Nick Spencer comments on Bede's vision for Wearmouth-Jarrow in the eighth century: "Monastic communities were not just pastoral communities that served the needs of their localities; they were also outward-looking missionary centres, in much the same way as modern theological colleges."[26]

Clearly, contextual models in their modern form cannot be seen as a panacea for the Church. Significant issues still require attention. Provisions for equitable financing of contextual placements needs to be worked out; the effect on the wider ecology of training and relations with secular universities needs to be borne in mind; time management on the part of students is a constant challenge (though this is good preparation for ordained life). However, contextual training does offer a potentially significant contribution to bridging the future leadership gap.

To return finally to the challenges named earlier, we may note promising signs thus far in each area. In terms of overall resources, contextual training is a lighter and more financially flexible model than residential training, with new contextual centres already helping rebalance the national distribution of training. The northern contextual pathways (including St Mellitus North West and contextual pathways run by the Yorkshire Ministry Course, Cranmer Hall and St John's, Nottingham) have already demonstrated a capacity to keep ordinands in the region who would otherwise have left. At its best, contextual training brings the added benefit of deeper local engagement and the reconfiguration of training from being a "student experience" to being participative leadership in a community of mission.

In terms of culture, the weaknesses inherent in traditional theological education were highlighted by the 1985 *Faith in the City* report: "Many would say that [the] monastic approach to preparation for the sacred ministry has itself become problematical. . . . [O]rdinands coming from working class backgrounds become involved in an educational enterprise familiar to professional people but strange to their home environment."[27] The particular contribution of contextual training is to link a new approach with the possibility of growing and planting local expressions of church. As the "Mission Shaped Church" report later expressed: "The critical factor will be our ability to identify and train emerging leaders in context . . . A pattern of training, mentoring and apprenticeship 'on the job' should be developed, rather than outside or apart from the mission situation where the leader (or potential leader) is exercising their ministry."[28]

In terms of developing new and younger leaders, St Mellitus College has already demonstrated the significant potential of this model to attract young ordinands. Importantly, there is evidence that this form of training raises vocation in others. The increased visibility, accessibility, and missional nature of this approach has made some potential candidates more open to the possibility of ordained ministry.

In terms of shared vision, one of the most rewarding aspects of pioneering this new model has been the creation of new kinds of conversation between regional partners. Dioceses have been enabled, if they so wish, to plan more strategically for retention of ordinands and for church planting. Training has been electrified by the practical context in a formational process that is more about cultivating sharpness for mission and depth of character than an institutionally-oriented notion of breadth. Through developments like those at SBTC, larger churches have been empowered to offer more of their strengths as gifts. An example of this is the extensive experience in missional discipleship and coaching at St Thomas Crookes, from which St Barnabas students benefit through our "huddles" for accountability and character development in place of the traditional college fellowship group.

Over twenty-five years ago, Lesslie Newbigin remarked, "It seems clear that ministerial training as currently conceived is still far too much training for the pastoral care of existing congregations, and far too little oriented toward the missionary calling to claim the whole of public life for Christ and his kingdom."[29] Newbigin's vision remains daunting in its scope, but the reversal of orientation he identifies is a vital one. As I write, the first ordinand to ever accept a place on our pathway is now 18 months into the task of helping to lead a turnaround project in a congregation that was facing critical decline. In partnership with the ordinand's sending church, this congregation has entered a new phase of life, already doubling in size and beginning to re-engage its community. This is what training should be. The North needs not just more people in training, but more missional training.

16.5.   LIFE IN THE BODY

The resurrection of Jesus Christ inaugurated a new kind of somatic existence. The physical body of Jesus became, and remains, the first truly fixed thing in the universe, operating according to the novel conditions of the kingdom. By the same token, the resurrection inaugurates a new set of relationships within the ecclesial body of Christ: relationships determined by God's economy of hope (Ephesians 1:10), founded on cultural and ethnic reconciliation (Ephesians 2:14–18), working together towards growth (Ephesians 2:19–22), and premised on receiving one another's giftedness (Ephesians 4:1–13).

Resurrection cannot therefore be claimed merely on the basis of statistical reversal, still less the veneer of success. Resurrection life participates in the ongoing love of the Trinity and as such it has a given quality, a certain somatic ecology, a way of being in the body together. There are signs of this quality in new developments in contextual training. Despite some concerns about the marketization of training in the Church of England's more permissive recent strategy, at a local level the evidence is that this has increased, not decreased, openness to collaboration. The gifted difference of the body of Christ is being seen in new ways as practical ministry interrelates with theological training, churches dialogue with colleges, and dioceses plan with local leadership teams. Where this happens, even when there are costs and setbacks, life is to be discerned. The criterion of collaborative body life applies to any genuine solution to the many pressing challenges to northern vocation.

If this analysis is correct, it also suggests a wider frame of reference for our reflections on the North. In Christ, North and South are related as parts of a body patterned by mutuality and honour (1 Corinthians 12:12–26). Gross inequality within the body is surely a blight, but the simple logic of equality is insufficient to describe somatic relations. The North is not to "match" the South, whatever that would mean. It is rather to relate to the South according to the pattern of gift, receiving and offering in mutuality and freedom. Southern gifts to the northern churches include the model for training pioneered by St Mellitus College in London and central funding for pioneering development. Northern gifts to the South include the lessons being learned in northern training contexts and whatever new models we ourselves have the courage to develop.

NOTES

1. Jonathan Owen, "Go Spread the Word of the Lord? Only Down South Says Choosy Church of England Clergy", *The Independent* (10 February 2014).

2. Madeleine Davies, "Clergy Flock to Fill Posts in Wealthy South East", *Church Times* (7 February 2014).

3. For example, Ian Paul, "Vicars are a Bunch of Self-Interested Southern Softies", <http://www.psephizo.com/life-ministry/vicars-are-a-bunch-of-self-interested-southern-softies/> (accessed 10 November 2014).

4. Statistics compiled for the Resourcing the Future report by the Resource Strategy and Development Unit, September 2014: for details, see <https://www.churchofengland.org/media/2139976/gs%201978%20-%20resourcing%20the%20future%20task%20group%20report.pdf> (accessed 20 October 2014).

5. *Resourcing Ministerial Education in the Church of England: A Report from the Task Group*, General Synod (January 2015) (GS1979).

6. David Ford, *The Shape of Living: Spiritual Directions for Everyday Life* (Baker, 1997), p. 19.

7. This and several of the other challenges noted were acknowledged in the recent "Resourcing the Future" report. The comments that follow draw on

reflections from several regional consultations looking into the issues raised by the report.

8. *Ibid.*

9. For example, David Goodhart, "The Big Divide that Politicians Ignore", *The Independent* (9 February 2014), and Philip Cowley and Mark Stuart, "If 60 per cent of Brits Live Within 20 Miles of Where They Lived When They Were 14, What About Their MPs?", *Revolts*, <http://revolts.co.uk/?p=727> (accessed 17 January 2015). The statistics are taken from the Economic and Social Research Council's Understanding Society project, <https://www.understandingsociety.ac.uk> (accessed 17 January 2015).

10. Alan Hirsch and Michael Frost, *The Faith of Leap: Embracing a Theology of Risk, Adventure and Courage* (Baker, 2011), p. 182.

11. For example, Linda Woodhead, "The Challenges that the New C of E Reports Duck", *Church Times* (23 January 2015).

12. Bob Jackson, *Hope for the Church: Contemporary Strategies for Growth* (Church House Publishing, 2002), pp. 168–181.

13. Quoted in Alan Hirsch, *The Forgotten Ways: Reactivating the Missional Church* (Brazos, 2006), p. 15.

14. Jackson, *Hope for the Church*, pp. 22–23.

15. "There will be no future for the broad church in the postmodern world. We will have to return to structures akin to the monastery, the religious community and the sect . . . [We need] to create sectarian plausibility structures in order for our story to take hold of our congregations and root them in the gospel handed down by our forebears", Andrew Walker, *Telling the Story: Gospel, Mission and Culture* (SPCK, 1996), p. 190.

16. Tom Smail, "The Ethics of Exile and the Rhythm of Resurrection" in Andrew Walker and Kristin Aune (eds.), *On Revival: A Critical Examination* (Paternoster, 2003), p. 60.

17. Smail, "The Ethics of Exile", pp. 57–58.

18. Jürgen Moltmann, *Theology of Hope: On the Ground and Implications of a Christian Eschatology,* translated by James W. Leitch (Harper and Row, 1967), p. 23.

19. "Talent Management for Future Leaders and Leadership Development for Bishops and Deans: A New Approach", *Report of the Lord Green Steering Group, September 2014*, <https://churchofengland.org/media/2130591/report.pdf> (accessed 15 January 2015).

20. Hirsch and Frost, *The Faith of Leap*, p. 132.

21. "Priests in the Church are called to enable the Church to play its priestly role of declaring the praises of Jesus Christ, the true High Priest, so that in turn the rest of humanity might be restored to its proper priestly dignity, and the whole earth resound to the joy of God", Graham Tomlin, *The Widening Circle: Priesthood as God's Way of Blessing the World* (SPCK, 2014), p. 114.

22. Jackson, *Hope for the Church*, p. 144.

23. Robert Banks, *Reenvisioning Theological Education: Exploring a Missional Alternative to Current Models* (Eerdmans, 1999), p. 111.

24. *Ibid.*, p. 123. Biblically speaking, training leaders by removing them from their context for extended periods has unhappy parallels. Arguably, the closest analogue would be the policy of cultural decapitation favoured by the Babylonian empire, as depicted, for instance, by the treatment of young leaders in Daniel chapter 1.

25. Banks, *Reenvisioning Theological Education*, p. 146.

26. Nick Spencer, *Parochial Vision: The Future of the English Parish* (Paternoster, 2004), p. 76.

27. Archbishop of Canterbury's Commission on Urban Priority Areas, *Faith in the City: A Call for Action by Church and Nation* (Church House, 1985), p. 122–127.

28. Graham Cray *et al*, *Mission-Shaped Church*, 2nd ed. (Church House Publishing, 2009 [2004]), p. 135 and p. 148.

29. Lesslie Newbigin, *The Gospel in a Pluralist Society* (SPCK, 1999), p. 231.

17. EVAPORATING THE MYTH OF "IT'S GRIM UP NORTH"

Nigel Rooms

No-one is quite sure where this rather hateful saying comes from; some attribute it to J. B. Priestley and his unhappy time researching his travel book on England in Tyneside in 1933,[1] while others suggest it simply arose in the industrial age, evoking as it does smoky, dirty, packed-in terraced houses and the hard life that went with them.

Let's take the saying apart first of all. "Grim" is derived from an Old English word, *grimm*, meaning "fierce, cruel, savage; severe, dire, painful", and it also survives in other modern languages descended from proto-Germanic, such as the German *grimm* "wrath, fury" and Swedish *grym* "cruel, ferocious". It has carried the sense of "bleak, dreary, gloomy" since the late twelfth century, especially when referring to place. However, we should not ignore its relationship with the picture of the "Grim Reaper", an image associated with imminent death, first attested in 1847—not unlike the way *sheol* is used in the Hebrew bible to describe a half-life, shadowy existence after death. So yes, perhaps people are closer to death in the North—and indeed mortality rates demonstrate this as we have seen elsewhere in this book.

What is more suggestive is that the North is "up" in this metaphorical saying, especially since this goes against conventional uses of up/down in metaphorical language. Lakoff and Johnson suggest that orientational metaphors are deeply embedded in our culture in the Western world and especially in English speaking countries.[2] They posit that this is due to the experiential and embodied nature of human life—for instance, living people are up[right] and dead people are down, literally on or in the ground. Thus normally such concepts as health, life, control, more, status, good, virtue, and rationality are all "up". The only exception to the general rule that positive concepts are "up" that they can find is that the unknown is "up" ("it's all up in the air") but what is known is "down" (since objects can be examined on the ground).

Given the earth's position in the solar system and the universe, there is no reason why maps are normally oriented with north at the top. I suggest that this is simply a consequence of history, as most of the power, resources, and wealth have been located in the northern hemisphere. England, therefore, upsets this normal orientational organizing of how we see the world since, as we know, the power, resources, and control are held in the South. This makes for interesting internet discussion forums about why one goes "up" to university (especially Oxbridge) and also to London.[3] The confusion is entirely understandable, however, given how our metaphorical worldview is organised. I wonder, therefore, whether "It's grim up North" is actually about the unknown nature of the North from the position of the South. It is "beyond the edge", the borders of what is known, safe, and good.

Elsewhere in this volume we have noted a similarity between the orientation of England and the land of the Holy One where Jerusalem, the power base, is in the south and Galilee the north. Jerusalem and its temple are ascended to on pilgrimage, but the one who is lifted up on the cross and raised in resurrection appears in Galilee.[4] Andrew Mayes has written eloquently about the marginality of Galilee at the time of the coming of the Christ.[5] Literally meaning the "circle of pagans", it buffers Jerusalem from foreign nations. Galileans like Peter were mocked for their recognizable accent and the place was despised and scapegoated.[6] It was haunted by poverty, where people were exploited by absentee landlords and became a base for rebellious insurgency against the Roman state; a liminal place which Jesus blesses with his presence in his life, ministry, and resurrection. Galilee was also grim. Quoting Freyne, Mayes concludes that Galilee is "a symbol of the periphery becoming the new non-localized centre of divine presence".[7] Jesus' critique of the "self-serving Jerusalem clerical elite" is possible from this place on the edge.[8] Mayes offers us a

beautiful paraphrase of the meaning of the risen Jesus going before the
disciples to Galilee:

> I will meet you in the liminal place, the land that is betwixt
> and between, caught between foreign countries and the
> religious centre; a place of opposition and protest. I will
> meet you places that need healing and encouragement.
> No need to look for me in the corridors of power or at the
> religious centre. I will be found among the poor, the broken
> and hurting. Find me among the rejected and stigmatized. I
> wait for you in situations of injustice and dehumanization. I
> *There* I will meet you.[9]

I believe it is therefore a gospel imperative to evaporate the myth that it
is "grim up North". This task can begin by overcoming the "unknown"
nature of the North by relating the two halves of our nation together
in new ways. Only by believing that Jesus is present in the marginality
of the North, that God is biased towards it, can we uncover the beauty,
goodness, and truth to be found there. Who will join in this task, this
call of God to go "beyond the edge"?

NOTES

1.   See <http://www.bbc.co.uk/news/uk-england-tyne-30152684> (accessed 20
     March 2015).
2.   George Lakoff and Mark Johnson, *Metaphors We Live By* (University of
     Chicago Press, 1980, reprinted 2003), pp. 14–21.
3.   "Going up to London" goes back at least as far as a reference in Charles
     Dickens' novel *Bleak House* and the general issues are discussed at <http://
     ask.metafilter.com/32837/Going-up-to-London-Why-on-earth> (accessed
     21 March 2015).
4.   Mark 14:28.

5. Andrew D. Mayes, *Beyond the Edge: Spiritual Transitions for Adventurous Souls* (2013, SPCK).

6. Mark 14:70; John 1:46, 7:52.

7. Mayes, *Beyond the Edge*, p. 112, quoting S. Freyne, *Galilee, Jesus and the Gospels: Literary Approaches and Historical Investigations* (Fortress Press, 1984, 1988) p. 54.

8. Mayes, *Beyond the Edge*, p. 112.

9. Ibid., p. 113 (emphasis his).

Lightning Source UK Ltd.
Milton Keynes UK
UKOW06f0500150316

270181UK00001B/21/P